Land Use and Cover Change

Editors

R.B. Singh
Jefferson Fox
Yukio Himiyama

Science Publishers, Inc.

Enfield (NH), USA   Plymouth, UK

SCIENCE PUBLISHERS, Inc.
Post Office Box 699
Enfield, New Hampshire 03748
United States of America

Internet site: *http://www.scipub.net*

sales@scipub.net (marketing department)
editor@scipub.net (editorial department)
info@scipub.net (for all other enquiries)

Library of Congress Cataloging-in-Publication Data

Land use and cover change / editors, R.B. Singh, Jefferson Fox,
Yukio Himiyama.
    p. cm.
  Includes bibliographical references (p.).
  ISBN 1-57808-147-5
  1. Land use—Remote sensing. 2. Land use—Data processing. 3.
Information storage and retrieval systems—Land use. 4. Geo-
graphic information systems. 5. Land use—Environmental as-
pects. 6. Land use, Rural—Environmental aspects. 7. Singh,
R.B., 1937-II. Fox, Jefferson, 1951-III. Himiyama, Yukio, 1949-

HD108.8.L36 2001
333.73—dc21

                           00- 067970

ISBN 1-57808-147-5

Published by Science Publishers, Inc., Enfield, NH, USA
Printed in India.

➤ Preface

Land-use and land-cover change is a focal theme and emerging issue in the study of global environmental change. Human modifications and alterations of the environment cause impacts on the surface of the earth, threaten global sustainability and livelihood systems, and contribute to changes in the biogeochemical cycles of the earth, which in turn affect atmospheric levels of greenhouse and other trace gases. Consequently the International Geosphere-Biosphere Programme (IGBP) and the International Human Dimensions Programme (IHDP) initiated land-use and land-cover change research (LUCC Programme) to develop a better understanding of the biophysical and human driving forces of land-use and land-cover change. In 1996 the International Geographical Union (IGU) established a study group on land-use and land-cover change (IGU-LUCC) to conduct research and to contribute to the LUCC Programme. Both the IGU-LUCC and LUCC initiatives have identified land-use and land-cover change as a major research topic with regard to global sustainability. Another major objective of IGU-LUCC is to coordinate comparative studies of land-use and land-cover changes in different regions, with a view to elucidating the nature and function of driving forces.

Leading scientists and researchers working on land-use and land-cover change have recently drawn attention to the need to 'socialize the pixel' or, in other words, to integrate research on monitoring land-use and land-cover change from space with research on the socio-economic causes of these changes. Remote sensing observations alone cannot explain the socio-economic and institutional factors that cause land-use and land-cover change, nor can they identify the factors that influence regional trends or local dynamics. These issues can only be addressed by using population and other social science data in a comparative framework. Geographic information systems (GIS) are used to merge social science variables spatially and temporally with physical science data. These analyses must then be supplemented by field research in order to understand the individual-level decision processes that produce the land-use and land-cover change.

The resurgence of research interest amongst scientists and geographers in these issues was reflected in an IGU-LUCC international seminar held at the East-West Centre in Honolulu, Hawaii in July 1999. Many research papers focused on land-use and land-cover change in relation to information bases, historical assessment, modeling and predication, remote sensing and GIS application, and environmental impact analysis. This book is a compilation of 24 papers presented and discussed at this international seminar. The papers have been edited and updated. A few invited papers have also been included in order to bridge gaps in research knowledge. The aim of the book is to promote a better understanding of land-use and land-cover change in the assessment and management of global environmental resources, and to develop a comparative framework for assessing these changes.

R.B. SINGH
JEFFERSON FOX
YUKIO HIMIYAMA
(EDS.)

➢ Contents

➤ List of Contributors

B.A. Alekseev Faculty of Geography, Moscow State University, Moscow, 119899, Russia

Shoichiro Arizono Aichi University, Toyohashi, Japan

Marina A. Arshinova Moscow State University, Moscow, Russia

Zhang Bai Changchum Institute of Geography, Changchun, 130021, China

Ivan Bicík Department of Social Geography and Regional Development, Faculty of Science, Universzita Karlova, 128 43, Albertov 6, Praha-2, Czech Republic

U.A. Chandrasena Department of Geography, University of Kelaniya, Kelaniya, Sri Lanka.

Jefferson Fox East-West Center, 1601 East-West Road Honolulu, Hawaii 96848-1601, U.S.A.

Yoshihisa Fujita Aichi University, Toyohashi, Japan

Desmond A. Gillmor Department of Geography, University of Dublin, Trinity College, Dublin 2, Ireland

Yukio Himiyama Hokkaido University of Education, Hokumoncho Asahikawa 070-8621, Japan

Manik Hwang Department of Geography Education, Seoul National University, Seoul 151-742, Korea

Takemasa Ishii Geological Survey of Japan; 1-1-3, Higashi, Tsukuba City, Japan

Nobusuke Iwasaki Dept. of Environmental Science & Technology, Tokyo Institute of Technology, Nagatuda-cho, Yokohama 226-8052 Japan

N.N. Kalutskova Faculty of Geography, Moscow State University, Moscow, 119899, Russia

Kazuyuki Konagaya Institute for Economic Research, Osaka City University, Osaka, Japan

K. Kok Wageningen Agricultural Univesity, P.O. Box 37, 6700 AA Wageningen, The· Netherlands

G.H.J. de Koning Wageningen Agricultural Univesity, P.O. Box 37, 6700 AA Wageningen, The Netherlands

Vladimir Kremsa Research Center for Applied Science and Advanced Technology (CICATA-IPN), Legaria 694, Col. Irrigacion Mexico City 11500, Mexico.

E.Yu. Lioubimtseva Faculty of Geography, Moscow State University, Moscow, 119899, Russia

Anjana Mathur Department of Geography, Delhi School of Economics, University of Delhi, Delhi-110007 India.

Irina Merzliakova Russian Conservation-Monitoring Center, Vavilova st. 41-1, 117312 Moscow, Russia

E.V. Milanova Faculty of Geography, Moscow State University, Moscow, 119899, Russia

Jag Mohan Department of Geography, Delhi School of Economics, University of Delhi, Delhi-110007 India.

Hidenori Morita Faculty of Engineering, Kagawa University, Japan

Kuninori Otsubo National Institute for Environmental Studies, Water and Soil Enviranmental Division 16-2 Onogawa Tsukuba, Ibaraki, 305-0053, Japan

D.A. Oyeleye Department of Geography, University of Lagos, Akoka-Yaba, Lagos, Nigeria.

Franci Petek Geographical Institute, Scientific Research Center of Slovenian Academy of Sciences and Arts, Gosposka 13, 51-1000 Ljubljana, Slovenia

Krishna P. Poduel Department of Geography, Tribhuvan University, Pokhra, Nepal.

J. Priess Wageningen Agricultural Univesity, P.O. Box 37, 6700 AA Wageningen, The Netherlands

Emma P. Romanova Moscow State University, Moscow, Russia

R.B. Singh Department of Geography, Delhi School of Economics, University of Delhi, Delhi-110007 India.

V.N. Solntsev Faculty of Geography, Moscow State University, Moscow, 119899, Russia

Alexandre Sorokine Regional Science Institute 4-13 Kita-24 Nishi-2, Kita-ku, Sapporo 001-0024, Japan

Vít Štěpánek Department of Social Geography and Regional Development, Faculty of Science, Universzita Karlova, 12843 Albertov 6, Praha-2, Czech Republic

Markus Stoffel Department of Geography, University of Fribourg, chemin du Musee 3, 1700 Fribourg, Switzerland

P.A. Tcherkashin Faculty of Geography, Moscow State University, Moscow, 119899, Russia

Vladimir S. Tikunov M.V. Lomonosov Moscow State University, Moscow 119899, Russia

Takashi Todokoro Takasaki City University of Economics, Takasaki, Japan

A. Veldkamp Wageningen Agricultural Univesity, P.O. Box 37, 6700 AA Wageningen, The Netherlands

P.H. Verburg Wageningen Agricultural Univesity, P.O. Box 37, 6700 AA Wageningen, The Netherlands

Qinxue Wang National Institute for Environmental Studies, Water and Soil Environmental Division 16-2 Onogawa Tsukuba, Ibaraki, 305-0053, Japan

Makiko Watanabe Dept. of Environmental Science & Technology, Tokyo Institute of Technology, Nagatuda-cho, Yokohama 226-8052 Japan

Leniana F. Yanvareva M.V. Lomonosov Moscow State University, Moscow 119899, Russia

Zhaoji Zhang National Institute for Environmental Studies, 16-2, Onogawa, Tsukuba City, Japan

CHAPTER 1

Chinese Land Use
Predicted by the GTR-model

(Kazuyuki Konagaya[1], Hidenori Morita[2]
and Kuninori Otsubo[3])

1. METHODS

1.1 Generalized Thünen (GT) Model or the GTA-model

The Generalized Thünen (GT) model is the extension of the traditional normative Thünen model, the exact fundamental theory of land markets. It enables us to explain the real land use ratio data. This new model successfully provides an exact theoretical interpretation to the intuitive picture of the movement of land use frontiers such as deforestation or desertification, and enables us to predict land use changes in the future.

The exact theory of land use (Thünen theory) predicts a concentric land use structure around a monocentric city as in the left diagram of Fig. 1. Although it is a normative model by which only one land use dominates in each area, and thus cannot be reconciled with the real ratio data, GT-model explains real land use mix based upon the exact land rent theory as in the right diagram of Fig. 1.

When applied to Indonesian data, the GT-model can explain the regularities observed in Sumatra land use change, and can predict 2025 land use profiles in Jawa which warn us of the danger of a loss of valuable forest on the axis between Jakarta and Bandung (Konagaya, 1999).

[1]Institute for Economic Research, Osaka City University, Osaka, Japan
[2]Faculty of Engineering, Kagawa University, Japan
[3]National Institute Water and Soil Environment Division for Environmental Studies, 16-2 Onogawa, Tsukuba Ibaraki 305-0053, Japan

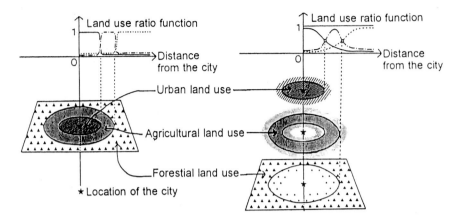

Fig. 1 Model of land use

The GT-model also reveals the realization of land use with a strong rent-bidding power. Urbanization driven by globalization is the prime factor producing land use changes. Thus, one of the environmental implications of the GT-model is on how to balance both globalization and sustainability. Generally speaking, the environmental impact of ordinary land use will tend to increase as its rent-bidding power increases. So it is important to search for land use acivities with low environmental impact and high rent-bidding potential.

$$K_i[a(p,c)] \equiv \left\{ \sum_j \exp\left(a(1,c) \cdot X_j - a(2,c) \cdot Y_{ij}\right) \right\}$$

$$R_i(c) = K_i[a(p,c)] \Big/ \sum_{c'} K_i[a(p,c')]$$

i: ($i = 1 \cdots ni$) land use grids, j: ($j = 1 \cdots nj$) cities, c: ($c = 1 \cdots C$) land use categories.

1.2 Generalized Thünen-Ricardo (GTR) Model

Currently, regions with rapid economic growth and environmental destruction are concentrated in China proper. Thus, effective land use models on China are needed urgently. Land in China has a larger scale in comparison to an island region in a South-East Asian country. Hence, various physical conditions need to be incorporated. The GT-model stated above is based mainly on economic conditions and influences from cities (urban driving force variables). However, micro physical conditions in each site (on-site variables) are needed to the model.

In this study, we extended the GT-model to the GTR-model integrating both variables to explain the Chinese land use structure. The GTR-model is derived from the bid-rent function of category c-land user to bid the land at i-grid economically based on j-city as

$$r_{ij}(c) = a(1, c) \cdot X_j - a(2, c) \cdot Y_{ij} + a(3, c) \cdot Z1_i + a(4, c) \cdot Z2_i + \varepsilon_{ij}$$

we can integrate this to produce the land use ratio function as

$$K_i[a(p, c)] \equiv \left\{ \sum_j \exp(a(1, c) \cdot X_j - a(2, c) \cdot Y_{ij}) \right\} \exp a(3, c) \cdot Z1_i$$

$$+ a(4, c) \cdot Z2_i)$$

$$R_i(c) = K_i[a(p, c)] \Big/ \sum_{c'} K_i[a(p, c')]$$

2. DATA SET

i: ($i = 1 \ldots ni = 22{,}789$) land use grids, j: ($j = 1 \ldots nj = 50$) cities,
c: ($c = 1 \ldots C = 3$) land use categories (c = 1: urban, 2: agricultural, 3: others (forest, steppe), etc.)
k: ($k = 1 \ldots K = 4$) parameters (k = 1: urban population, 2: distance, 3: elevation, 4: slope, etc.)

The most important feature of the GTR-model is that it has two kinds of explanatory variables (Fig. 2).

(1) *Situation variables (Urban driving force variables)*: It represents the influence of far located cities on the land use of the grid, the driving forces. This consists of the indicator to gauge the agglomeration economies of cities (such as urban population of the j-city, X_j, and the indicator to gauge the deterioration effect of space (such as distance between the j-city and the i-grid, y_{ij}). The influence of these situation variables is presented as the { } factor of the above formula, which is called 'Thünian Component'.

(2) *Site variables (On-site variables)*: It represents the conditions of the same location as the grid, which control the influence of driving forces. This time we take the elevation Z1 and the slope Z2 variables. The influence of these site variables is presented as the exponential factor of the above formula, which is called the 'Ricardian Component'.

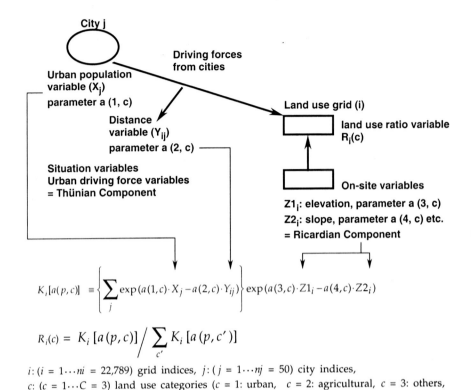

$$K_i[a(p,c)] \equiv \left\{ \sum_j \exp(a(1,c)\cdot X_j - a(2,c)\cdot Y_{ij}) \right\} \exp(a(3,c)\cdot Z1_i - a(4,c)\cdot Z2_i)$$

$$R_i(c) = K_i[a(p,c)] \Big/ \sum_{c'} K_i[a(p,c')]$$

i: ($i = 1 \cdots ni = 22,789$) grid indices, j: ($j = 1 \cdots nj = 50$) city indices,

c: ($c = 1 \cdots C = 3$) land use categories ($c = 1$: urban, $c = 2$: agricultural, $c = 3$: others, etc.)

k: ($k = 1 \cdots K$) parameters

Urban driving force variables ($k = 1$: urban population, $k = 2$: distance, etc.)

On-site variables ($k = 3$: elevation, $k = 4$: slope, etc.)

Fig. 2 GTR-model, structure of land use weight function

3. CALIBRATION RESULTS

The optimized model is as follows:

$$K_i[a(k,1)] = \left\{ \sum_j \exp(10\cdot X_j - 8.7\cdot Y_{ij}) \right\}$$

$$K_i[a(k,2)] = \left\{ \sum_j \exp(9\cdot X_j - 3\cdot Y_{ij}) \right\} \exp(0.3\cdot Z1_i + 1.3\cdot Z2_i)$$

$$K_i[a\,(k,3)] = \left\{ \sum_j \exp\,(5 \cdot X_j - 2 \cdot Y_{ij}) \right\} \exp\,(1.3 \cdot Z1_i + 1 \cdot Z2_i)$$

This model predicts land use profiles of 22,789 grids of China with $R^2 = 0.776$.

Forestial land use is usually in higher locations than the urban and agricultural land.

4. 2025 PREDICTION

4.1 Calculation

We can predict the 2025 land use by increasing the populations of 1992 by 1.464 times. Figure 4.1 shows the agricultural land use at present and the 2025 profiles and Fig. 4.2 shows the other land uses (forest, steppe, etc.) at present and the 2025 profiles.

4.2 Interpretation

The most drastic change in the 2025 map is the great expansion of agricultural land in north and north-eastern regions, and at the same time the conversion and decrease of others (forest, steppe, etc.) in north and north-eastern regions. This trend is most successfully captured by the Thünen-type model family (GT-model or GTR-model). In the Thünen-type models, cities not only play a simple role in determining the urban land use (housing, industry, commercial and so on), but also play a more important role of influential drivers to order all the other land use around their locations, such as quasi-concentric zones of

urban land use → agricultural land use → forestial land use → other land use.

Additionally, the Thünen-type model explains that the same phenomenon had occurred in Japanese land use structures. In Japan, the most typical production center of rice crops ('Kome-dokoro') is north and north-eastern regions ('Hokuriku-chiho' and 'Tohoku-chiho'). Seemingly this contradicts with the tropical origin of rice, however, the idea of Thünen-type model helps one to understand this overturn. In Japan, after the WW2, urban land use has developed in the southern region ('Pacific industrial belt') which is the growth center of economic development. Thus, north and north-east regions far from 'Pacific industrial belt' are suitable for rice production based on the rent-bidding ability.

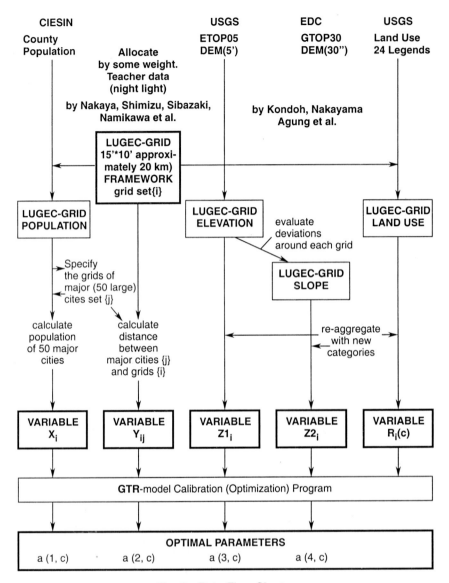

Fig. 3 Data Flow Chart

Similarly southern China has been the center of agricultural production until now. However, as urbanization based on rapid industrialization will proceed in the south, agricultural land use is pushed toward north, which turns the large scale structure of Chinese land use.

Agricultural Land Use 1992–93 (Present Status)

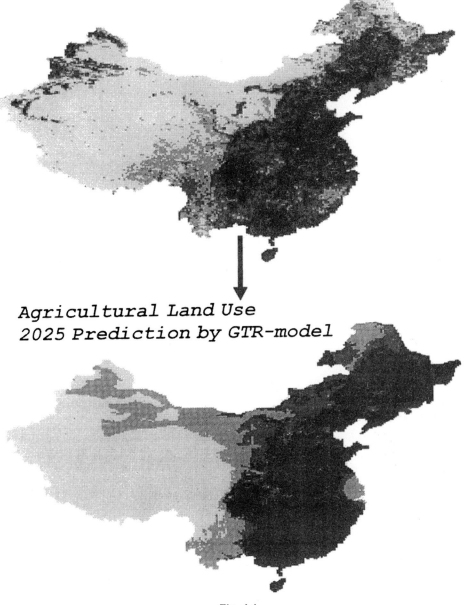

Fig. 4.1

Other Land Use (Forest, Steppe, etc. 1992-93 (Present Status)

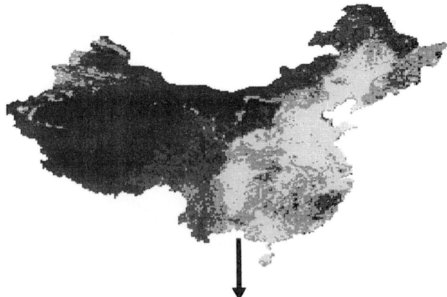

Other Land Use (Forest, Steppe, etc.)
2025 Prediction by GTR-model

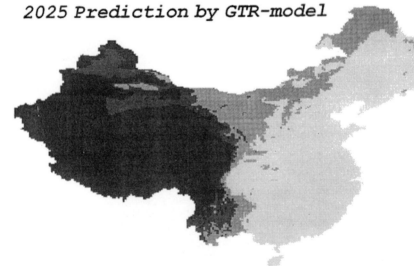

Fig. 4.2

REFERENCE

Konagaya, K.U. (1999). The Generalized Thünen-Alonso Model for Land Use Change in Sumatra Island', *Geographical & Environmental Modelling* 3-2.

CHAPTER 2

The CLUE Modelling Framework: An Integrated Model for the Analysis of Land Use Change

(P.H. Verburg, G.H.J. de Koning, K. Kok,
A. Veldkamp and J. Priess[*])

1. INTRODUCTION

Research shows that human-induced conversions (e.g. deforestation) and modifications (e.g. changing land use management such as fertilizer use and irrigation practices) of land use have great significance in the functioning of the earth system with impact on the biogeochemical cycles (Turner et al. 1994). The dynamics of greenhouse gas emissions are to a large extent determined by natural ecosystems. Ecosystem conversion results in changing these gas dynamics. Land use changes can also have an impact on the water and energy balance, directly affecting climatic conditions. The impact of these land use changes becomes globally significant through their accumulative effects.

Apart from affecting environmental sustainability, land use change also has an effect on food security. Conversion of cultivated land to non-farm uses such as housing, factories and infrastructure in combination with a growing population is regarded as a serious threat to future food sufficiency (Brown, 1995). Thus, studies that explore land use changes are very relevant.

In land use change studies, it is essential to link land use changes to their driving forces. These driving forces (e.g. population or

[*]Wageningen Agricultural University, P.O. Box 37, 6700 AA Wageningen, The Netherlands

development), mediated by the socio-economic setting (e.g. market economy, resource institutions) and influenced by the existing environmental conditions or context, lead to changes in land use through the manipulation of the biophysical conditions of the land (Turner et al. 1995). Understanding the trends of land use change in relation to the driving forces will provide essential information for land use planning and sustainable management of resources.

Until now, only few models have attempted to assess the spatial patterns of the process of land use change (Hall et al. 1995). Broad scale, highly aggregated analysis of land use change at the national level provide us with information on the extent of land use change; however, it does not provide us with the spatial information needed to calculate the consequences of land use changes. The highly aggregated data obscures the variability of situations and relationships, which can cause the underestimation of the effects of land use change for certain regions and certain groups of the population.

Spatially explicit information on land use change is needed when the environmental consequences of land use changes are assessed. The amount of carbon-dioxide released due to deforestation can cause significant differences depending on the biomass level of the primary forest (Brown et al. 1994). So, not only the amount of deforestation, but also the location and associated biomass level are required for reliable assessments of carbon-dioxide release. Also for the calculation of changes in nutrient balances and subsequent assessments of sustainability of agroecosystems (Smaling and Fresco, 1993), spatially explicit land use change data are required.

To make land use change models spatially explicit, one has to understand the spatial structure of land use. This paper presents a modelling framework to explore the spatial patterns in land use. This modelling framework, CLUE (the Conversion of Land Use and its Effects), was first applied in Costa Rica (Veldkamp and Fresco, 1996, 1997a,b; Kok and Veldkamp, 1999). Current research was carried out in Ecuador (de Koning et al. 1999), Honduras, China (Verburg et al. 1999a) and Indonesia (Verburg et al. 1999c).

1.1 Socio-economic and Biophysical Driving Factors of Land Use Change

Land use changes are clearly driven by human activities (Skole and Tucker, 1993). However, the biophysical conditions of the land such as soil characteristics, climate, topography and vegetation, to a large extent determine the spatial pattern of land use and land use changes (Turner et al. 1993). An integrated approach to study the spatial pattern of land use (change) is difficult because of the complexity of the interactions between socio-economic and biophysical factors, and the different ways that these interactions unfold in particular areas of the world. Many studies at detailed scales have been undertaken which offer detailed insights into specific cases that unfortunately cannot be generalized. Literature is weak in quantitative assessments that analyse the influence of socio-economic and biophysical driving factors on land use at coarser scales. Causal relations between actors and land use change, as identified at detailed scales (Groot and Kamminga, 1995), can often not be used at coarser scales. At coarse scales we need to use factors that represent or proxy the driving factors identified at the actor level. For example, to describe the process of deforestation we can use parameters like roads density, population density and average incomes as proxies for the actual drivers of land use change. Detailed studies are essential to identify the factors which can be used as proxies to avoid the problem of unknown causalty (does deforestation cause roads or do roads cause deforestation?).

The relations between land use and its driving factors is dependent on the scale of observation (Veldkamp and Fresco, 1996). Hall et al. (1995) found that, at detailed scales, land use in tropical rainforest areas is strongly correlated with topography. However, at a coarser scale, land use was strongly correlated with precipitation and cloud cover. Most often coarse scales are useful to reveal the general trends and relations between land cover and its determining factors. Factors that influence land cover over a considerable distance (like cities) can only be observed at these coarse scales. However, the high level of aggregation at these coarse scales can obscure the variability of units and processes and is therefore considered inaccurate for detailed scale and local assessments. A multi-scale approach which identifies and quantifies the determinants of land cover at multiple scales gives the most complete description of the structure of land use.

2. DATA AND METHODS

2.1 Data

For the three different study areas (China, Costa Rica and Ecuador) biophysical and socio-economic data, that were considered as potential explaining factors of the structure of land use, were collected. The potential explaining factors were selected based on literature review and knowledge of the country specific situation. The data on land use and the socio-economic conditions were obtained from the population and agricultural census of the countries. Census data are useful for a study of this kind as they contain relative extensive sets of data covering the whole country. The biophysical parameters were obtained from different maps (Nuhn, 1978) or digital datasets (UNEP/DEIA, 1997), containing information on soil conditions, relief and climate. Census data can be implemented in a Geographical Information System by mapping the administrative units for which the data are derived. Because these units only rarely coincide with biophysical units, a grid-based system is used to facilitate analysis. Grid size was selected based on the estimated average district sizes, the most detailed spatial scale for the census data, resulting in grids of 7.5 × 7.5 km for Costa Rica, 8.5 × 8.5 km for Ecuador and 32 × 32 km for China.

In contrast to most grid-based approaches derived from maps which represent land use by cells with one dominant land use type, we characterized land use by the relative cover of each land use type in each grid cell, e.g. a grid cell can contain 30% cultivated land, 40% grassland and 30% forest. This way of representing the data is a direct result of the information contained in the census data.

In order to allow a systematic analysis of spatial scale effects, the grid data was aggregated into larger grids, composed of 4, 9, 16 and 25 basic grid units respectively, making five additional aggregated spatial scales. The new aggregated grid values were averages of the included basic grids.

2.2   Statistical Methods

A stepwise regression procedure was used to identify the factors that contribute significantly (at 0.05 level) to the explanation of the land use structure. This way it was possible to distinguish the potential factors which have relevance in the spatial pattern of land use. Expert knowledge and literature review are used to explain the relations found. Figure 1 summarizes the followed procedure. The stepwise procedure was repeated for the different aggregation levels to allow new variables to enter the regression equations at the aggregated scales. Standardized betas were calculated to allow a comparison of the relative importance of the different identified factors.

2.3   Modelling

2.3.1   General structure of the model

The results of the statistical analyses give quantitative insight in the multi-scale structure of land use. The next step is the modelling of

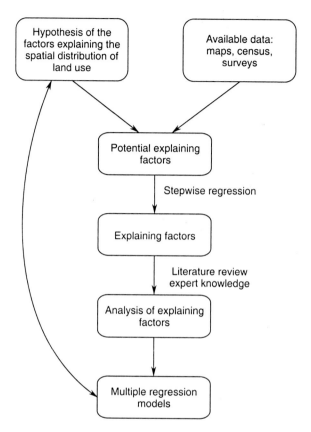

Fig. 1 Overview of the procedure used to derive multiple regression models for the explanation of the distribution of land use

possible future land use change scenarios. This is the actual CLUE model, that can broadly be divided into a demand and allocation module (Fig. 2) which interacts with a population and yield module (Verburg et al. 1999b). In the demand module, the national demand for agricultural commodities is estimated for a series of years in future on the basis of different projections of the factors determining this demand. The allocation module calculates local changes of different land use type areas on the basis of changing demands, using the results of the statistical analysis and applying the multi-scale approach by looking at regional and local driving forces for land use change. The model produces results with time steps of one year, and aims at future exploration of about 20 years.

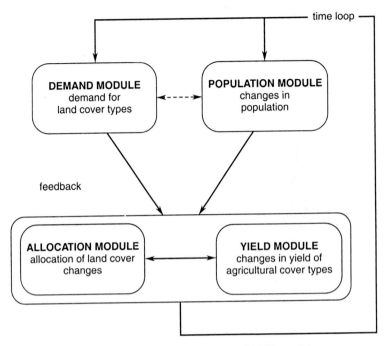

Fig. 2 General structue of the CLUE model.

2.3.2 Demand module

In the CLUE demand module, the total area needed for different land use types is calculated on the basis of national demand for separate commodities. The demand for these commodities is the sum of domestic consumption and export volumes. Export volumes can be related to international prices and national subsidies. Domestic intake is a function of population size, population composition and consumption patterns. Consumption patterns can be related to macro-economic indicators like gross domestic product, purchasing power and price levels. Historic data are used to calibrate the commodity volume demand functions. Future developments are hard to predict, and therefore different possible development scenarios are being formulated, taking into account varying projections of future population development and diet patterns.

Commodity demands calculated as production volumes are translated into areas through crop specific yields (for animal products, production per animal and stocking densities are used). Different developments of yield for separate crops can be included through the yield module. On the basis of the calculated areas for separate crops, the needed areas for broader land use types are calculated.

2.3.3 Allocation module

In the CLUE allocation module, the area demand for separate land use types is allocated to the basic grid cells using a nested scale approach. The idea behind the allocation procedure is that local land use change is determined by local biophysical and socio-economic conditions, as well as by conditions at higher scales. This is related to the fact that decisions at the local level are the result of local processes, but also by processes that operate over large distances.

In the allocation module, the national demand for each land use area is allocated first to the cells at the higher aggregation levels in order to establish the comparative advantages between these larger cells, representing regions. Then, within these larger cells, local changes of all land use types in the smallest cells are calculated on the basis of their locally specific biogeophysical and socio-economic conditions, but taking into account the conditions in the larger cells in which these cells are nested.

The actual calculation of the expected area changes at the different scales is done by using the scale-specific regression equations from the statistical analysis. The area of a certain land use type in a cell, is determined by the multidimensional space made up by the land use drivers. If a cell has less area of a certain land use type than expected on the basis of the regression equation, area increase of that land use type is considered feasible (and vice versa). The actual fraction of change allowed is established through an iteration procedure in which a new equilibrium is calculated. This is done simultaneously for all land use types, accounting at the same time for competition between land use types within cells.

The changes of biophysical and socio-economic drivers are also taken into account, thereby changing the multidimensional space within which land use is situated and calculated. For Ecuador, for example, the changes in local population densities are included.

In the multi-scale allocation procedure, the top-down and bottom-up effects are mimicked. The demand is allocated from national to intermediate and local levels, but local conditions can constrain increases in land use, thereby forcing other areas to grow or even prohibit the national demand to be allocated. In the model, local effects like the protection of areas through national parks or areas becoming unsuitable due to deterioration of biophysical resources can be included as different scenarios.

3. RESULTS

3.1 Statistical Analysis

3.1.1 China

Table 1 shows the main factors that contribute to the explanation of the spatial distribution of cultivated lands and grasslands in China for the situation in 1990. The distribution of cultivated land can be explained reasonably well, while only 56% of the spatial variation in the distribution of grassland can be explained by a model that needs 12 different factors. The relatively poor model fit for grassland can be attributed to the wide variation in grassland types in China ranging from dry steppe in desert areas to artificial or improved grassland for livestock grazing and cutting of grass. The different types of grasslands are related to different biophysical and socio-economic environments. A subdivision of grassland types would be needed to find better relations between the grassland distribution and the biophysical and socio-economic environment.

Table 1   Multiple regression models (factors and standardized regression coefficients (stb)) explaining the area devoted to cultivated land and grassland in China for 1990

cultivated land $\text{adj. } r^2 = 0.77$		grassland $\text{adj. } r^2 = 0.56$	
Factor	stb*	Factor	stb*
rural population density	0.56	illiterate population (%)	0.39
poorly drained soils (%)	0.19	poorly drained soils (%)	−0.35
rural population (%)	0.17	deep soils (%)	0.35
suitable soil for rainfed maize (%)[1]	0.14	temperature in coldest month	−0.27
mean altitude	−0.13	yearly precipitation	−0.24
rich fertility soils (%)	0.12	soils with low moisture storage (%)	0.24
distance to city	−0.08	moderately drained soils (%)	−0.23
		rural labour force (% of total labour force)	0.22
		rural population density	−0.18
		agricultural households (%)	−0.17
		level land (%)	0.16
		rich fertility soils (%)	0.09

*all coefficients significant at 0.05.
[1] Soils suitable for the cultivation of rainfed maize according to FAO, 1995. Digital Soil Map of the World and Derived Soil Properties, Version 3.5.

The distribution of the rural population is the main determinant of the distribution of the cultivated lands and needs no further explanation. Cultivated lands are positively correlated with poorly drained soils while grasslands have negative correlations with poorly and moderately drained soils. This can be explained by the relatively large share of rice farming, which requires poorly drained soils, and the vast areas of steppe occurring on well drained soils. Cultivated land is found on soils that have a relatively high natural soil fertility and at low altitudes. The negative relation with the distance to cities can be explained by the difficulties of transporting food crops over long distances and the lack of infrastructure in remote areas. Climatic variables were included in the analysis but not retained in the stepwise regression procedure, indicating that the large climatic differences in China do not influence the distribution of cultivated lands structurally. This does not imply that climatic variation does not have an influence on the distribution of land use at all; the negative correlation with altitude is probably mainly due to the unfavourable conditions for land use in the mountains.

The distribution of grasslands, however, is strongly correlated to climatic conditions. The negative regression coefficients for temperature and precipitation indicate that grasslands are mainly found in the colder and dry regions; the northern steppe regions and grasslands on the Qinghai-Tibetan plateau. In these areas it is indeed climate that makes grassland the climax vegetation while the areas are unsuited for cultivation. The distribution of grassland is positively correlated with the percentage of the population older than 15 years that is illiterate and negatively correlated with the rural population density. We can interpret these results by considering the percentage illiterate population a proxy of the remoteness of the area. Sparsely populated areas at large distances from the cities often have higher percentages of illiterate population. These are the areas where grasslands are found.

3.1.2 Ecuador

A multiple regression analysis for different land use types was done for Ecuador at 6 different aggregation levels (de Koning et al. 1998). The lowest aggregation level consisted of grid cells of 9.25 × 9.25 km, while the higher levels were aggregations of 2 × 2 cells up to 6 × 6 cells. Analysis was done unstratified for the whole country, as well as stratified for the three main eco-regions—Pacific coast,

Land Use and Cover Change

Andean Highlands, and the Amazon. Table 2 provides the results for the unstratified analysis of the land use type arable crops at three aggregation levels, giving the 7 main factors in the regression models.

Table 2   Multiple regression models (factors and standardized regression coefficients (stb)), explaining the area of arable crops in Ecuador for 1991 at different aggregation levels

1 grids (9.3 × 9.3 km) $r^2 = 0.48$		3 grids (27.8 × 27.8 km) $r^2 = 0.65$		5 grids (46.3 × 46.3 km) $r^2 = 0.77$	
Factor	stb*	Factor	stb*	Factor	stb*
rural population	0.31	rural population	0.43	rural population	0.57
average soil fertility	−0.26	rural illiteracy	0.27	precipitation	−0.23
rural illiteracy	−0.25	precipitation	−0.23	total population	0.20
precipitation	−0.21	average soil fertility	−0.22	rural illiteracy	0.19
sandy soils	0.20	steep slopes	−0.17	agric. labour force	0.16
urban distance	−0.17	river distance	−0.13	steep slopes	−0.15
steep slopes	−0.17	total population	0.10	river distance	−0.10

*all coefficients significant at 0.05.

The correlation coefficient increases with the aggregation level. At all levels a strong positive relation was found with rural population density. At the higher aggregation levels total population density becomes increasingly important, indicating the influence of urban population in the area. The positive relation with rural illiteracy (that can be considered a proxy of access to information and education) indicates the occurrence of arable crops (most of which are subsistence crops) in the less endowed areas. A fairly constant negative relationship is found between arable crops and a high percentage of steep slopes which are difficult to cultivate and have high erosion risks. Less arable crops are grown in areas with high precipitation, like the tropical climate zones in the Amazon and northern part of the Pacific coast. Soil fertility and texture only contribute to explanation of the area of arable crops at the lower aggregation levels. The preference for proximity to urban centres is likely to be related to access and size of urban markets, while rivers offer transport, access and irrigation opportunities.

It can be concluded that the regression factors and their relative contribution to the explanation of the area of arable crops vary with the aggregation level.

3.1.3 Costa Rica

Veldkamp and Fresco (1997a) constructed multiple regression models for the spatial structure of land use in Costa Rica for the situation of 1973 and 1984. At the finest level of data aggregation a stepwise regression procedure was used to identify which factors could be used to describe the land use distribution. Based on these factors multiple regression models at different aggregation levels 1, 4, 9, 16 and 25 grid cells respectively) were calculated. This procedure keeps the same parameters in the analysis for the different aggregation levels instead of allowing new factors to enter at other aggregation levels, as was possible in the Ecuador case-study described above. Table 3 gives the results of the multiple regression for the distribution of permanent crops in 1973. The factors that contributed to the explanation of the distribution of permanent crops were the size of the agricultural labour force, the urban population density and the amount of relief.

Table 3   Multiple regression models (factors and standardized regression coefficients) explaining the area devoted to permanent crops in Costa Rica for 1973 at different aggregation levels

Factor	1 grid (56 km^2) r^2=0.45	4 grids (225 km^2) r^2=0.40	9 grids (506 km^2) r^2=0.67	16 grids (900 km^2) r^2=0.72	25 grids (1406 km^2) r^2=0.66
agricultural labour force	0.78	0.61	0.70	0.90	0.84
urban population	−0.18	0.11	0.22	−0.02	−0.02
relief	−0.05	−0.04	−0.09	−0.07	−0.06

The agricultural labour force has a strong positive relationship with permanent crops at all aggregation levels, whereas urban population has alternating negative and positive relationships, and relief displays only a slight negative relationship with permanent crops. The same pattern was observed for the 1984 data (not displayed). From the data it is clear that the permanent crops are mainly found in relatively flat areas (negative relation with relief) and in areas with a substantial agricultural labour force. The changing contributions of urban population may be explained by a spatial scale effect. Permanent crops are not found too near the urban centres (negative relationship at detailed scales), but preferably at a convenient transportable distance from the urban population (positive contribution optimum at aggregation level of 9 grids).

3.2 Overall Interpretation of the Case-studies

The three case-studies presented on the spatial distribution of land use indicate that it is possible to explain the spatial structure of land use as a function of biophysical and socio-economic factors. All three case-studies illustrate the importance of the extent of rural population or agricultural labour force for the distribution of cultivated land. The biophysical conditions, especially soil conditions and topography, also have an important, but less pronounced, influence on the distribution of land use. Surprisingly, the influence of climate is not very structural.

The case-studies from Ecuador and Costa Rica reveal that the level of aggregation of data influences the results. This scale dependency of the land use system results in changes in the factors contained in the multiple regression models (Ecuador) and in changes in the contribution of the different factors. The Costa Rica case showed that a contribution can even change from negative to positive depending on the level of aggregation. The changes with aggregation level can be attributed to changes in variability. At the detailed scales the relationships are strongly influenced by the variability in observations while at the coarser scales the general trends have a larger contribution because the variability is obscured by the high level of aggregation. The Costa Rica case indicated that the scale dependency is also caused by factors that act over a considerable distance such as urban population concentrations. Depending on the scale of analysis these factors will affect the relationships found.

As a consequence of the scale dependency in land use systems one should use relations derived at a certain aggregation level only for analysis and implementation at the same aggregation level. Errors will be induced when relations derived at detailed scales are used at highly aggregated scales or the other way around.

However, the scale dependencies do not restrict our research possibilities, they also contain valuable information. By combining coarse and detailed scale analysis a more complete description of the land use system is obtained including general trends, local variations and factors that influence land use over some distance.

3.3 Modelling Results

An example of the results of model simulations is shown in Fig. 3 for the changes in grassland area in a base scenario. This example shows a growing grassland area due to increased demand for animal

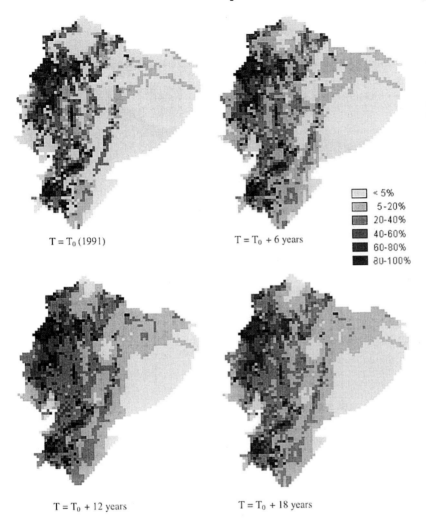

$T = T_0 (1991)$ $T = T_0 + 6$ years

☐	< 5%
☐	5-20%
▨	20-40%
▩	40-60%
■	60-80%
■	80-100%

$T = T_0 + 12$ years $T = T_0 + 18$ years

Fig. 3 Changes in grassland area under a baseline scenario. Percentage of the cell area under grassland is indicated in the figure legend

products that is the result of a growing population. It should be realized that here only relative cell surface fractions of one land use type are given. For a complete interpretation of land use changes, the other land use types have to be taken into account as well. The actual data can be analyzed and specific areas of interest can be located. A selection of the results can be seen at the website: *http:/ /www.gis.wau.nl/~landusel/clue.html.*

4. CONCLUSIONS

This paper indicates the importance of understanding the dynamics of land use change in a spatial explicit way. To incorporate spatial explicit information on land use in a dynamic model, the spatial structure of land use needs to be understood. A stepwise regression procedure was presented that identifies and quantifies factors that explain the structure of land use from a large set of potential explaining factors. The factors comprise both socio-economic and biophysical parameters such as soil conditions, altitude, population density and population composition. The different case-studies indicate that the spatial structure of land use is strongly scale-dependent. The multi-scale analysis allows for a more complete description of land use. Implementation in a dynamic land use change model will be useful to explore the spatial pattern of land use change under different scenarios of population growth and food demand. In combination with studies based on quantitative land evaluation methods and multi-criteria models such as interactive linear-programming models (de Wit et al. 1988; WRR, 1992) and studies exploring yield potentials (Penning de Vries et al. 1995) this approach will lead to a more complete description of land use and land use changes.

5. ACKNOWLEDGEMENTS

This research was supported by the Dutch National Research Programme on Global Air Pollution and Climate Change (NRP).

REFERENCES

Brown, L.R. 1995. Who will feed China? Wake-up call for a small planet. The Worldwatch Environmental Alert Series. New York.

Brown, S., Iverson, L.R. and A.E. Lugo. 1994. Use of GIS for estimating potential and actual forest biomass for continental South and Southeast Asia. In: *The effect of land-use change on atmospheric CO_2 concentrations*, V.H. Dale (Ed.), Springer-Verlag, New York.

Groot, W.T. de and E.M. Kamminga. 1995. Forest, People, Government. A policy-oriented analysis of the social dynamics of tropical deforestation. Main report of the project 'Local Actors and Global Tree Cover Policies'. Centre of Environmental Science. CML report No. 120. Leiden.

Hall, C.A.S., Tian, H., Qi, Y., Pontius, G. and J. Cornell. 1995. Modelling spatial and temporal patterns of tropical land use change. Journal of Biogeography 22: 753-757.

Kok, K. and Veldkamp, A. 1999. Multi-scale land use change modelling using the CLUE framework. In: *Tools for land use analysis at different scales* B.A.M. Bouman, H.G.P. Jansen, R.A. Schipper, H. Hengsdijk and A. Nieuwenhuyse, *With case-studies from Costa Rica*. Kluwer Academic Publishers-Dordrecht.

Koning, G.H.J. de, Veldkamp, A. and L.O. Fresco, 1998. Land use in Ecuador: a statistical analysis at different aggregation levels. Agriculture, Ecosystems and Environment 70: 231-247.

Koning, G.H.J. de, Verburg, P.H., Veldkamp, A. and L.O. Fresco, 1999. Multi-scale modelling of land use change dynamics in Ecuador. Agricultural Systems 61: 77-93.

Nuhn, H. 1978. Atlas Preliminar de Costa Rica, Informacion geografica regional. San José, Costa Rica.

Penning de Vries, F.W.T., Keulen, H. van and R. Rabbinge. 1995. Natural resources and limits of food production in 2040. In: *Eco-regional approaches for sustainable land use and food production*, J. Bouma et al. (Eds), 65-87.

Skole, D. and C. Tucker. 1993. Tropical deforestation and habitat fragmentation in the Amazon: satellite data from 1978 and 1988. Science 260: 1905-1910.

Smaling, E.M.A. and L.O. Fresco. 1993. A decision-support model for monitoring nutrient balances under agricultural land use (NUTMON). Geoderma 60: 235-256.

Turner (II) B.L., Ross, R.H. and D.L. Skole. 1993. Relating land use and global land cover change. IGBP Report No. 24, HDP Report no. 5., 65 pp.

Turner (II) B.L., Meyer, W.B. and D.L. Skole. 1994. Global land use/land cover change: towards an integrated study. AMBIO 23: 91-95.

Turner (II) B.L., Skole, D., Sanderson, S., Fischer, G., Fresco, L. and R. Leemans. 1995. Land-Use and Land-Cover Change; Science/Research Plan. IGBP Report No. 35; HDP Report No. 7.

UNEP/DEIA 1997. Spatial Data Sets for Environmental Assessment: Towards Bridging the Data Gap—UNEP/DEIA/TR.97-4 A. Singh, E. Fosnight and R. Rykhus (Eds), Division of Environment Information and Assessment. United Nations Environment Programme.

Veldkamp, A. and L.O. Fresco. 1996. CLUE-CR: an integrated multi-scale model to simulate land use change scenarios in Costa Rica. Ecological Modelling 91: 231-248.

Veldkamp, A. and L.O. Fresco. 1997a. Reconstructing Land Use Drivers and their Spatial Scale Dependence for Costa Rica (1973 and 1984). Agricultural Systems, Vol. 55, No. 1, 19-43.

Veldkamp, A. and L.O. Fresco 1997b. Exploring Land Use Scenarios. An Alternative Approach Based on Actual Land Use. Agricultural Systems 55: 1-17.

Verburg, P.H., Veldkamp, A. and J. Bouma, 1999a. Simulation of changes in the spatial pattern of land use in China. Applied Geography 19: 211-233.

Verburg, P.H., G.H.J. de Koning, K. Kok, A. Veldkamp and J. Bouma. 1999b. A spatial explicit allocation procedure for modelling the pattern of land use change based upon acutal land use. Ecological Modelling 116: 45-61.

Verburg, P.H., A. Veldkamp and J. Bouma. 1999c. Land use change under conditions of high population pressure: The case of Java. Global Environmental Change 9: 303-312.

Wit, C.T. de, Keulen, H. van, Seligman, N.G. and I. Spharim. 1988. Application of interactive multiple goal programming techniques for analysis and planning of regional agricultural development. Agricultural Systems 26: 211-230.

WRR (Netherlands Scientific council for Government Policy). 1992. Ground for choices. Four perspectives for the rural areas in the European Community. Report to the Government 42, SDU Uitgeverij, The Hague, 144 pp.

CHAPTER 3

Information System for Monitoring of Land Use/Cover Changes

(Vladimir Kremsa*)

1. INTRODUCTION

Landscape development results from five broad natural processes: geomorphology, climate, the establishment of plants and animals, soil development and natural disturbances.

Human influences increase landscape heterogeneity in three primary ways: (1) rhythms of natural disturbances, ranging from one day to a few centuries long, are modified through agricultural and forestry practices; (2) the methods of landscape modification have increased in number and effectiveness (constructing buildings and communication routes, developing agriculture, extracting renewable resources, etc.); (3) the aggregation process is related to the centralization of necessities, the diversification or specialization of human roles, the construction of sacred and other monuments, and the development of politics.

2. LANDSCAPE ECOLOGY

2.1 Landscape Ecology Concept

Landscape ecology focuses on three characteristics of the landscape: 1) *structure*: the spatial relationships among the distinctive ecosystems (elements) present (the distribution of energy, materials, and species in relation to the sizes, shapes, numbers, kind and configurations of the

*Research Center for Applied Science and Advanced Technology (CICATA-IPN), Legaria 694, Col. Irrigacion, Mexico City 11500, Mexico

ecosystems); 2) *function*: the interactions among the spatial elements (the flow of energy, materials, and species among the component ecosystems); and 3) *change*: the alternation in the structure and function of the ecological mosaic over time.

2.2 Landscape Ecology Research

Landscape studies have always posed difficult quantitative problems for ecologists (Lipsky and Kremsa, 1994). Although different variables may be measured, repeated observations in time and space are often not available at the landscape scale.

Landscape ecology emphasizes large areas and the ecological effects of the spatial patterning of ecosystems. Specifically, it considers the development and dynamics of spatial heterogeneity, interactions and exchanges across heterogeneous landscapes, the influences of spatial heterogeneity on biotic and abiotic processes, and the management of spatial heterogeneity.

Quantitative methods that link spatial patterns and ecological processes at broad spatial and temporal scales are needed both in basic ecological research and in applied environmental problems for monitoring land use/cover changes.

2.3 Scale in Landscape Ecology

Landscapes can be observed from many points of view, and ecological processes in the landscape can be monitored and studied at different spatial and temporal scales. The consideration of spatial patterns distinguishes landscape ecology from traditional ecological studies, which frequently assume that systems are spatially homogeneous.

Several studies have suggested that the landscape has critical thresholds at which ecological processes will show dramatic qualitative changes. Current theoretical research also suggests that different landscape indices may reflect processes operating at different scales.

The dramatic expansion of the spatial and temporal scales at which landscape-ecological problems are to be considered has presented another difficult quantitative challenge. Ecologists now face a series of problems that require landscape, continental and global levels of information and an understanding of both short- and long-term consequences.

This problem has created new demands to understand the effect of spatial heterogeneity and to make broad-scale predictions by extrapolating from fine-scale measurements.

3. INFORMATION SYSTEM FOR MONITORING OF LAND USE/COVER CHANGES

3.1 The Role of Information System

The development of an information system that handles landscape-ecological data of a variety of scales in a hierarchical fashion which can be used in applied landscape ecology (e.g. land use/cover change monitoring) is of great importance. Such system should support the following functions. 1) It should provide a database structure for efficiently storing and managing landscape structure (land use/cover) data over a large regions; 2) enable aggregation and dis-aggregation of land use/cover data between multiple scales (regional, landscape and plot); 3) assist in the location of study plots and ecologically sensitive areas; 4) support spatial statistical analysis of ecological distributions; 5) improve remote-sensing information-extraction capabilities; and 6) provide input data/parameters for landscape, ecosystem and land use/cover modeling.

3.2 Database Structure

Research data management in landscape ecological research requires an integrated approach that involves a clear understanding of the purposes of the research program and the types of land use/cover data expected. It also involves organizational scheme which facilitates retrieval and use of land use/cover data. Awareness of technological tools which are available is also absolutely essential as also an appreciation for the future value of the database.

3.3 Hierarchical Format

The range of spatial and temporal scales of landscape (land use/cover) and ecosystem processes and the desire to assess ecological structure at the local, landscape and regional level, gives rise to the need to integrate hierarchical aspects of ecological theory and database formats.

A multi-scale information system can provide a mechanism for performing empirical evaluation of scale variations of landscape and ecosystem structure and function. Such an information system should be built on the principles of multi-stage sampling. One approach of creating a multi-scale information system is through the use of quad-tree structures.

3.4 Location Analysis

Coarsest resolution level of a hierarchical information system database can be used for location analysis, especially for locating field plots for sampling the variables. Elevation, soil and vegetation type layers are often useful for locating study plots in a manner that representatively stratifies the ecological diversity of the region.

Coarse resolution elevation data covering large areas may be readily obtained from existing digital elevation models (DEM); by digitizing small-scale topographic maps; or by generating a DEM from small-scale stereoscopic aerial photographs or stereoscopic SPOT high resolution panchromatic images.

3.5 Remote Sensing Analysis

Beyond the representation of landscape features, information system is useful in predicting consequences of an action being considered (e.g. possible impact of land use/cover change). It is also useful in evaluating results of actions that have already been taken (real impact of land use/ cover change); and for comparison of alternative actions (scenarios of land use/cover change). Certain data layers in an information system (terrain, soil, vegetation, etc.) can be useful for improving information extraction capabilities from remotely sensed data (Kremsa, 1985, 1986).

Geo-coded and terrain corrected remotely sensed image data are useful as a graphical backdrop when displaying and analysing computerized information system coverage. It can be also used to assist verification of remote sensing results and also in image processing.

3.6 Spatial Analysis

The spatial encoding structure and a large number of data elements inherent in the information system make it particularly amenable to the supporting spatial statistical analysis. Most ecological applications of such analyses assess the spatial interrelationship between environmental variables.

Information systems can be also exploited for spatial statistical analysis which compare ecological structure (e.g. land use/cover) between positions in a landscape or between regions.

To address phenomena that depend on spatial pattern, we must find better ways to quantify patterns of variability in space and time and to understand the causes and consequences of pattern (land use/cover) and how patterns vary with scale.

3.7 Temporal Analysis

An a-temporal information system describes only one state of land use/cover data. This means that historical states are essentially forgotten and the anticipated or forecast future land use/cover cannot be treated.

A temporal information system, in contrast, would trace the changing state of a study area (land use/cover monitoring), storing historic and anticipated geographic/ecological states.

By storing temporal information on-line, a temporal information system could respond to the following queries. Where and when did landscape (land use/cover) change occur? What types of landscape (land use/cover) change occurred? What is the rate of landscape (land use/cover) change? What is the periodicity of landscape (land use/cover) change?

Given access to these types of data, the software might asses: whether temporal patterns exist; what trends are apparent; what processes underline the landscape (land use/cover) change, etc. Such assessment could form the basis for understanding the causes of landscape (land use/cover) change, leading to a better understanding of the processes at work in a landscape.

3.8 Intelligent Information System

The utility of conventional information system can be greatly expanded by adding artificial intelligence methodologies. The resulting product is an intelligent information system. The artificial intelligence environment can enhance the functionality of an information system in three principal ways: 1) automation of interpreting relations within and among landscape (land use/cover) data themes; 2) selection of appropriate analytical solutions of landscape ecological problems (e.g. land use/cover changes); and 3) guidance in use of the system.

3.9 Landscape Modeling

Landscape ecological modeling can be described as involving the following general steps: 1) collection of coordinated biological and environmental data over the full range of environmental situations possible, 2) construction of a general model of land use/cover change based of the full range of environmental data; 3) simulation of land use/cover change, using a large environmental database, in order to depict the geoecology of the situations; 4) quantification and other interpretation of results of land use/cover change monitoring; 5) validation of land use/cover change model, using independent hard data from many situations.

The advent of bigger and faster computers, remote sensing, and the detection of long-term changes in ecosystem and landscape patterns has allowed the development of a new class of dynamic spatial simulation models of ecosystems and landscape (land use/cover). Landscape models have the potential to map the flow of energy, matter, and information; designate source, sink, and receptor areas; predict succession in two- and three-dimensional space; determine cumulative thresholds for anthropogenic substances, etc.

Models in landscape ecology applied to land use/cover monitoring can also be used to quantitatively describe spatial landscape level phenomena (e.g. land use/cover distribution); predict the temporal evolution of landscapes (e.g. land use/cover future changes); and integrate between and among spatial and temporal scales. A dynamic information system provides the basis of simulation modeling of dynamic (i.e. time-dependent) landscape processes.

4. CURRENT TRENDS IN ADVANCED TECHNOLOGIES

4.1 Geographical Information Systems

Current trends in GIS are increasing availability of digital data sets; increased system processing power and software functionality; increased initial awareness of the costs and benefits of GIS for update of large spatial data; increasing concern regarding issues of accuracy and precision; improvement in riser interfaces to GIS; hardware-small stand-alone machines with large memories; substantial computation power and high resolution color graphics displays; increase in the complexity of problems and increased demand for GIS capabilities and development of GIS industry; potential for exponential growth in the volume of geo-referenced data in the next decade GPS satellites, remote sensing; increase of hardware and peripherals capability and decline in cost (communications, networking, distributed processing, etc.); the proliferation of powerful systems because of combined impact of hardware, software, communications and data volume; lack of trained personnel; important role of network in facilitating corporate objectives; faster and cheaper hardware components as a result of processor miniaturization and densification; popularity of object oriented programming; need for system integration; corporate-wide approaches required by organizations; and data quality.

4.2 Remote Sensing

Current trends in remote sensing show an exponential increase in the quality of data and range of data types being produced by earth observing satellites; increase in the spatial, spectral and temporal resolution and in the precision of the recording of such data; significant improvements in our capacity to store and manipulate the large data sets; growing availability of local satellite data receiving stations and of global communication network; increasing sophistication of software packages to analyze remotely sensed data; and increasing demand for user training.

4.3   GIS/Remote Sensing Integration

The following trends in GIS/RS integration could be identified: end products of remote sensing are increasingly being produced in digital formats to be used with GIS; the most promising areas that have emerged recently can be associated with automated DEM (digital elevation model) generation, change detection and database productions; satellite imaging can be used with DEM to produce realistic perspective views of the ground (landscape modeling, terrain visualization) even simulating passage using video recording; manufacturers have started offering integrated solutions and/or standard interfaces between different systems to facilitate data integration; the automated integration process accelerated by recent developments based on artificial intelligence and expert systems; the progress in display systems, storage devices, advanced computing architecture (workstations, parallel computing, networking) may shift the focus from vector-based systems to raster and/or hybrid GIS/RS systems.

4.4   Ecological Modeling

The current trends in eco-modeling can be identified as the increasing availability of generic models known to be effective for specific problems over a wide range of regions; increasing use of qualitative models, and models mixing rules and functional relationships; the embedding of models of comprehensive GIS in decision system; and use of expert systems to aid users in gaining the full power of such integrated systems.

4.5   Modeling/GIS Integration

The employment of dynamic simulation models in connection with GIS offers the following perspectives: system state changes can be registered in the spatial and temporal dimensions; backward linkages and spatial interactions of processes can be registered; the calculation of three-dimensional transport process is done on the basis of a relief-substrate model; prognosis of the occurring processes in the temporal and spatial dimensions; scenarios for the derivation of alternative procedures; studies of the spatial variability of structural values enable statements concerning the accuracy of results of simulation calculations; due to the increasing availability of multi-temporal remote sensing data, more space-related data for dynamic GIS methods will be available in the future.

5. CONCLUSIONS

Future directions in quantitative landscape ecology in general are discussed in Naveh and Lieberman (1993), Kremsa (1989, 1990, 1993, 1995, 1996), and in previously cited sources.

The questions that landscape ecologists need to ask about the landscape structure (land use/cover) and the human impact upon it are complex and highly demanding of intellectual frameworks. Land use/ cover change is only one example. The growth of the discipline has in recent years been stimulated by access to the new technologies for handling spatial and temporal information, which may help us to overcome some of the practical difficulties we face.

But investment in technology is only worthwhile if it allows us to solve outstanding scientific problems or to look at the landscape (land use/cover) change in new and more perceptive ways. Future research should be oriented toward testing land use/cover change hypotheses in actual landscapes. Theoretical and empirical work should progress jointly, ideally through an iterative sequence of land use/cover change model and field experiment.

New technologies are increasingly being used in combination. These interdisciplinary approaches already provide promising tools for efficient storage, query, information extraction and integration of remotely sensed data. The function of advanced technologies is especially seen as one of the key research fields in spatial and temporal data handling over the next decade.

Key issues in the future use and development of these information technologies include: the question of scale in scientific analysis and policy making; infrastructural investments for the successful adoption of technologies; accuracy in physical measurement and in interpretation and transformation; standardization of transfer formats for spatial data; timeliness of access to data; trends in technological progress; and clear and wider understanding of the role of science and technology in human affairs (e.g. land use/cover change).

REFERENCES

Kremsa, V. 1985. Remote Sensing of Agricultural Landscape Ecology. In: *2nd Remote Sensing Conference* Proceedings, Czechoslovak Society for Science and Technology, Prague, pp. 183-192 (In Czech).

Kremsa, V. 1986. *Remote Sensing Information for Management of Ecological Activities in Agricultural Landscape on Local and Regional Levels.* Czechoslovak Academy of Sciences (In Czech).

Kremsa, V. 1989. Applications of Remote Sensing in Landscape Ecology. In: *Methods of Landscape Ecological Analysis and Synthesis.* Conference Proceedings, Institute of Landscape Ecology, Academy of Sciences, Ceske Budejovice. pp. 77-93 (In Czech).

Kremsa, V. 1990. Remote Sensing in Landscape Ecology Projects. In: *Landscape Ecology.* Proceedings of the International Conference, Institute of Landscape Ecology, Czechoslovak Academy of Sciences, Ceske Budejovice, pp. 19-21.

Kremsa. V. 1993. Advanced Technologies for Landscape Ecology and Management. In: *GIS for Environment.* Jagiellonian University, Krakow, Poland, 25-27 November 1993. pp. 123-127.

Kremsa, V. 1995. Landscape Monitoring: Trends in Advanced Technologies. In: *Historical Changes of Ecological Situations In People-Environment Relationships.* Symposium Proceedings of the IGU (International Geographic Union) Commission Historical Monitoring of Environmental Change, Prihrazy, Czech Republic, 18-21 August, 1994. pp. 113-117.

Kremsa, V. 1996. Information System for Landscape Ecology. In: *I Foro sobre Aplicación de los sistemas de información geográfica. Universidad Autónoma de Estado de México, Facultad de Geografía, Toluca, 23 de oct.-5 de noviembre de 1996,* 55-63 pp.

Lipsky, Z. and Kremsa, V. 1994. Landscape (ecological) mapping in the Czech Republic. In: *Remote Sensing in Landscape Ecological Mapping.* European Collaborative Programme Workshop Proceedings. Katholieke Universiteit Leuven, Leuven, Belgium 17-19 March 1994, pp. 153-161.

Naveh, Z. and Lieberman, A.S. 1993. *Landscape Ecology. Theory and Application.* Springer-Verlag, New York, Berlin & Heidelberg. 2nd Edition.

➢ **4**

Spatial Patterns of Land Use and Cover Change:
Processes, Causes and Consequences in the Republic of Ireland

(Desmond A. Gillmor*)

1. INTRODUCTION

The processes of land use and cover change can vary over short distances and even within a small country. The extent and ways in which these changes in various parts of a country differ, hidden by national trends, are often ignored. The variations may be due to land users in different areas responding differently to national influences depending on particular circumstances, or they may be the outcome of certain regional and local influences, or there may be a combination of these. Whatever the reasons, differential spatial changes combine to yield aggregate national trends, so that determining them would contribute to a better understanding of land use and cover change at the national level.

The purpose of this paper is to investigate patterns of land use and cover change within the small state of the Republic of Ireland at the spatial level of the county over the twentieth century. This timespan was chosen in accordance with the view of the Land Use and Cover Change Programme that a historical perspective over a significant time is desirable (Turner (II) et al. 1995).

The land uses for which data from the beginning to the end of the century were available were selected for investigation. There has never been a land use survey of the Republic of Ireland and the only land cover mapping was done using remote sensing under the

*Department of Geography, Trinity College, University of Dublin, Dublin 2, Ireland

European Union CORINE Project in the early 1990s. Thus, this paper relies mainly on the detailed agricultural census returns for the years 1900 and 1997. The latter is the last year of the century for which statistics are available by county but figures for pigs and poultry have not been released since 1993. Agriculture accounts for over 70% of the land in the Irish Republic and a further 8% is under forest cover, for which some data are included in the agricultural census. The remaining land comprises principally rock, heath, bog, marsh, roads, recreational land, rural buildings and urban development, none of which has appropriate available data.

Agriculture in the Republic of Ireland comprises essentially mixed livestock production based on grass with some arable cropping. The dominance of grass in Irish agricultural land use is indicated by the fact that of the total area farmed in 1997, 51.3% was pasture, 28.7% was grass conserved as silage and hay and 10.7% was rough grazing, whereas only 9.3% was under arable crops. Farm output is dominated by livestock and livestock products, with a high level of specialization in dairying and beef production. The percentage structure of gross agricultural output in 1997 was: milk—33.9, cattle—33.2, crops—11.8, pigs—7.7, sheep—6.2, poultry—4.5 and horses—2.6. The farming system is essentially based on small to medium sized family farms, with almost universal owner occupancy.

Despite the small size of the country and the high level of national specialization, there are distinct spatial patterns in contemporary Irish agriculture (Horner et al. 1984). Farm size diminishes towards the west and this tends to be in direct relationship with declining land quality. Arable farming is confined largely to the east and south, where the climate is driest and sunniest and soils are most favourable. Dairying is most intensive in the southwest and to a lesser extent in the northern area but dairy farms are seen in most parts of the country. Beef cattle production is the most widespread enterprise, being practised on most farms, though reliance on cattle is greatest in the midlands and west. Sheep are very important in and adjacent to the upland areas which fringe the country but there are substantial numbers on the lowlands too.

2. AGRICULTURAL LAND

The area covered by crops and pastures is the best indicator of agricultural land in the Republic of Ireland. Combining arable crops and grass, it corresponds with the improved or enclosed agricultural land. Some additional land is used for agricultural purposes, mainly rough grazing for sheep and cattle on mountain, hill and bog land. In 1997 there were 473,900 ha of rough grazing, covering 6.9% of the state. Data on rough grazing are available for only a few years during the twentieth century and they are not comparable. This relates in part to interpretation of the boundary between rough grazing and improved pasture. The definition of what constitutes crops and pasture has been changed several times. This renders the decline of 22% in crops and pasture imprecise, though it is certain that the area has diminished. While the magnitude of change may be uncertain, much more reliance can be placed on the spatial pattern portrayed in Fig. 1, as the definition and alterations to it have been at the national level.

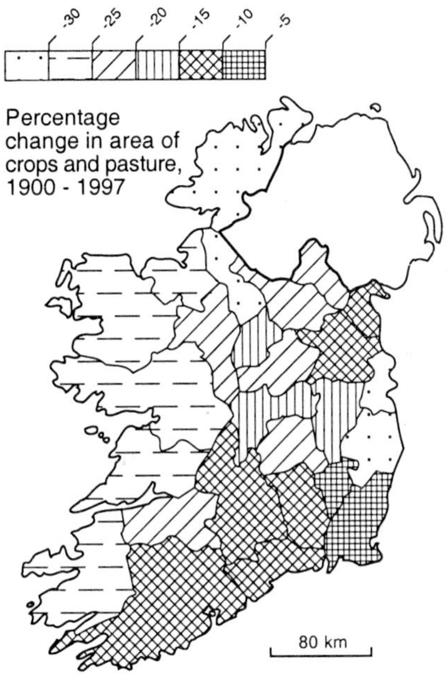

Decline in crops and pasture has mainly represented retreat

Percentage change in area of crops and pasture, 1900 - 1997

Fig. 1   Change in area of crops and pasture, 1900-1997

of agriculture from land least suited to it physically, principally on the mountains, hills and bogs. The areas with this poorer land are also those which have experienced the greatest loss of rural population. This correspondence between land type and population trend is a major influence accounting for the fact that the decline in crops and pasture was substantially greater in the west and northwest than in the south and east (Fig. 1). The loss was least in the high-income arable cropping and dairying areas of the southeast and south. The cause of the decline in agricultural land on the mideast coast was very different from that in the west, being attributable mainly to urban expansion in Dublin and north Wicklow, though retreat from unfavourable land was a contributory factor in the mountainous part of Wicklow.

While there was a decrease in agricultural land as a whole, the constituents of arable crops and grassland contributed differently, the rates of decline being 43 and 19% respectively. This shift represents the strong reinforcement of pastoral emphasis in Irish farming in the twentieth century. It had a markedly differing spatial expression, however, as indicated by the huge variation in the pattern of change in arable cropping by county (Fig. 2). While the area of tillage declined by 91% in the western province of Connacht, it increased by 3% in the eastern province of Leinster. Irish environmental conditions are less favourable for the growth of arable crops than for the growth of grass and so tillage is much more concentrated in those parts of the country where the climate is driest and sunniest and where soil conditions are most suitable for cropping. Another consideration is the interrelationship between farm size and technological change. With increasing mechanization, there has been a shift in arable cropping towards the larger farms and fields which are predominant in the east. Decline in crop growth for use on the farm has been another factor in the process of spatial change, this subsistence element is greatest on western farms.

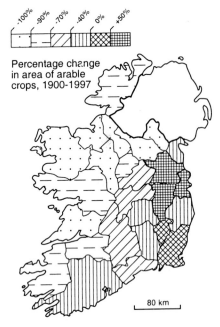

Fig. 2   Change in area of arable crops, 1900-1997

3. CATTLE AND SHEEP

Cattle and sheep have been the major growth sectors of Irish agriculture over the twentieth century, numbers expanding by 101 and 106% respectively. They are increasingly dominating Irish land use and agricultural output. This reflects differential price trends in favour of livestock and livestock products when compared to arable crops, combined with the increased tendency to exploit the country's comparative advantage in grass-based production. Major expansion of sheep has been more recent than that of cattle; the latter grew with the development of the Irish agricultural economy from 1960 whereas sheep numbers increased rapidly only from 1980 with improved EU (European Union) support and market conditions. The spatial patterns of these changes have differed substantially (Figs. 3 and 4).

Change in the distribution of all cattle combined is shown in Fig. 3 as no clear and consistent distinction between the dairy and beef sectors is possible over the century. Additionally the two enterprises are closely

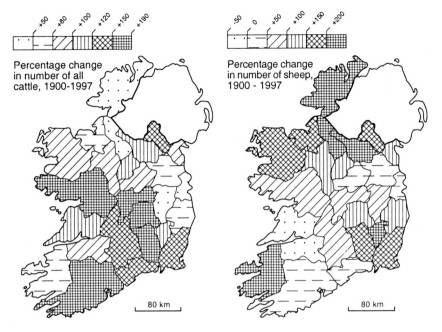

Fig. 3   Change in number of all
cattle, 1900-1997

Fig. 4   Change   in   number   of
sheep, 1900-1997

integrated in Ireland in that dairy herds provide substantial numbers of stock which are reared for beef purposes. With beef cattle being kept on most farms and in all parts of the country, its spatial pattern is the one which has undergone least change amongst all farm enterprises.

Traditional dairy farming regions have been in the southwest within the province of Munster and a less intensive belt extends across the northern counties. In the 1960s and 1970s dairying extended into many other parts of the country as it offered financial benefits and was actively promoted. Dairy cows, kept mainly to produce milk for human consumption, were first distinguished from other cows in the agricultural statistics in the 1970s. Between 1980 and 1997, the proportion of the national dairy herd in Munster increased from 56 to 60%, indicating a reversal of the earlier dispersal tendency as many marginal producers withdrew from dairying and the enterprise became more concentrated on specialized farms. These locational trends in dairying have contributed to the pattern of change in total cattle scenario over the century (Fig. 3), in that the highest growth rates were not in the intensive core dairy area of Limerick and parts of adjoining countries, where densities were already high, but instead in a belt of encircling countries. The northern dairying belt contracted as the enterprise declined in the western half and intensified within Cavan and Monaghan.

The only county in which there was a decline in the number of cattle was Dublin, a consequence of urbanization and the conversion from grass to arable crops. Dairying expanded in adjoining mideastern counties, initially to supply the Dublin market, but there had been high densities of other cattle in this traditional cattle fattening region, so that growth in total cattle over the century was low. Another explanatory factor was the increase in arable cropping there too (Fig. 2). The other area of low growth in cattle numbers, in the northwest, represents very different farming circumstances. It reflects the lesser level of agricultural development in general in that area with difficult environmental conditions and a small farm size.

In the northwestern area, conversely, there were high growth rates in sheep numbers, though it should be recognized that in the interior this increase was from a small base (Fig. 4). The growth resulted in part from the tendency for sheep production to become more concentrated in upland areas, where the comparative advantage of sheep was greatest under difficult environmental conditions, while dairy and beef production were expanding on the lowlands. This occurred also in the other upland areas of the west and southwest. The effect on the figure for the western county of Galway was concealed by the fact that there had been already a high density in the traditional sheep grazing area on the dry limestone lowland in the east of the county. These spatial trends reflect in part the fact that cattle and sheep are competitive enterprises in the use of available grassland. As the competitive position of sheep production increased considerably relative to beef cattle in the 1980s, numbers expanded on the lowlands also. The only area of decline in sheep numbers over the century was Limerick-Clare, all the more striking because densities were low there at the outset. This reflects the fact that sheep are not favoured on heavy soils where dairying is important.

4. PIGS AND POULTRY

The most pronounced spatial changes in agricultural production were seen in the intensive enterprises of pig and poultry production. This resulted mainly from the structural transformation that occurred in these industries. Traditionally they had been regarded as the farmyard enterprises, with the animals and birds occupying small houses in the farmstead and using the farmyard and land adjacent to it. They were associated especially with small farms, the densities of pigs and poultry diminished with the increased size of the holding. Major change occurred in the second half of the century as output came to be concentrated increasingly in large intensively managed production units. As efficiency and output increased, market prices diminished in relative terms, so that production in small units became increasingly uneconomical and most producers withdrew from these enterprises. The outcome has been a greatly increased spatial concentration in those areas where the large production units have been established. Concentration has occurred in particular in the northern counties of Cavan and Monaghan, where development may be interpreted as a southward extension across the border of industries which are much more important in Northern Ireland. The spatial concentration has occurred to the extent that statistics by county have not been released since 1993 because of fear of breach of confidentiality with regard to individual large pro-ducers, so that change is restricted to 1900-1993 in Figs. 5 and 6.

The most striking feature of Fig. 5 is the extent of the decline in pig production in the western counties. Their small-scale production

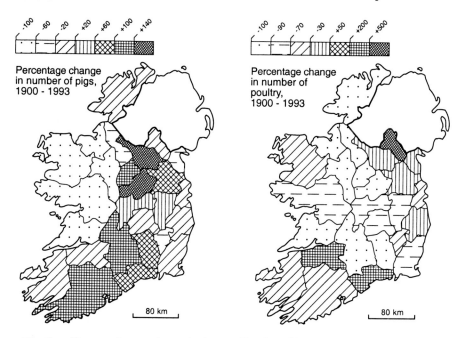

Fig. 5   Change in number of pigs, 1900-1993

Fig. 6   Change in number of poultry, 1900-1993

diminished but the west was less suited to the establishment of large units than places to the east which were nearer to feed supplies and markets and where more enterprise and capital was available. The two adjacent coun-ties with the highest increases are very different in that the five-fold increase in pigs in Cavan was in a county where production had been important traditionally, whereas the three-fold growth in Westmeath was from a low base and was mainly an extension of activity southward from Cavan. In 1900, 5% of the pigs in the state were in Cavan and by 1993 the proportion had risen to 23%. This has involved the development of a specialized area of pig production with a substantial number of large units in the east of county. Elsewhere the distribution pattern that has evolved is a patchy one with dispersed individual units, though there has been significant expansion in the southern county of Cork which traditionally had one of the highest densities of pigs.

Spatial concentration has been even more striking in poultry production (Fig. 6). Most notable has been the increase in Monaghan's share of the national flock from 5% in 1900 to 46% by 1993. This is the highest degree of spatial concentration of any main farm enterprise in the Republic of Ireland. Monaghan had already been the leading poultry county, so this impetus and traditional skills combined with the involvement of employees of a feed compounding firm and the development of marketing and processing linkages seem to have contributed to its position of preeminence. The remaining two counties in which there was substantial growth over the period, involving more than a doubling of poultry numbers, were Waterford and Limerick. This has been the result of associated production and processing develop-ments around one centre in each county. The only other counties in which there were not substantial declines were the three adjoining Monaghan and also Wicklow, in which the position is attributable to one large firm.

5. INTENSITY OF AGRICULTURAL LAND USE

From consideration of the individual land uses, it is evident that there has been increased spatial concentration of farm enterprises over the twentieth century, as was shown to have occurred during the shorter time period of 1960-1980 (Gillmor, 1987). Furthermore, while the patterns of spatial change of the individual agricultural land uses have differed from one another, comparison of the maps suggests that some parts of the country have experienced greater overall growth in the intensity of land use than others. In order to investigate further and quantify, it is necessary to combine the enterprises in some way.

As livestock dominate Irish agricultural production, this combination can be done to a considerable extent through the use of livestock units. These units provide the most satisfactory method of equalizing the very different types of livestock based on estimated dry matter intake as indicated by physiological body weight. The coefficients applied here were based on those used by Gillmor (1970). Differences between the statistics for 1900 and the 1990s in the subdivisions within the livestock categories made full and uniform application of the detailed coefficients impossible. Instead a composite coefficient for each category of livestock had to be calculated. This was done separately for 1900 and 1993/97, using the different subdivisions of the statistics within each category of livestock, and the mean of the two values for each category was taken to provide the coefficient for this study. These mean livestock unit values were: cattle 0.67, sheep 0.16, pigs 0.18 and poultry 0.008. Application of these coefficients to the livestock numbers in 1900 and 1993/97 enabled the change in total livestock over the intervening time to be quantified by province and by county.

While the number of livestock units increased greatly in all provinces, there were substantial differences in the extent of growth even at this broad level, with the increase in Munster (108%) in the south being two-fifths larger than that in Connacht (78%) in the west. An inter-mediate rate of livestock growth in Leinster (90%) in the east was compen-sated to some extent by the fact that arable cropping expanded there. Clearly the trends in the intensity of agricultural land use were least favourable in Connacht, in that the growth in livestock units was substantially less than in the other provinces and the loss of arable cropping was greatest there.

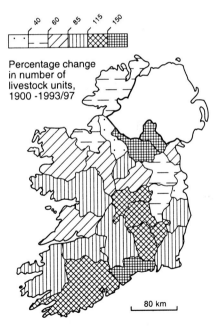

Fig. 7   Change in number of live-stock units, 1900-1993/97

Within the provinces, there was substantial variation between counties in livestock trends (Fig. 7). The only county in which there was a decline, with a loss of almost one-third, was

Dublin. The increase in livestock units was small in the adjoining counties of Meath and Kildare. These are the three counties which had the greatest expansion in arable cropping, so that their lesser livestock growth must be attributable at least in part to the conversion from pastrol to arable farming, in addition to the effect of urbanization in Dublin. Very different is the other area of low growth in livestock units in the northwest, where there was major loss of arable cropping and farming conditions are much less favourable. Expansion throughout the west was relatively low to moderate, with only Galway exceeding the national average. In marked contrast were Monaghan and Cavan in which, although part of the small-farm region, there had been a major expansion of livestock. This resulted mainly from growth in dairying and in pig and poultry production. The other counties in which there was the largest growth were concentrated in south midlands and the south.

The spatial change in the intensity of agricultural land use over the twentieth century in the Republic of Ireland indicates a major locational shift within farming towards the east. The shift has been furthest east in arable cropping and somewhat less far east in livestock production. It has been a move towards larger farms and more favourable environmental conditions for agriculture. Furthermore, investigation of the individual land uses indicates that the west has lost proportionately more of its intensive and remunerative land enterprises, principally arable cropping, dairying, pigs and poultry, accentuating the comparative disadvantage of farming in the region.

The underperformance of the west has major adverse implications not only for the farm population of the region but also for its wider economy in which agriculture plays an important role in the western society. These are the areas of greatest physical disadvantage, of smallest farm size, of substantial population decline over the century and of lowest income levels. It is the part of the country, and in particular the northwest, where rural poverty is greatest. The outcome of the spatial changes in agricultural land use has been to accentuate regional disequilibrium, despite the existence of measures to address the problems of the less developed areas.

6. FORESTS

Deforestation had occurred to the extent that less than 2% of the Republic of Ireland was under woods and plantations at the beginning of the twentieth century. Although this privately owned woodland was depleted further, active state and more recently private afforestation have led to the forest cover now being 8%. The change in forest cover over the century has been the outcome of government policies and the decisions of private landowners, both of which have varied over time and over geographic space.

Afforestation has been predominantly on land of low agricultural value, principally mountain, hill and peatland together with some farmland. Planting during the first half of the century was at a moderate rate, it was almost entirely by the state and it was principally on the lower hill land of east and midlands. Introduction of new cultivation technology and tree species after the Second World War enabled planting to increase greatly and to extend onto land with less favourable physical conditions. This was mainly up-mountain slopes, onto peat bogs and especially into the west of the country. Afforestation had been almost a state monopoly until the mid 1980s but thereafter private planting escalated in response to EU incentives. Farmers have tended to plant only land which they consider to be of low agricultural value and private afforestation in general has been substantially greatest in the west. Throughout most of the century, state policy was to minimize potential conflict between forestry and agriculture by not planting land which might be used for agriculture but this has changed with EU promotion of conversion of farmland to forestry in the 1990s.

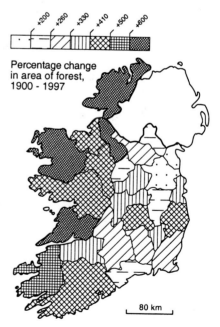

Percentage change in area of forest, 1900 - 1997

The fact that both state and private afforestation have been principally on land less suited to agriculture mainly accounts for the pattern of spatial change over the century (Fig. 8). While increases were recorded in all counties, the lowest growth rates were in the northeast, where there is least unimproved land, and the highest rates were in western counties with large areas of poor quality land. More than ten-fold growth occurred in the forest area of four of these western counties. These are areas where there has been major population decline and where the performance of agricultural land use has been below average.

Fig. 8   Change in area of forest, 1900-1997

7. ENVIRONMENTAL CONSEQUENCES

The spatial changes in the patterns of land use and cover change over the twentieth century have had substantial environmental consequences. The extension of the forest cover has been beneficial from a global perspective, with the rate of afforestation relative to the preexisting cover perhaps being higher in Ireland than anywhere else in the world. In the Irish context, however, there are detrimental dimensions to afforestation and to its concentration in certain areas. This is mainly due to the fact that, while the diminishing cover at the beginning of the century was mainly of deciduous woodland, afforestation has been largely by coniferous monoculture, dominated by sitka spruce. Effects include the imposition of monotonous geometric stands of dark trees on the landscape, the blocking of scenic views, the destruction of wildlife habitats and archaeological features, the restricted wildlife content of the new forests and the acidification of water bodies with consequent effects on aquatic life. The impact is greater due to the concentration of afforestation in places of high environmental quality in the upland and bog areas and particularly the west.

While the environmental impact of Irish agriculture is low compared to countries with more intensive and arable farming systems, the detrimental effects have been accentuated by the spatial changes which have involved greater concentrations and localizations of farm enterprises. Significant impact is associated with arable cropping, including the effects of chemical applications, of machinery usage and of hedgerow removal. These increased in intensity with the much greater concentration of tillage in the east and southeast. Fertilizer usage on arable crops and on grassland, especially on dairy farms, has contributed to the pollution of rivers and lakes, as has silage effluent and cattle waste. The expansion in silage making has been associated most closely with dairying; silage accounted for 78% of the conserved grassland in Munster as compared with 67% in Connacht in 1997 but with the differential having lessened from earlier years. The most acute localized problem of livestock waste has been in the concentrated area of pig and poultry production in Cavan and Monaghan. In this area of drumlin topography with water-retentive gley soils there has been severe eutrophication of the many lakes and rivers. A different and more widespread but nonetheless acute environmental problem has resulted from the large growth in sheep numbers in upland areas of the west. Overgrazing by sheep has led to serious land degradation through erosion of soils, peat and vegetation on hill and bog land.

The eastward shift in the intensity of agricultural land use in the twentieth century has a number of environmental implications. The expansion of production and its associated impacts have been less in the west. Thus there have been environmental benefits for the west as against the economic and social disbenefits of locational change. The disadvantages are now being compensated to some extent by the Rural Environment Protection Scheme (REPS) introduced in 1994, under which farmers undertaking environmentally sound farming techniques receive payments per hectare upto a maximum of 40 ha. While the scheme is available everywhere, participation is substantially higher in western counties. This is principally because adaptation to meet the requirements of the scheme are less with their more extensive dry cattle and sheep enterprises and the financial incentive is proportionately greater on the smaller farms. Conversely the REPS is least attractive to those farms on which the environmental benefits would be greatest, that is large intensive holdings, especially those in arable cropping and dairying, and these are mainly in the east and south. Thus an outcome of the REPS may be to reinforce the environmental consequences of the spatial shift in the intensity of agricultural land use.

8. CONCLUSION

While there has been continuity in the geography of land use and cover in the Republic of Ireland, substantial spatial change has occurred over the twentieth century. The changes have involved processes of areal specialization and concentration. They have incorporated a general shift from west to east in agricultural land use and in the opposite direction in forest cover. The economic, social and environmental consequences of these changes in land use and cover suggest that they should be recognized and addressed in public policy and in particular there is an urgent need for a national land use plan.

REFERENCES

Gillmor, D.A. 1970. Spatial distributions of livestock in the Republic of Ireland, Economic Geography, 46(4): 587-597.

Gillmor, D.A. 1987. Concentration of enterprises and spatial change in the agriculture of the Republic of Ireland, Transactions of the Institute of British Geographers, NS12, 204-216.

Horner, A.A., Walsh, J.A. and J.A. Williams. 1984, Agriculture in Ireland: a census atlas. Department of Geography, University College, Dublin.

Turner (II) B.L., Skole, D., Sanderson, S., Fischer, G., Fresco, L. and R Leemans (Eds), 1995. Land-use and land-cover change science/research plan. The International Geosphere-Biosphere Programme Report No. 35 and The Human Dimensions of Global Environmental Change Programme Report No. 7, Stockholm and Geneva.

CHAPTER 5

Land Use and Land Cover Change in Montane Mainland Southeast Asia

(Jefferson Fox*)

1. INTRODUCTION

Montane Mainland Southeast Asia is an isolated upland area constituting approximately one-half of the land area of Cambodia, Laos, Myanmar, Thailand, Vietnam, and Yunnan Province (China). The region harbors an immense wealth of natural resources including globally important stocks of biological diversity. It is home to a rich heritage of indigenous cultures and is also the headwaters of many major river systems of mainland Southeast Asia. Many parts of the region have only recently been reopened to outside influences and large portions of the physical environment as well as many social, political and economic institutions are experiencing profound and widespread change in the transition to modernity.

Shifting agriculture or swidden cultivation has been practised for centuries, if not millennia, across this region. Swiddening involves cutting living vegetation in the dry season, letting it dry, burning it late in the dry season, and then planting a crop in the ashes early in the wet season.

Swidden agriculture and its associated stages of secondary vegetation pose particular problems for monitoring because they are not captured well in traditional land cover classes of agriculture, plantation, forest, etc. Studies (Potter et. al. 1994; Kummer and Turner, 1994; Game-Tropics, 1996) suggest that between 26 and 49% of all land in Southeast Asia can be classified as 'other' where *other* is defined as

*East-West Center, 1601 East-West Road Honolulu, Hawaii 96848-1601, USA.

shrub, brush, pasture, waste and other land use categories, most of which is actually secondary vegetation.

2. METHODOLOGY

Spatial databases were developed using aerial photographs as well as Landsat Thematic Mapper images. Aerial photographs were manually interpreted and classified into 5 classes—secondary growth, swidden, paddy, cash crops and plantations, and miscellaneous. The photographs were registered to base maps and land cover categories digitized and entered into a geographic information system (GIS) database (Arc/Info software on a Sun Sparc workstation). The Landsat images, except Vietnam, were classified using an unsupervised image classification algorithm into the same land cover categories and registered to the same base maps as the photographs. For the Vietnam site a supervised land cover classification was used. Table 1 provides more information on the types of images and methods of analyses used in each study.

Table 1   Spatial data used in the 5 case-studies

	Northern Thailand Ban Pang Khum	Northeast Cambodia Ban Lung	Southern Yunnan, China Baka	Southern Yunnan, China Mengsong	Northern Vietnam Tan Minh
Aerial photographs					
Year (first set)	1954	1953	1965	1965	1952
Scale	1:50,000	1:40,000	1:35,000	1:32,000	1:40,000
Method of analysis	Manual	Manual	Manual	Manual	Manual
Field checked	No	No	No	No	No
Year (second set)	1983	1996	1992		
Scale	1:15,000	1:25,000	1:35,000		
Method of analysis	Manual	Manual	Manual		
Field checked	No	No	No		
Landsat TM images					
Year				1993	1995
Image classification				Unsupervised	Supervised
Field checked				No	Yes
Accuracy assessment					95%
Base map					
Scale	1:50,000	1:50,000	1:25,000	1:25,000	1:50,000

With the exception of Vietnam, neither the results of the manual interpretation of the aerial photographs nor of the image classifications were field checked. Hence accuracy assessments of these results could not be conducted. The researchers familiarity with the sites and the extensive field interviews conducted with residents suggest that these results are reasonably accurate and the directions in change are correct. The accuracy assessment of the Vietnam image correctly found 95% of 155 checkpoints classified after accounting for GPS surveying and image registration error.

The secondary growth or successional vegetation was further subdivided into 3 classes—closed-canopy forest, open-canopy forest, and grass, bamboo, and bushes. Given the long history of swidden cultivation throughout this region we consider it unlikely that forest conditions in any of the sites were in any way 'primary'. Secondary growth is not a simple or uniform phenomenon, but consists of a wide variety of vegetation types. Species composition and structure of secondary forest change rapidly in the course of succession and only experienced observers are able to distinguish mature secondary forest from primary forests. Young secondary forests and other formations such as grass, bamboo, and bushes can be recognized more easily as products of human pressure (Schmidt-Vogt, 1998).

The socioeconomic databases were developed through interviews with local residents as well as government officials. Researchers documented changes in national and regional policies influencing land use (e.g. tenure, taxation, credit, import and export regulations) as well as changes in infrastructure (roads and markets). Researchers conducted semi-structured informal interviews in order to identify the socioeconomic and institutional factors influencing use and management decisions regarding land use and land cover.

3. RESULTS

Table 2 (a) and (b) shows changes in land cover, size of land cover fragments, and population density. Table 3 shows the annual rate of change in land cover and human population. And Table 4 shows the annual rate of change in the mean fragment size. These tables indicate that secondary growth remained fairly stable throughout this period at all sites with the greatest change found in northern Thailand. Within the secondary growth classes, closed-canopy cover tended to be lost while the open-canopy and grass, bamboo, and bush categories tended to grow. These results also show a slight increase in the amount of land devoted to cash crops including paddy. Mean fragment sizes

Table 2(a)   Elevation, annual rainfall, and major forest types

	Northern Thailand Ban Pang Khum	Northeast Cambodia Ban Lung	Southern Yunnan, China Baka	Southern Yunnan, China Mengsong	Northern Vietnam Tan Minh
Elevation (m)	750-1850	100-400	530-1700	530-1700	800-1000
Annual rainfall (mm)[1]	3000	2000	1400	1800	1600
Major forest types[1]	Montane rain	Lowland monsoon	<1000 m lowland monsoon >1000 m broadleaf evergreen	< 1000 m lowland monsoon >1000 m broadleaf evergreen	Lowland monsoon

[1]Collins et al. 1991.

Table 2(b)   Changes in land cover mean size of fragments and human population

Land Cover	Northern Thailand Ban Pang Khum 9500 (ha)				Northeast Cambodia Ban Lung 18,500 (ha)				Southern Yunnan Baka 8800 (ha)		Southern Yunnan Mengsong 10,000 (ha)				Northern Vietnam Tan Minh 740 (ha)			
	1954		1983		1953		1996		1965	1992	1965		1993		1952		1995	
	%	Mean size (ha)	%	Mean size (ha)	%	Mean size (ha)	%	Mean size (ha)	%	%	%	Mean size (ha)	%	Mean size (ha)	%	Mean size (ha)	%	Mean size (ha)
Secondary Growth	97	24	88	11	78	129	77	44	81	83	95	70	95	17	92	37	85	2
Closed-canopy	76	219	56	84	63	250	56	41	31	76	38	198	15	63	11	20	3	1
Open-canopy	11	10	14	9	6	38	18	18	18	—	22	33	37	14	54	78	15	3
Grass, bamboo, bushes	10	6	18	3	9	47	3	7	32	7	35	71	43	17	27	22	67	2
Swidden	1	2	5	1	21	23	14	4	18	12	2	3	2	3	7	1	10	1
Paddy	1	2	2	1	—	—	<1	4	<1	<1	3	65	2	71	1	8	5	1
Cash/plantation	1	11	5	11	—	—	4	13	—	4	—	—	1	7	—	—	—	—
Miscellaneous	—	—	—	—	1	4	4	16	—	—	—	—	—	—	—	—	—	—
Total	100	17	100	8	100	58	100	14	100	100	100	51	100	16	100	13	100	2
(People/sq. km)[1]	6		16		7		30		13	32	17		30		10		75	

[1]Historical population data were available in Mengsong, Baka, and Tan Minh. At Ban Pang Khum and Ban Lung, we estimated historical population using an assumed growth rate of 3.5% per year.

Table 3 Annual rate of change in land cover and in human population

	Northern Thailand Ban Pang Khum (%) 1954/1983	Northeast Cambodia Ban Lung (%) 1953/1996	Southern Yunnan Baka (%) 1965/1992	Southern Yunnan Mengsong (%) 1965/1993	Northern Vietnam Tan Minh (%) 1952/1995
Secondary growth	-0.3	<-0.1	0.1	<0.1	-0.2
Closed-canopy	-1.0	-0.3	3.4	-3.2	-3.3
Open-canopy	0.9	2.4	—	1.7	-3.0
Grass, bamboo, bushes	2.1	-2.1	-5.2	0.8	2.0
Swidden	4.8	-0.9	-1.7	0	0.8
Paddy	2.5	17.0	0	-2.1	4.3
Cash/plantation crops	4.7	4.0	35	—	—
Miscellaneous	—	3.0	—	9.0	—
Human population	3.3	3.4	3.4	2.0	4.8

Table 4 Annual rate of change in mean fragment size

	Northern Thailand Ban Pang Khum (%)	Northeast Cambodia Ban Lung (%)	Southern Yunnan Mengsong (%)	Northern Vietnam Tan Minh (%)
	1954/1983	1953/1996	1965/1993	1952/1995
Secondary growth	–2.7	–2.5	–4.9	–6.6
Closed-canopy	–3.3	–4.1	–4.0	–6.7
Open-canopy	–0.4	–1.7	–3.0	–7.3
Grass, bamboo, bushes	–2.4	–4.3	–5.0	–5.4
Swidden	–2.4	–4.0	0	0
Paddy	–2.4	—	0.3	–4.7
Cash/plantation crops	0	5.0	—	—
Miscellaneous	—	—	—	—

throughout this period decreased in all but two cases (paddy in Mengsong and plantation crops in Ban Lung). Human population density also increased at all sites with the greatest growth occurring in Vietnam. While overall secondary growth remained stable (ranging from an annual change of – 0.3% in northern Thailand to 0.1% in Baka, Southern Yunan), large differences were observed within the sub-classes of secondary growth among the 5 sites.

4. DISCUSSION

These studies suggest that swidden cultivation has remained the dominant land use practice in this region throughout the last 50 years. This is despite the fact that every country in the region has attempted to 'control' swidden cultivation through polices that include banning shifting cultivation, declaring forest reserves from which people are excluded, resettling people into the lowlands, and introducing settled agriculture either *in situ* or in a new location.

At the gross level of secondary growth after swidden cultivation, land cover has remained stable across the region throughout this 50-year period. This level of abstraction, however, hides the major changes that have occurred within the subcategories of secondary vegetation as well as in the size of number of land cover fragments.

In the Thai, Baka-Yunnan, and Cambodia sites we see evidence that national policies that force people to restrict the area they use for swidden cultivation can work. In Mengsong-Yunnan we see evidence that state policies played a key role in the degradation of forests through poorly thought-out efforts to manage local economies. At the Vietnam site, population growth appears to have been the major factor affecting land cover. In Baka-Yunnan, however, the human population grew at about the same rate as the closed-canopy tree cover increased (3.4% per year). Hence, while population growth can cause land cover change in this region this is not always the case.

These studies also suggest that the minor amount of land use change that has occurred in the region has been a change from swidden cultivation to cash crops including both paddy rice and plantation tree crops. The number of hectares planted to these crops has remained relatively inconsequential. But in some cases the annual rates of change have been significant. In Baka-Yunnan, cash crops while not measurable (<1%) in 1965 had grown to 4% of the landscape in 1992. This represents a rate of change of approximately 35% per year. At the Cambodia site, the amount of land devoted to paddy rice grew at a rate of 17% per year. The area suitable for paddy, however, is limited to the river and stream bottoms, whereas the area suitable for plantation crops is much more extensive.

These results suggest that in most of Montane Mainland Southeast Asia two forces will increasingly determine land use systems. First, national land tenure policies—the nationalization of forest lands and efforts to increase control over upland resources by central governments—will provide a push factor making it increasingly difficult for farmers to maintain their traditional swidden land use practices. And second, market pressures—the commercialization of subsistence resources and the substitution of commercial crops for subsistence crops will provide a pull factor encouraging farmers to engage in new and different forms of commercial agriculture. Combined, these forces will eventually cause a major change in land use practices from swidden agriculture to commercial crops, and a change in land cover from secondary vegetation to monocultural agriculture.

5. CONCLUSION

These case-studies as well as other studies of swidden cultivation in Southeast Asia repeatedly conclude that the moist tropical forests of this region are impressively resilient. Under the right conditions, these forests regenerate and gradually recover after both human induced distrubances (swidden cultivation, clear-cutting) and natural events (hurricanes, landslides, lightning) (e.g. Schmidt-Vogt, 1998; Fox et. al. 1995; Cannon et al. 1998; Lawrence et al. 1998).

Natural resource managers and government planners need to recognize the benefits as well as the costs of swidden agriculture systems. A chief benefit of swidden systems may be their long-term stability. Systems of multiple landholders (such as those found in these studies) each with a small multipurpose, multispecies plot can manage a sustainable forest cover until the introduction of cash crops upsets this balance (Schmidt-Vogt, 1998).

Another argument for swidden systems may be emerging from studies of carbon dioxide levels in the US and South America. Fan et al. (1998) and Philips et al. (1998) suggest that much more carbon dioxide is absorbed in North America and the Amazon than previously believed. They suggest that earlier studies failed to note this absorption because they were based on forest inventories which missed a lot of forest regrowth on abandoned farmland and formerly logged forests and also failed to account for carbon stored in soils and wetlands. As this and other studies demonstrate (Schmidt-Vogt, 1998; Fox et al. 1995; Canon et al. 1998; Lawrence et al. 1998), upland areas of Southeast

Asia are in a constant state of flux among old growth forest cover, various forms of secondary growth, and open swidden fields. Failure to account for forest regrowth on fallow swidden fields throughout Southeast Asia could well mean that scientists are missing another important carbon sink.

These studies reinforce a new paradigm in the management of tropical biodiversity that extends conservation to human-impacted lands (Chazdon, 1998; Pimentel et al. 1992; Janzen, 1998). Government planners and resource managers in Asia must recognize that swidden cultivation, rather than being the hobgoblin of tropical biodiversity, may be the most ecologically appropriate and culturally suitable means available for preserving biodiversity in many upland areas of Southeast Asia. To do this, planners and government agents should stop trying to eliminate swidden cultivation systems and start seeking to improve swidden systems through greater investments in research on methods of maintaining the biodiversity associated with fallows while increasing the productivity and soil sustaining properties of these lands.

6. ACKNOWLEDGEMENTS

I would like to acknowledge the financial support for my fieldwork from The Ford Foundation and the Rockefeller Brothers Fund. I am also thankful for support in Thailand from the US Man and the Biosphere Program; in Cambodia from the International Development Research Center, Canada; and Associates in Rural Development, World Bank funded Forest Policy Reform Process Project; and in Vietnam from the National Science Foundation, the John D. and Catherine T. MacArthur Foundation, and the Global Environment Forum.

REFERENCES

Cannon, C.H., Peart, D. and M. Leighton. 1998. Tree species diversity in commercially logged Bornean rainforest. Science 281: 1366-1368.

Chazdon, R. 1998. Tropical Forests—Log'Em or Leave'Em. Science 285: 1295-1296.

Collins, M., Sayer, J. and A. Whitmore. 1991. The Conservation Atlas of Tropical Forests. Asia and the Pacific. New York: Simon Schuster: 256.

Fan, S, Gloor, M., Mahlman, J., Pacala, S., Sarmiento, J., Takahash, T., and P. Tans. 1998. A large terrestrial carbon sink in North America implied by atmospheric and oceanic carbon dioxide data and models. Science 282: 442.

Fox, J., Krummel, J., Yarnasarn, S., Ekasingh, M. and N. Podger. 1995. Land use and landscape dynamics in northern Thailand: Assessing change in three upland watersheds AMBIO 24(6): 328-334.

Game-Tropics. 1996. Draft Implementation Plan of GAME-Tropics, website: http://climate.gsfc.nasa.gov/~taikan/GAMET/Imple2e/imple2e.html#3221.

Janzen, D. 1998. Gardenification of wildland nature and the human footprint. Science 279(5355): 1312.

Kummer, D.M. and B.L. Turner (II). 1994. The human causes of deforestation in Southeast Asia. BioScience 44(5): 323-328.

Lawrence, D., Peart, D. and M. Leightor. 1998. The impact of shifting cultivation on a rainforest landscape in West Kalimantan: Spatial and temporal dynamics. Landscape Ecology 13: 135-148.

Philips, O., Malhi, Y. and J. Grace. 1998. Changes in the carbon balance of tropical forests: Evidence from long-term plots. Science 282: 439.

Pimentel, D., Stachwo, U., Takacs, D., Brubaker, H., Dumas, A., Meaney, J., O'Neil ,J., Onsi, D., and D. Corzilius. 1992. Conserving biological diversity in agricultural/forestry systems. BioScience 42: 354-362.

Potter, L., Brookfield, H. and Y. Byron. 1994. The Sundaland region of Southeast Asia. In: J.X. Kasperson, R. E. Kasperson, B.L. Jarun (II), (Eds), Regions at Risk: Comparisons on Threatened Environments. Tokyo: United Nations University Press, 460-518.

Schmidt-Vogt, D. 1998. Defining degradation: The impacts of swidden on forests in northern Thailand. Mountain Research and Development 18(2): 135-149.

CHAPTER 6

Anthropogenic Factors of Transformation of the Natural Landscapes in Europe

(Emma P. Romanova and Marina A. Arshinova*)

1. INTRODUCTION

The evolution of the European territory has resulted in formation of the 'present-day landscapes' which are functioning and developing under the complex influence of both natural and anthropogenic factors. Throughout the history of the human civilization, natural landscapes bore permanent or sporadic impact of human activities and anthropogenic structures, which differed in trend and intensity. The anthropogenic pressure produces a number of effects including the qualitative changes of natural components and the internal structure of landscapes, as well as the development of specific natural-anthropogenic back pogenic processes. The results of the anthropogenic transforma-tions are accumulated and stored in the 'memory' of landscapes, becoming a factor which controls landscape stability, acuteness of the environmental problems and possible solutions.

The present-day landscape is a complicated system consisting of two subsystems namely the natural and anthropogenic ones (Fig. 1).

The natural subsystem is a result of the interaction of the natural components such as tectonic structures, surface deposits, relief, climate, natural waters, soils, vegetation, etc. It is characterized by a specific internal structure and natural-resource potential, including climatic, water, land, mineral and other resources, which is utilized by the human society.

*Faculty of Geography, Lomonosov Moscow State University, Vorobievy gory, 119899, Moscow, Russia

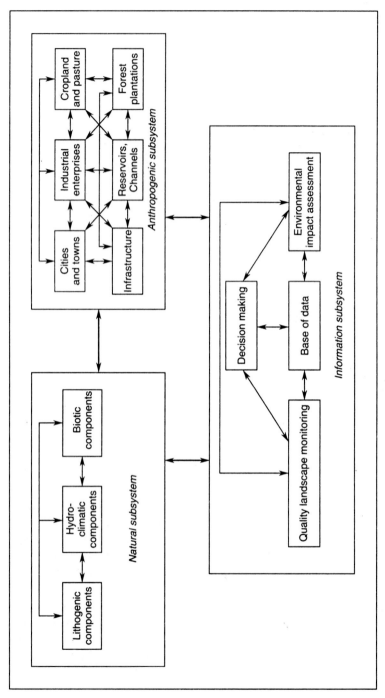

Fig. 1 Model of the present-day landscape

The anthropogenic subsystem is complicated as well. It includes the material objects of human existence being the sources of anthropogenic influence on the natural subsystem. These are the settlements, industrial objects, roads, canals, agricultural and forest lands, etc. They are responsible for the nature and the intensity of the anthropogenic impact and govern the consequences evolving within the natural subsystem. These consequences produce the so-called natural-anthropogenic processes, as a response of the natural subsystem to the external impact it has experienced (Romanova, 1997).

The development of the European[1] landscapes has been in many respects unique as compared with other large regions of the world.

2. URBAN TERRITORIES

The European region is densely populated—with more than 105 inhabitants per sq. km. According to the UN data, there were 510 million people living in Europe in 1995, i.e. 8% of the world population. About 75% of them are urban dwellers (UN Demographic Yearbook, 1999). The population of large cities shows the highest rates of growth; in the nineties 23 European cities hosted 141 million people, i.e. almost a third of the European population. The areas of urban settlements are rapidly spreading (CEC 1992). During the last 30 years they have nearly doubled, while the urban population has increased only by 30%. It is estimated that today various settlements occupy about 20 million ha or 4.2% of the European area, and the urban pollution could be traced over another 2.4 to 5 million ha of surrounding territories. The expansion of urban territories is predicted to be ahead of the urban population increase in the future. Each decade, Europe sacrifices about 2% of the total area of fertile agricultural lands to cities. During the twentieth century the area of the urban landscapes has increased ten times. At present we estimate the area of landscapes dominated by large urban agglomerations or high concentration of urban settlements to be above 60 million ha.

2.1 Functioning of Urban Geosystems

Cities are specific structures within the natural landscapes. They are characterized by construction of various technogenic objects such as buildings, industrial structures, roads, squares, artificial reservoirs, etc. Urban geosystems accumulate immense flows of energy and different products, which are taken up and processed within the urban area.

---

[1]Hereinafter the name "Europe" means the region outside Eastern Europe, i.e. to the west of the European part of the former USSR.

Then the environment receives the equally extensive flows of various wastes. These energy and material flows, typical of the metabolic processes within each urban system, differ according to the area of the city, its population numbers, as well as its economic and social functions (Table 1).

The impact of urban objects results in the vast amount of wastes which are the end-products of the metabolic processes of an urban system. These wastes are deposited within the limited territory of the enclosing natural landscape or sometimes within far removed landscapes as well. According to the UN European Economic Commission (OECD, 1993), in early nineties there were about 2 billion tonnes of wastes produced annually within the European territory (except the radioactive ones). This large amount included 150 million tonnes of household wastes (10% of the total), 330 million tonnes of industrial wastes (21%), 700 million tonnes of agricultural wastes (44%), 360 million tonnes of mining wastes (23%) and 27 million tonnes of energy objects wastes (2%). About 620 million tonnes of sludge are accumulated at waste treatment facilities, and there are 259 million tonnes of construction wastes and 46 million tonnes of displaced ground as well.

Table 1   Energy and material inflows into the urban environment of the European cities (early 1990s)

Energy and material inflows	London	Prague	Madrid	Barcelona
Population (.000 of inhabitants)	6680	1212	3010	1635
Area (sq. km)	1578	495	607	99
Energy consumption				
Total (GWt-hours/years)	26562	4000	9400	4773
%: in households	36			
in trade	24			
in industry	11			
on transport	29			
person (KWh/person/year)	3977	3300	3122	2919
Import of materials				
Foodstuffs (million tonnes)	2.4	4.6		
Production of wastes				
CO_2 (million tonnes)	13.6	16.1	15.7	8.5
SO_2 (thousand tonnes)	248.1	46.1		
O_x (thousand tonnes)	174.2	23.0		
Household waste (t/pers./year)	0.5	0.3	0.5	0.4
Water consumption, (l/pers./day)	—	540	91	220

Source: Europe's Environment: Statistical Compendium, 1995. Stannes and Bordeau (Eds), 205-206, 257 pp.

The analysis of the natural components of landscapes dominated by large cities suggests that these landscapes could be certainly classified as technogenic ones, because all natural links and components are radically transformed within them. This is equally true for climatic conditions, natural waters and soil and vegetation cover. The urban geosystems are characterized by unique energy and material flows.

3. IMPACT OF AGRICULTURE

Europe has a rather limited area of land suitable for cultivation. According to FAO (outside the former USSR territory) Europe occupies 472.7 million ha, including 138.5 million ha of arable lands (29.3%), 83.1 million ha of meadows and pastures (17.6%), 157.3 million ha of forests (33.3%) and another 93.8 million ha of the so-called 'other' lands [OECD, 1993; Stanners and Bordeau, 1995). The other lands are settlements, transport routes, mining areas, etc. as well as wastelands. By comparison, the arable lands of the world covers 11% of the total land area of the Earth, 26% are under pastures, 30% are forests and 33% belong to the category of 'other' lands. As to the Index of Agricultural Use (IAU), showing the percentage of arable lands within the whole area of a region, Europe ranks first among all the continents.

Natural conditions in Europe are rather unfavorable for cultivation. According to our estimates, only 6% of the whole European territory could be used for crop farming without amelioration (Table 2). Nevertheless, with the scarcity of food becoming acute at a global scale and with the majority of countries experiencing increasing food deficit, the European countries have ensured a safe level of self-supply and also provide extra foodstuff. This has become possible due to the application of complex ameliorations, namely chemical, hydrotechnical and

Table 2 Landscapes of Europe suitable for cultivation

Belt	Area of landscapes					
	Suitable for cultivation		Limitedly suitable for cultivation		Unsuitable for cultivation	
	0.000 ha	%	0.000 ha	%	0.000 ha	%
Cold		0		0	49,200	100
Cool		0	39,800	66	15,100	34
Temperate	29,100	11	131,850	49	108,420	40
Warm	—	—	31,790	34	61,950	66
Total	29,100	6	183,340	39	260,260	55

biological, introduction of high-yielding crops and new agrotech-nologies, and utilization of specialized agricultural machinery (FAO, 1997).

The rates of fertilizing in the European countries are among the highest in the world. In the 1990s, an area of 138 million ha received 27 million tonnes of nitrogen, phosphorous and potassium compounds, i.e. 192 kg of biophile elements were added to each hectare of arable lands in Europe (FAO Fertilizer Yearbook, 1997). This is about twice as high as in the USA, four times higher than in South America and 10 times higher than in Africa. The yields of main crops are respectively high in the European countries: in 1996 the yield of cereals was about 4,6 centners per ha in Europe and 28.2 centners per ha in the world (World Resources, 1998-99). Despite extremely high costs of such agriculture, a number of European countries rank first in the world as to crop yields and specific animal production. Thus, the natural landscapes have been radically transformed by anthropogenic factors.

In some regions of Europe, unsuitable for agriculture or with extremely low agricultural potential, high-productive agrolandscapes have been created due to the application of complex amelioration measures. These are the polders of the Netherlands or the irrigated plantations on terraces in the mountainous areas of Valencia and Andalucia in Spain. Within such landscapes, the local climate and soils are deeply transformed, the natural vegetation is removed, thus changing the whole natural subsystem. The functioning of such landscapes is supported by the permanent anthropogenic intervention, therefore they should be classified as technogenic ones (Mayer, 1984).

4. FOREST LANDS

The most obvious result of the anthropogenic influence on the natural environment in Europe is practically the total transformation of the natural vegetation. Formerly the forests covered 80 to 90% of the territory; at present their area is only 155 million ha or 33% of the total area. The percentage of forest lands varies from 6% in Ireland to 66% in Finland. The main cause of deforestation of the European landscapes is the clearing for croplands, pastures, settlements or mining, as well as logging for fuel and construction. Practically all existing forests in Europe are transformed by forestry, however, to a variable degree. Among them there is a technogenic category as well—these are forest plantations with introduced, rather than indigenous, species. The soils and grounds of such plantations are actively ameliorated by irrigation and drainage, fertilization and liming. This category of forests is constantly increasing in the area.

4.1 Degree of Economic Transformation

According to the degree of economic transformation all natural complexes are classified into several categories (Table 3).

Table 3   Areas of transformed landscapes in Europe (thousands of hectares)

Belt	Sector, zone	Area of landscapes	Areas of landscape categories			
			Modal	Derivative	Anthropo-genically modified	Technogenic
Sub-Arctic belt		13,662	12,161	961	540	
Temperate belt		365,065	34,761	56,963	207,323	66,018
	Boreal					
	Taiga	83,771	27,129	50,017	1,544	5,081
	Subboreal humid Mixed forets	10,550		252	8143	2155
	Broad-leaved forests	77,119	383	1526	57,635	17,575
	Subboreal semihumid Mixed forests	12,537			9,147	3,390
	Broad-leaved forests	161,159	7,249	4,483	116,122	33,305
	Semiarid					
	Steppes	19,929		685	19,244	
Subtropical belt		94,013		599	88,539	4875
	Semiarid Xerophytic forests	76,701		599	71,227	4875
	Subarid Woodlands and steppes	17,312			17,312	
Europe		**472,740**	**46,922**	**58,523**	**296,402**	**70,893**

4.1.1 Modal Landscapes

They are quasi-natural, or primary landscapes corresponding to the zonal types of landscapes. They did not experience the direct impact of human activities or sometimes they undergo only occasional local impacts which do not cause qualitative changes. In Europe, this group includes the Arctic landscapes of Spitsbergen, Sub-Arctic ice and stone deserts of Iceland, as well as some protected territories like the national parks. Nevertheless, all these landscapes are now under the influence of transboundary air pollution, thus they cannot be classified as 'natural', even in the absence of visual transformation.

4.1.2 Natural-anthropogenic landscapes

This category includes all other landscapes of Europe, to a variable degree transformed by the human activities. According to the degree of transformation of their natural subsystem these landscapes are classified into the following groups.

4.1.2.1 *Derivative*—incorporating rather stable complexes which are rather difficult to distinguish from the natural ones and capable of further existence and evolution without the anthropogenic intervention. Their development is a result of an 'over-exploitation' of natural landscapes in the past, namely over-grazing, frequent fires, excessive forest cutting, etc. The vegetation cover of such landscapes is dominated by maquis, garriga, tomillara, as well as forests with modified species composition. As a rule, they are more arid than the primary landscapes.

Both modal and derivative landscapes may have local areas with a certain anthropogenic impact, i.e. agricultural, pastoral or forestry. However, the scale and degree of transformation of the natural basis of landscapes are of minor importance and do not cause irreversible changes.

4.1.2.2 *Anthropogenically modified*—profoundly transformed natural complex under the direct economic impact. These are the regulated, deeply transformed landscapes, intensively exploited by humans. The most common are the landscapes with agricultural, namely arable ameliorated, plantation, orchard-plantation, pastoral and other, and forestry modification, which occupy up to 80 to 90% of the area in some regions, as well as their combinations (forest-arable, pasture-arable, etc.). Altogether 19 types of the anthropogenically modified landscapes have been identified in Europe.

4.1.2.3 *Technogenic*—natural-anthropogenic complexes with the most radical transformation by the human activities. All natural components of such landscapes are transformed, including lithogenic, climatic and biogenic ones; the internal landscape structure is corrupted or abated. The existence of these complexes is possible only under intensive and permanent human intervention. The processes of self-regulation are totally blocked, so they are not capable of recovering. The category of technogenic landscapes includes five types: 1) urban agglomerations (above 1 million inhabitants) and large objects of the infrstructure; 2) concentrations of smaller cities; 3) water management and mining complexes; 4) agricultural structures (polders, terraced lands, etc.); and 5) forest plantations.

The principles of the classification of present-day landscapes have been used to classify and map the landscapes of Europe at a scale of 1:5,000,000. The calculation of the areas of transformed landscapes with the help of the GIS 'Landscapes of Europe' suggested the following results. The modal, i.e. slightly transformed, landscapes occupy only 47 million ha or 10% of the total area, and are concentrated in Sub-Arctic regions and within the boreal subbelt of the temperate zone. The rest of the European territory is dominated by the natural-anthropogenic landscapes with different trends and degree of transformation due to human activities. More than 70 million ha, or 15% of the total area, are covered by technogenic landscapes, both urban and agricultural, with the most profound transformation. In Central Europe they account for 21% of the area (more than 60 million ha), while in Southern Europe there are only 5 million ha of such landscapes or 5% of the area. Unlike the primary natural landscapes, the technogenic ones receive an immense flow of energy and materials, namely fuel, electricity, raw materials and products. At the same time these complexes produce gaseous, liquid and solid wastes, unknown with the natural landscapes.

REFERENCES

Romanova, E.P. 1997. Present-Day Landscapes of Europe, Moscow, 308 p. (in Russian).

UNEP. 1987/88. Agricultural Production and the Environment, Vol I-III, Moscow.

OECD. 1993. Environmental Data Compendium, Paris.

Stanners, D. and Ph. Bordean. 1995. Europe's Environment. The Dobřis Assessment, Copenhagen, 205-206, 257 pp.

FAO Fertilizer Yearbook. 1997. Rome.

FAO Production Yearbook. 1997. Rome.

Mayer, H. 1984. Wälder Europas. Stuttgart.

CEC. 1992. The Future of European cities. Brussels.

UN Demographic Yearbook. 1999.

World Resources. 1998-99. New York–Oxford, 1998.

CHAPTER ➤ 7

Land Use/Land Cover Change in Russia

(E.V. Milanova, B.A. Alekseev,
N.N. Kalutskova, E.Yu. Lioubimtseva,
V.N. Solntsev, P.A. Tcherkashin and L.F. Yanvareva*)

1. INTRODUCTION

The latest political and socio-economic changes in Russia have had a considerable impact on the land use structure due to the increasing rate of land conversion. Analyses, mapping and modeling of these new trends in vegetation and land use change are needed for their understanding, forecasting and efficient land use management.

Russia has a long background in the study of environmental science and land use/cover mapping through remote sensing data (space imagery Meteor-Priroda, Cosmos, and other meteorological and resource satellites, Salyut and Mir stations, and airborne data). Expertise and considerable data sets accumulated in Russia and other NIS countries in this domain represent enormous potential interest for the international community, and must be accessible worldwide.

Recently the research project, carried in the framework of INTAS/ VEGETATION Programs at the Faculty of Geography, Moscow State University, aims at assessing and mapping land use, vegetation and landscape cover of Russia using satellite data, traditional maps, and field survey results as geographical indicators of environmental status and dynamics (Milanova, 1992; Milanova et al. 1993).

This research is the first attempt of mapping and analyses of land use/vegetation cover dynamics of Russia using combination of remote

*Faculty of Geography, Moscow State University, Moscow 119899, Russia.

sensing and in-field data of different spatial and temporal resolution. Coarse, medium and high resolution imagery from several satellite systems (NOAA-AVHRR, RESURS-01-3/MSU-SK, RESURS-F/MK-4,) have been processed, interpreted and analysed.

Satellite data were interpreted in order to update existing cartographic data, to fill information gaps, to identify new areas of change, and to reveal the degree of vegetation disturbance. False color photographic images (made by MK-4 onboard RESURS F) prove efficient for detailed land use/land cover classification and definition of territorial units (Gedymin, 1960, 1964).

2.   RUSSIAN INPUT INTO A PILOT WORLD ATLAS ON LUCC

It will consist of 3 parts: 1) Scale-dependent LUCC applications using satellite data of different resolution, 2) Land use/land cover long-term and short-term dynamics for Russia, and 3) GIS database as a reference for landscape mapping of Russia. Series of maps and satellite imageries will be included in the Atlas.

2.1   Scale-dependent LUCC Applications Using Satellite Data of Different Resolution

2.1.1   Geographical scope and scaling

One can often come across the geographical term 'landscape scale' which actually means the scale of visual landscape perception in a field. However, landscape aggregations of different hierarchical levels can be detected at a number of scales from a global or a continental (landscape zones and sectors) to a regional or a local scale (stows and facies). Since landscape is basically a scale-dependent phenomenon we prefer to avoid the term 'landscape scale', which can be a reason of confusion, and suggest usage of terms like 'macroregional or continental scale' (1:1-1:10 M), 'regional scale' (1:500-1:1M) and microregional or 'local scale' (1:100-1:500 M). Accordingly different types of remote sensing data were analysed in order to test their suitability to detect land cover/land use patterns at different scales.

For country (macroregional) level scale, the entire Russian territory was studied. Russia occupies 17.1 million sq. km and comprises enormous landscape diversity. However, natural intact ecosystems can be found mainly in Eastern Siberia, Arctic or the high mountains. In contrast, landscapes of the European part of Russia (EPR), where the major part of the population is concentrated, have been subjected to strong human impact and transformation since the nineteenth century.

A territory of Central part of European Russia between 33-42° eastern longitude and 53-60° northern latitude was chosen as study area on a regional level. Local level mapping was carried out on the basis of field data validation for several test areas with distinctively different land-cover composition and configuration. The following features defined the selection of this territory as case-study area for the investigation:

1. Consequential diversity of types of land cover and their territorial combinations.
2. Good coverage (comparing with other parts of Russia) with traditional and remotely sensed data.
3. Huge amounts of attribute and spatial data from traditional sources (topographic and industrial maps, government fund materials, field work results, etc.).

This gives us an opportunity to investigate the characteristics of land cover through remote sensing and check the accuracy and efficiency of the results with a set of independent data sources.

For a local scale, several test areas were chosen for field data validation with distinctively different land cover composition and configuration.

2.1.2 Methodology and definitions

Landscape approach to the environment as a combination of hierarchically subordinated geosystems (present-day landscapes) is very useful for realistic understanding of land use/land cover dynamics and changes. It provides a base for the perception of the world as a system of interrelated territorial samples with different environmental situations. The way people use the land has become a source of widespread concern for the future of the world. The inability of many countries in balancing environmental and production needs as well as land cover capability and anthropogenic stress present 'mega-scale' issues. Therefore, the need for rational planning of land use/cover development to make optimal use of the land resources is felt more than ever before.

Present-day landscapes (PDL) are territorially defined units of land surface characterized by a structurally organized combination of natural and economic components whose close interactions result in spatially distinct and temporally stable territorial system (Fig. 1).

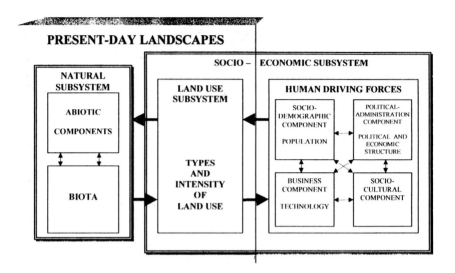

Fig. 1   Natural and socio-economic subsystems of PDL

PDL approach provides a base for the perception of the world as a system of interrelated territorial samples with different environmental situations. In response to this issue, a hierarchical landscape classificatory scheme is proposed for scale-dependent landscape applications. The main points of landscape monitoring and assessment are inventory and diagnosis of their status, based on the scale-dependent mapping and GIS (Eastman, 1992).

Recent work in the field of landscape ecology has provided a number of fundamental concepts of landscape or land unit, that proved important for the diverse environmental assessment applications. 'Land (scape) unit' is described as an ecologically homogeneous tract of land at the scale of issue. It provides a basis for studying topological as well as chorological landscape-ecology relationships. There are two meanings for landscape: (1) the common meaning that concerns a physiognomic category that, when used in the scientific language, was worded as a visual landscape; (2) the scientific language meaning, a rather specific one, used by physical geographers as an equivalent of geoecosystem as a territorial category (natural territorial complex).

Anthropogenic alteration of natural land cover patterns is quite well known. Through activities like agricultural practices, urban development and forestry, the natural land cover is removed and replaced by managed systems of altered structure. Presently very few territories of the world can be classified as natural landscapes. Most of them are influenced by human-induced phenomena such as acid rains and global climate changes. The resulting landscape is generally a mixture of natural and human-managed patches of different sizes and shapes.

The term 'landscape' is commonly understood by the geographic and landscape-ecological research community at large as a general territory that integrates different components of the geobiosphere and the socio-economic sphere. Any landscape system of any spatial dimension currently represents a complex ecological-economic system, where two subsystems—natural and anthropogenic— coexist and interact within the boundaries of their comparatively stable natural basis. The present-day peculiarity of any landscape system is expressed in the character of the anthropogenic transformation of its natural pattern.

The notion of 'land cover' accepted by the International Geosphere-Biosphere Program—Human Dimensions Program (IGBP-HDP) Land Use/Cover Project as an object of studies relating land use and land cover change has proved to be a close synonym of the recently defined hierarchical concept of PDLs .

The PDL concept stresses that the natural foundation of any specific landscape should be regarded as an indispensable basis for specific economic activities on a local and regional scale; in order to achieve optimal environmental management, economic structures and processes have to fit the mobile-equilibrious natural structures. Ignoring this local compatibility principle proves to be a major cause for most local and regional ecological problems. The PDL approach emphasizes the elaborate definition and comprehensive consideration of the whole global hierarchy of the existing landscape organization, since preserving the natural spatial landscape structure of the globe is a major guarantee of the relative sustainability of the present-day geobiosphere.

2.1.3 Satellite data sets and processing

The most sufficient source of NOAA-AVHRR NDVI images for continental-scale feasibility study was Global Ecosystems Database (GED), Version 1.0 (on CD-ROM) by EPA Global Climate Research Program, NOAA/NGDC Global Change Database Program (Kineman and Ohrenschall, 1992). Monthly Global Vegetation Index (GVI) from Gallo Biweekly Experimental Calibrated Global Vegetation Index (April 1985-December 1990) with 10' resolution was used for this study (principal investigator: Kevin P. Gallo, USGS EROS Data Center and the

NOAA National Environmental Satellite, Data, and Information Service). This data set contains Normalized Difference Vegetation Index (NDVI) from AVHRR sensor on NOAA-9 and NOAA-11 satellites (Kidwell, 1990). For this particular research, a total of 60 images over a period of 1986-1990 with a 10 km resolution was obtained from the database (Eidenshink and Faundeen, 1994).

Two principal sources of satellite imagery were used for data simulation on a regional level over Central Russia: AVHRR images of 1 km resolution over the whole area of study and photographic high and medium resolution images acquired by MK-4 and MKF-6 instruments on board of Russian satellites of RESURS-F1 series and orbital stations Soyuz and MIR were used. Complimentary ancillary data incorporated into geographical information system were analysed in order to aid image interpretation.

The following computer techniques are currently found to be most efficient for different types of lad categorization based on AVHRR data: classification (supervised and unsupervised) and principal component analysis (PCA). Both supervised and unsupervised classification methods are based upon statistical parameters such as mean and standard deviation.

2.1.4   Results of multi-level data simulation

Experiments with PDL mapping and classification done on the basis of remote sensing at the macroregional (for the whole of Russia) level have shown the features of the natural zonal structure and the anthropogenic transformation of land cover.

According to our analysis of vegetation biomass, seasonal dynamics based on 10 km resolution data set, zonal stratification of forest landscapes on the north of Russia differs from the traditionally drawn vegetation and landscape maps.

In the macroregional scale, according to vegetation seasonal dynamics and biomass, there must be a different stratification of forest landscapes in the north of Eurasia in comparison to the existing one. Only two zones should be determined on the basis of the humidity of the landscapes: a) extra-humid forest zone, it corresponds with the existing zone of northern taiga, but also includes tundra and central taiga; b) zone of optimal humidity forests, that corresponds with the zone of south taiga and mixed forests. Both the newly determined zones have set sub-latitude appearance through most of the Eurasian continent (which cannot be said about traditional zones). Even the south of the forest zone, step zones should also be stratified based on the humidity and warmth (normal humidity, dry, extra dry). These zones will not strongly correspond with the existing structure and will have better sub-latitude appearance, than the existing zones, because they are based on real dynamics of energy and water input, shown in vegetation dynamics, and not on the floral characteristics of the land cover.

Anthropogenic transformation of natural zones was also studied at the macroregional level of landscape applications. Experiments in this sphere show that human activity has, in some cases, changed the picture of natural zones. The oil and gas exploration region of Russia in Western Siberia is one such area. Severe exploitation of natural resources in this region has caused irreversible global scale changes of vegetation and land cover. Another area of active anthropogenic influence, that may be seen and analyzed by the use of remote sensing technique is an area of intensive artificial irrigation to the north from Black Sea near Dnieper and Kuban rivers. These humid steppe differ a lot in vegetation from the dry steppe of Volga region and West Siberia, though traditional vegetation and land cover maps write them in one zone. Finally, the well-known area of ecological disaster around the Aral sea should also be analyzed with the use of remote sensing techniques.

The use of remote sensing data allows one to determine a new scheme of natural zones with anthropogenic corrections. Different quantitative mathematical methods will be used for post-classification analysis that will provide a complete geographic characterization of each of the zones.

For the regional scale, 5 major cluster categories were determined by applying unsupervised classification. By visual interpretation and analysis of attribute data and case-studies, these primary clusters were defined. The image containing these clusters was then analysed using vast traditional cartographic and text data about land cover particularly of the study area as well as land use on it. Finally, the selected cluster categories were described as: water bodies, dry agricultural lands, dry forests, wet forests and agricultural lands, low-vegetated urban and rural lands. Comparitive analysis of classified image with the ground data shows that patterns of major land cover types coincide. Mutual analysis of traditional and remotely sensed data allows the determination of the following, sometimes contradictory, patterns of land use/cover dynamics: extemporaneous recovery of forests, Anthropogenic recovery of forests, Controlled deforestation, agglomerations and transport channels, Changes in species composition of forests (through clearance of valuable wood), Urban development over agricultural lands, and Waterlogging of arable and forest lands next to wetlands.

2.2   Land Use/Cover Dynamics Study of European Russia

2.2.1   Long-term (100-years) dynamics of land-use trends

Currently, the European part of Russia is the most highly cultivated part of the country. During the last 100 years, the vegetation cover has gone through natural evolutionary changes, but alteration under human impact—mostly the agriculture and the timber industry, was considerably higher.

Retrospective analysis is used to study land use for time against the last 20 years (before remote sensing data became available), that involve cartographic and statistical data with a different level of reliability.

Major methodological steps include data collection, analysis and assessment of reliability for different time periods. The goal was to design a GIS database from the existing data about land use and land cover changes for EPR.

The following methodological approaches are used to analyse land cover dynamics:

- Statistical
- Cartographic
- Case-studies

The following data have been collected:

(1) Statistical data of land use parameters (area of forests, arable lands, pastures) on 1881 and 1979 for 2 levels:
- (a) gubernia (1881) and oblast (1979) level as large administrative units;
- (b) uezd (1881) and rayon (1979) as small administrative units.
(2) Traditional (on paper) maps of administrative divisions for the respective years (1881, 1979)
(3) As additional source—traditional maps of land use (1862 and 1985).

The maps of administrative divisions have been digitized and transformed to the map projection currently used in Russia. Then the statistical data have been put in the relational tables for each unit for each year and thematic maps have been designed.

The patterns of administrative units for these time slices were different, but changes were also different in different parts of the regions. So it was decided to design the grid with formal polygons 30, to 30, and recalculate all the data to this grid taking into account the source data type.

The grid was automatically designed and the data was recalculated. It was found that land use with the territory of European Russia was developing in a centrifugal manner. Central regions were characterized by longest exploitation of lands (up to 1000 years), southern, south-eastern and northern by the shortest (100-150 years). Starting from the end of the nineteenth century, the area of agricultural lands has doubled (from 34.6 to 63.4% of the total area).

Data comparison had brought out some patterns of land cover distribution. In particular, significant variances were determined at the level of agricultural development between different landscape zones as well as provincial variance inside zones. Analysis also showed variance in directions of the process of agricultural development in different regions.

2.2.2 Analysis of land cover transformation on EPR between 1970-1992

To analyse 20-years of land use dynamics, two maps were overlaid using OVERLAY module in ARC/INFO to produce a map with difference in forest contours on the maps:

1. Forests map derived from AVHRR data
2. Traditional map of the forests

There was a-15 year difference in between the production of maps and during this period dramatic changes have taken place. Only one layer from each map was compared—forest contours. (Milanova, et al. 1994).

A series of on-ground checks took place in key points of disagreement between the layers of information to determine the factors of disagreement. These checks have shown that significant changes have taken place in the land cover of Central European Russia in the last 2 decades due to changes in agriculture that investigations like this can reveal. The following changes were detected:

2.2.2.1 *Deforestation*—There are certain regions, that may be easily interpreted on the attached map, that traditional maps show as forest cover and more recent remotely sensed images show as open land. We have investigated several big areas of possible deforestation in the area near Moscow. The major factor for possible change of land cover in these areas is the vast level of urban construction that took place in these areas in the last 20 years. After citizens of the Moscow metropolis obtained a permit to build a country summerhouse, thousands of small households, usually from 600 to 2,000 sq. meters in size, formed a 'dacha belt'.

2.2.2.2 *Forest regeneration*—There are areas within the study territory that had experienced secondary forest regeneration during the last 2 decades, according to the results of map overlay. Mostly this process take places in the marginal arable areas and was mostly intensive in early 1990s during the period of stagnation.

2.3   GIS Database as a Reference for Landscape Mapping of European Russia

Building a landscape database requires extraction of information on landscape components from available thematic maps. Each thematic layer (coverage) was digitized separately so that the following thematic 16 vector layers were created: hydrological network, relief (6 classes); phytomass (7 classes); mortmass (9 classes), production (7 classes); typologic and ecophytocenologic subdivisions of climax vegetation (48 types and 127 groups respectively); pedological types and genetic groups (25 and 41 respectively), land use categories (57 classes); railways, roads (3 categories); urban canters (5 categories), and administrative regions. This primary data was necessary for interpretation and mapping physiographical, ecological and socio-economic landscape components and form a core information in the database.

All cartographic data were stored and processed in Arc/Info GIS environment (Arc/Info, Ver. 7, 1995).

In order to provide complete superimposition of all information layers they were all transformed to the same projection (conic equidistant projection Nefedova). Deformations, initially introduced to thematic maps by imperfect registration and geodetic control, were geometrically corrected by edge matching, and computing links for adjusting erroneous data using a considerable number of control points.

Data layers based on typological classifications of one of the landscape parameters (e.g. vegetation, soils, and land use), where qualitative characteristic are expressed by alphanumeric codes were processed in the vector format that allows one to retain information on horizontal spatial relationships between territorial units and their elements (polygons, arcs and points), which is very important in analyzing spatial organization of horizontal landscape structure. However, vector cartographic model brings an assumption that polygon contours are sharp and not fuzzy as in the reality. In our case, when almost all data were taken from hand-drawn broad-scale maps, mainly with qualitative parameters, such assumption is quite acceptable and a vector model is more appropriate. Layers containing continuous qualitative information (more specifically, climatic parameters and satellite imagery) were acquired and stored in a grid format. The latter seems to be more convenient when arithmetic and logical operations on data should be undertaken.

The database structure meets the logic of landscape differentiation by various factors and components. The layers are organized as 'themes'—directories containing thematic vector coverages, grids, and associated attribute and database tables. In turn, each directory includes subdirectories and files, containing information on the layer's thematic content, geographical and topological information.

Assemblage and analyses of cartographic, field and remote sensing data on landscape components of European Russia allowed us classification and mapping of the present-day landscape of this macro region at the reference scale of 1:4-1:8 M. A series of natural and anthropogenous factors define the landscape structure of the area: climate, relief, hydrological network, potential vegetation and soils, and human impact. The main advantage of landscape maps produced by GIS tools is that they can be easily corrected, updated or modified according to the requirements of specific applications.

3. CONCLUSION

Landscape concept could enrich land use/cover situational assessment and help in delineating landscapes as a complex system with different patterns of relationships. Together with computer quantitative methods, landscape concept may serve as a scientific base for long-term development of ecologically sound and economically efficient agriculture in Russia as well as for the development of ecologically sound agriculture. Such agriculture will help use natural potential more effectively and avoid unfavorable consequences of land degradation.

A universally acceptable database on land use is not an easy undertaking, both in conceptual and in computer programming terms. Such a database can only function if it forms part of a wider context of related databases in land resources and is used in the framework with clearly defined societal goals and constraints. The important part of Russian input for a pilot Atlas should be an assessment of the socio-economic feasibility and acceptability of the options for land use development and their impact.

REFERENCES

Eastman, J.R. 1992. IDRISI Technical Reference and User's Guide, Version 4.0 (rev.1). Clark University, Graduate School of Geography, Worcester, Massachusetts, 01610, USA.

Eidenshink, J.C. and J.L. Faundeen. 1994. The 1 km AVHRR global data set: first stages in implementation. *International Journal of Remote Sensing*, 3443-3462.

Gedymin, A.V. 1960. Experience of application of data from General Survey in Russian Empire in agricultural studies. *Geographic Issues*, 50: 147-171.

Gedymin, A.V. 1964. Use of old cartographic materials for landscape analysis. Recent questions of geography, Moscow, 298-302.

Kidwell, K. 1990. NOAA Polar Orbiter Data User's Guide. NCDC/SDSD, National Climatic Data Center, Washington D.C.

Kineman, J.J. and M.A. Ohrenschall. 1992. Global Ecosystems Database. Version 1.0 (on CD-ROM). Documentation Manual. EPA Global Climate Research Program. NOAA/NGDC Global Change Database Program.

Milanova, E.V. 1992. Geographical Approach to the Studying and Mapping of Agrolandscapes. In: *Comparison of Landscape Pattern Dynamics in the European Rural Areas, MAB UNESCO*, 274-282.

Milanova, E.V., Kushlin, A.V., and N.J. Middleton (eds). 1993. World Map of Present-Day Landscapes, M. Soyuzkarta, 1-33

Milanova, E.V., Kushlin A.V. and P.A. Tcherkashin. 1994. Landscape Mapping and Assessment (GIS Methodology). In: *InterCarto: GIS for Environmenal Studies and Mapping, MSU/InterCarto*, Moscow, 141-144.

CHAPTER 8

Land Use Changes in Pamiro-Alai

(Irina Merzliakova[1] and Alexandre Sorokine[2])

1. INTRODUCTION

An analysis of the former USSR's history shows that changes in political organization usually lead to the transformation of the economic structure at a regional level. This in turn reflects land use changes of the local territories and could inflict changes in the land cover, ecology as well as the well-being of the local communities. The study of land use changes in Pamiro-Alai mountain region between 1949-1991 (Soviet period), conducted by the Institute of Geography, Russian Academy of Sciences, in 1990/95 confirmed this.

The territory studied covers the lower and central part of Surkhob valley (Pamiro-Alai environmental province). This area is greatly affected by exogenic processes due to seismic and anthropogenic activity. The Khait earthquake with a magnitude of 10 on the Richter scale occurred in 1949. Settled agriculture first appeared here in the ninth century and was introduced everywhere 150 years ago (Kisliakov, 1966). The population reached 120,000 (the whole Surkhob valley) at the turn of the century but has decreased then on due to forced resettlement after 1949. In 1992/95 this territory faced severe

[1]Russian Conservation-Monitoring Center, Kedrova st., 8/1, #3, 117874, Moscow, Russia
[2]Regional Science Institute, 4-13 Kita-24 Nishi-2, Kita-ku, Sapporo 001-0024, Japan

military tension[*] and now urgently requires strategic planning for economic development.

2. EVOLUTION OF ECONOMIC STRUCTURES

Between 1949-1991, two types of economic structures existed in Surkhob valley. The semi-nomadic husbandry of Kirgizians with the kitchen-garden culture replaced the ancient nomadic husbandry of Kirgizian tribes with seasonal sites at the bottom of the valley and in the upper slopes. By the beginning of the twentieth century, Kirgizian grazing grounds shifted to the upper sections of Jasman and Jarkhich tributaries and stows in alpine zone of the Peter the Great ridge. Husbandry predominates only in Jirgatal district to the East from the demarcation line between Tajik and Kirgiz lands. The line was established 150 years ago by the military agreement, signed in Khait and corresponds to the modern boundary between Tajikabad and Jirgatal districts.

Traditional intensive settled agriculture of Tajiks expanded from the bottom of the valley and from paths to slopes and side valleys and was managed by local neighbourhood-patronimical communities. Distribution of arable land followed the main directions of Tajiks settling in Karategin, after they were evicted from the plains. Subsidiary irrigated agriculture had vertical specialization and was oriented to isolated basins. It was maintained by the relative-neighbourhood 'mutual assistance system', operating along vertical axes according to the agricultural calendar. Husbandry traditionally played a secondary role despite the presence of the alpine zone. The main limitation was the lack of fodder in winter and generally straw predominated over hay. (Fig. 1).

---

[*]Direct military conflicts occurred in Garm and Tajikabad in 1993. The roots of the civil war and current tensions were in measures taken by Stalin in the early years of Soviet rule. They included the forced resettlement of population groups from northern to southern Tajikistan, pursuing the goal to suppress the resistance of *basmach* groups and to satisfy labor requirements for cotton cultivation. This aggravated clan and ethnic sensitivities and culminated in conoslidation of power of opposition groups composed of Pamir and Garm regional clans (some supporters of Islamic Revival Party, JRP) and thus resulted in the civil war. The presence of an entrenched, armed and militant opposition in the heart of the country in the Karategin valley has further served to isolate a significant population from the rest of the country, geographically, economically and politically, affecting economic spheres and land use (World Food Program, 1996).

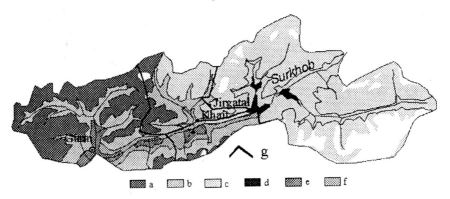

	1949	1954	1991
a	1	5	5
b	3	5	5
c	1	1	1
d	2	2	2
e	3	4	7
f	3	5	6

Types of economic structures

1—Nomadic Kirgizian husbandry.

2—Kirgizian kitchen-garden culture.

3—Traditional intensive settled agriculture of Tajiks.

4—Large-scale mechanized agriculture combined with large scale horticulture oriented to export.

5—Seasonal grazing of outsider herds in highlands with transit migrations.

6—Large-scale mechanized agriculture and individual horticulture with kitchen-gardens and fragmental fields.

7—Large-scale horticulture oriented to export.

Fig. 1 Evolution of main economic structures in Surkhob valley between 1949 and 1991 (g: *administrative boundaries; the isoline marks the absolute height of 3000 m*).

Coexistence of the above-mentioned economic structures within a single resource utilization scheme in Surkhob valley was formed during the development of Karategin independent state and further to its joining the Bukhara emirate in 1876. It was slowly transforming until 1949 when the first collective farms were established on the basis of communities.

Cardinal transformation of economic structure was a result of political restructuring in Soviet period, the shift towards planned economy and new scheme of husbandry migrations introduced according to the government order in 1927. It envisaged the transfer of highland grazing grounds to the temporal ownership of southern collective farms and into the category of State Land reserve. Since that time only 1/5 of highland pastures (440,000 ha in Garm district) was used by the indigenous population. After 1949, when the catastrophic Khait earthquake inflicted great damages to arable lands at the bottom of Jasman and Jarkhich valleys, the government used it as a reason for resettlement of mountain dwellers in the southern cotton growing districts. Depopulation on both sides of the river was followed by the establishment of large state farms managed from outside the region and oriented to export of agricultural products. These processes promoted complete deterioration of traditional community resource utilization schemes and cardinal changes in land use.

Since 1949, traditional economic structures were replaced due to collectivization with:

- Large-scale mechanized agriculture with semi-distant grazing husbandry in collective and state farms. This system assumes development of export oriented grain agriculture, vegetable and potato growing. Main areas of arable lands were situated at the bottom of the valley along roads.
- Seasonal grazing of outsider herds in highlands with transit migrations along the bottom of Surkhob valley.
- Large-scale horticulture oriented to export.
- Another result of the planned economy was the appearance of individual plots sizing 0.2-0.7 ha size (the largest private land ownership in Surkhob valley in the nineteenth century was up to 100-200 ha and the average 1-2 ha). They included the kitchen-garden, micro-fields and gardens mainly within or near settlements. These plots were the main source of agricultural products for local dwellers.

The recent transformation of economic structures was related to modern changes of political organization towards autonomization just before the civil war in 1992/93. It is represented with shifts towards 'individual plot agriculture' and the community farm system based on the rent of state lands with small-scale horticulture combined with strictly economically specialized large state farms.

Modern and future changes in economic organization are predetermined by conditions of civil war and depend now on the international humanitarian activity. They will reflect the perspectives of post-war rehabilitation and the introduction of decision-making scheme oriented to local community.

Lack of data allows us to just speculate on modern trends in agricultural orientation of the territory. Full destruction of large state farms, loss of agricultural machinery and manpower lead to orientation towards the 'community agriculture' growing fruits, vegetable, potato and cereals, granted by international funds.

All these transformations of the economic systems, predetermined by the political restructurization lead to the changes in land use: composition of land use types and its spatial structure. We analyzed land use changes inflicted under the centralized Soviet management to see if they are justified with available resources, able to support local population (i.e. provide ecological stability and economic prosperity) in comparison to traditional land use managed by the local community. This question is still important, because the process of autonomization in peripheral regions interrupted now by war will continue. Revision of resource utilization strategies, land use schemes and decision-making approaches will be required to overcome political instability, economic backwardness and environmental degradation. Under war conditions, such an analysis helps one to find out the agricultural capacity of the region.

In order to study the consequences of economic and political restructurization in detail, we have created an extensive three-tier database of environmental and socio-economic information with levels that correspond to three different map scales.

Basic layers (digital elevation model; physiograph units; exogenic proceses; land use, settlements and road network) were compiled based on different sources of information within Arc/Info 6.1 and 3.4 D+. We used aerial photography of panchromatic spectral range and scales: 1:17,000; 1:32,000 for 1949, 1954-56, 1988-91 (produced by Tajikistan Kosmogeodesia and analysed manually); topographic maps of 1:25,000 to 1:100, 000 scales; materials of field studies; data from archives and census statistics for 1954, 1970, 1989. The core of the socio-economic database is formed with land use type distribution, demographic data, transportation network and crops productivity information.

The middle level includes synthetic layers devoted to land suitability, land use dynamics, exogenic vulnerability of slopes that were prepared using GIS. GIS allowed one to combine a great amount of diverse information and is considered to be the most flexible method for studies on the sustainable development in the mountains. Geographical retrospective analysis and geographical regionalization according different schemes, helped us compare spatial and temporal changes in land use and resource utilization on the whole that were inflicted by earthquake and those referring to decision-making in the post-stress stage.

Spatio-temporal analysis resulted in a set of maps for three time slices (1949, 1954, 1991). Maps show ratios between parameters, mean indices and compliance with assessment criterion. They are built on the basis of regionalization according groups of watersheds (or districts), which are the traditional basis for community economy.

On the basis of spatio-temporal analysis of land use types' changes in 1949-1997, we have estimated absolute and relative changes of ratio between fields and pastures (intensively used by local dwellers) for two periods: 1949-1954 and 1954-1991 (Merzliakova, 1996b). We analysed the changes in distribution of land use types due to damages inflicted by earthquake and changes due to resettlement and economic restructurization. We realized that during the studied period, area of arable land had sharply decreased. Also, inspite of decrease of the total field area in districts damaged by earthquake (the right bank of Surkhob), in 1954 they were still leading in dominance of arable lands. During the next period, cultivated area continued to decrease on both sides of the main valley. By 1991 dominance of pastures over fields at the right bank shows dramatic reorientation of economy when compared with the beginning of the discussed period (Fig. 2). The reasons and consequences of these changes are discussed below in detail.

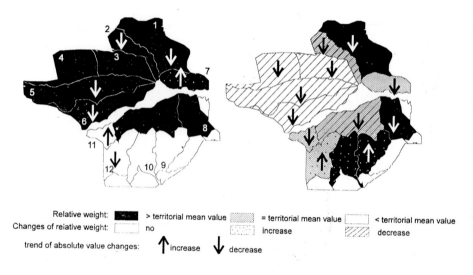

Relative weight: █ > territorial mean value ▓ = territorial mean value ☐ < territorial mean value
Changes of relative weight: ☐ no   ▓ increase   ▨ decrease
trend of absolute value changes: ↑ increase ↓ decrease

Fig. 2   (a) changes of field to pasture ratio just after earthquake (1949-54)
(b) changes of field to pasture ratio within the period 1949-91.

3.   TRADITIONAL LAND USE

3.1   Structure and Specificities

As estimated, environmental conditions governed the differences in economic specialization of the right and left banks (see above) and the formation of vertical land utilization system, which corresponds to the settlement system (Fig. 3).

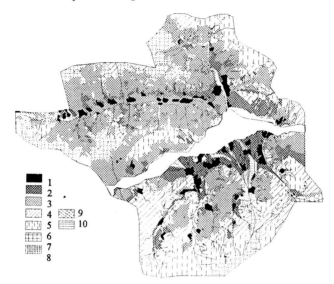

Fig. 3 Land use in 1949: 1. settlements; 2. large fields; 3. small terraced fields; 4. fields and hays; 5. pastures; 6. pastures and unused land; 7, 8. unused lands; 9. erosion; and 10. landslides and mudflows.

Specialization of households of the left bank was as follows: husbandry over 2400 m; horticulture with hays and small terraced fields on slopes, cropping in the bottom of the valley (terraces and cones) and on the local watersheds. Economy of the right bank orients to cropping and secondly on pasturing on tops of ridges and in the upper sections of the valleys. The share of fields and pastures on the right bank was positive whereas on the left it was negative (Fig. 4).

The horizontal structure was presented with sub-concentric zones of agricultural activity within watersheds (with different land use type composition). They could be determined by distances from settlements (Mukhiddinov, 1984). In traditional spatial structure of community agriculture, these distances determine the regime for seasonal activity (irrigation and manuring of fields): the zone of adjacent fields lies within the settlement boundary or can extend up to 200 m, the zone of remote fields lies within 1 km radius, and the zone of remote territories with fragmented fields lies more than 1 km from the settlement (Fig. 5).

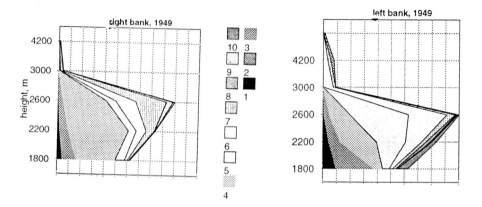

Fig. 4 Vertical structure of land use in 1949 (land use types proportional to the square of vertical belt): 1. settlements; 2. gardens; 3. large fields; 4. small fields; 5. hays; 6. pastures; 7. fragmental pastures; 8. erosion; 9. unused lands; and 10. landslides and mudflows.

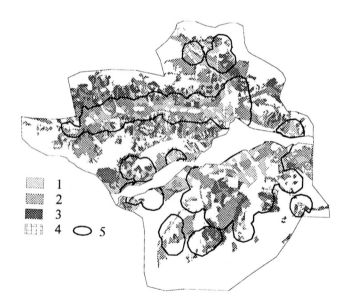

Fig. 5 Lands of different quality being ploughed before 1949: 1. favourable; 2. suitable; 3. of limited suitability; 4. unfavourable; and 5. boundary between adjacent and remote fields with different regime of irrigation and manuring.

This type of organization of the territory, differences in specialization under conditions of local market in Khait and the presence of social regulators of resource utilization (neighbourhood and relative 'mutual assistance system', taxes, penalties, religious rites) provided a high degree of utilization of suitable lands for agriculture (60-70%), a stable exogenic situation and prosperity of the local population.

All suitable (according to local ideas) patches of the territory were ploughed and the productivity of land was high. In 1878, Arandarenko (1878, 1883) called this territory 'the valley of cereal landscape' (with the productivity of wheat and barley 9-10 centner/ ha under irrigation and 6-7 c/ha rainfed). Even after 1923, all slopes were ploughed, but in the present only remnants of terraced fields were seen everywhere.

3.2 Transformation of Land Use Due to Earthquake

An earthquake with its epicenter in Darakhavz valley with a magnitude 8-10 on the Richter scale inflicted great damage to the land use system. It caused severe rockfall which covered the bottom of the valley with 150 m of material.

Degradation and loss of fields buried under landslides and mud flows at the bottom of the valley lead to a decrease of field share in comparison to pastures in Jasman and Jarkhich valleys that were less damaged (3 to 54% of fields on right bank of Surkhob). But this does not change the relative weight of the regions at the right bank and the fields dominated there (Fig. 2a).

3.3 Transformation of Land Use Due to Resettlement

Further transformation of land use structures continued due to the forced resettlement of local inhabitants from the right bank of the main river. The valley of Surkhob was considered to be an 'unperceptive' economic zone and the government stopped support to its further development. This resulted in a reduction of a number of collective farms and their enlargement. Ten collective farms were eliminated by 1954 in the Jasman and Jarkhich valleys and only two were left. Collectivization along with depopulation of the upper sections of the valley led to complete deterioration of the individual agricultural sector (Table 1). All this led to a sharp fall in the grain production between 1949 and 1997.

According to Arandarenko (1883), and then Vasiliev (1888) the family or community (clan) could provide for themselves

Table 1   Individual sector

Vertical belt, m	Size of individual plots		Number of households per settlement		Population number per settlement		Population density	
	1949	1991	1949	1991	1949	1991	1949	1991
1400-1800	1-60 ha	0.1-0.15 ha (2-15 ha) rent	100	300	800	1500	25	Upto 100 and more
1800-2400	1-1.5 ha	0.07-0.08 ha	70	15	400	100	10	less
2400-3000	1-1.5 ha	0.06-0.05 ha	30	3	200	20	4-5	0

comfortably with agricultural products and bring the surplus to the market. It related both to cereals and meat. By our estimations, the harvest of cereals (quite stable per year per person) was four times greater in 1878 than the World Food Programe (1996) nutrition norms (73 kg to 400 kg annually per person). Even in 1944, before cardinal restructurization of the economy, collective farms produced about 220 kg of wheat grain per person (Fig. 6)

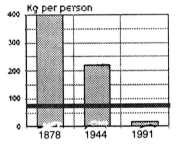

Fig. 6   Decrease of annual grain production per person in Surkhob valley (the line shows nutrition norms suggested by WFP).

In 1991, only two sacks of flour (120 kg) was supplied to each household (an average of 7 persons) by the government (Merzliakova, 1996a). Due to lack of land only few families could grow enough wheat at their individual plots. It was especially devastating to regional agriculture when the governmental and collective farms were destroyed and the individual sector could hardly compensate for this process.

The total negative changes in land use since 1949 account for around 34 percent. They mostly comprised transformationed of fields into pastures, abandoned or wastelands. At a glance, the earthquake seems to be the main factor of land use transformation. But the negative changes in land use were observed on both territories, damaged and not damaged by earthquake. If damage by earthquake was obvious up to 2400 m, then by 1990 abandoned lands appeared even on high slopes and on the left bank (Fig. 7).

Land use was transformed more on the right bank of Surkhob (Fig. 2b, regions 3, 4 and 5). Productive lands at the bottom of

Jasman valley were transferred to the State Land reserve and later given for grazing to the southern collective farms. A local husbandry state farm was organized there in 70th. As a result, Jarkhich and Jasman valleys lost their agricultural importance. Both of them before 1949 provided agricultural products to the local market in Khait (Fig. 8).

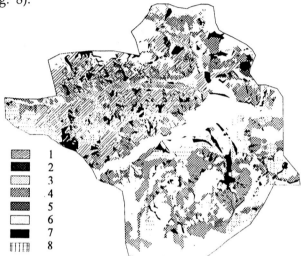

Fig. 7 Transformation of land use 1949-1991. *Lands damaged by earthquake*: 1. recultivation not complete; 2. to badlands; 3. no changes recultivated. *Lands not damaged by earthquake*: 4. negative changes; 5. no changes; 6. no changes–badlands; 7. positive changes.

Fig. 8 Transformation of arable lands in Jasman valley (1949-1991): 1. abandoned fields; 2. fields destroyed in 1949; 3. fields recultivated by 1991; 4. long standing fields; 5. new fields; 6. the zone with 1 km from paved roads.

Now, on the contrary, the left bank is dominated by arable lands and sends some crops including potato to the market in Dushanbe. On the left bank, the traditional agricultural belt (1400-1800 m) lost its agricultural importance due to large-scale horticulture development on low river terraces.

Arable area decreased and fields shifted to the bottom of the valley, concentrating along roads. Accessibility factor and presence of lands suitable for cropping without reclamation became the main factors for economic development. It means that the shift shown on cartograms (Fig. 2) reflects not only horizontal changes of agricultural specialization but also transformation of the vertical land use system.

Formation of abandoned lands, utilization of former fields as poor pastures lead to erosion development and soil degradation. Fall in grain production along with a good resources potential necessitated recultivation of abandoned lands. Using the described diagrams, while planning an agricultural strategy, we can determine districts needing more attention. In our case Jasman valley with the greatest potential is not being used now. On a detailed level, we accounted a modern status of this potential in relation to exogenic process development and accessibility. Such analysis for Jasman valley gave us an average 15% of abandoned lands that need to be recultivated before cropping (Fig. 9).

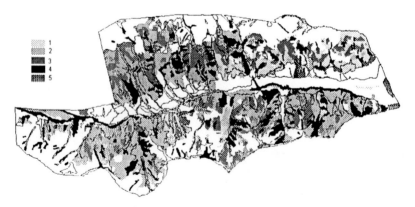

Fig. 9 Potential for arable land development in Jasman valley: 1. favourable;
2. suitable; 3. of limited suitability; 4. unfavourable, but ploughed before
1949; 5. modern exogenic processes: erosion screes and small surface landslides.

4. CONCLUSION

Using the described approaches, it was concluded that the transformation of the vertical resource utilization and spatial shift in economic specialization are not reasoned by the natural factors. They represent the most negative results of changes in decision-making policy to a centralized planned economy and the establishment of the centralized political power in the region. All these aggravated the consequences of the environmental catastrophe.

Currently continuing repatriation of mountain dwellers, presence of abandoned lands in a relatively good condition, total fall of grain production at the country level all call for wide scale reclamation of arable lands. According to our study Jasman valley is the most promising area within the upper section of Surkhob basin.

Reconstruction of agriculture in the region under modern conditions can occur only on a small-scale and has to be oriented at a community level. According to the analysis of the recent governmental policy by WFP experts, it still continues to prioritize cotton production (for export) on the Southern state farms. That is the reason why rates of recovery of peripheral agriculture and land privatization are low. Acute shortage of fuel and spare parts leads to deterioration of mechanized agriculture and irrigation systems in mountain regions. Consequent degradation of state farms and a universal lack of high quality seeds lead to increased use of marginal rain-fed upland for grains. Rural populations have responded to the shortage of cereals by planting wheat wherever possible. Kitchen-garden and vegetable growing become more important due to considerable lack of cereals that is not covered by humanitarian aid. Also taking into perspective the small gardens on the slopes, they prevent erosion development, but are too young to give enough harvest.

Planning future resource utilization schemes and land use development at local and regional level is a complicated task. Comparative analysis of territories by set of parameters and evaluation of their relative importance could be used as additional illustrative means for decision-making purposes. A preliminary rough spatio-temporal analysis of resource utilization needs to be conducted in order to realize problems and relative trends while planning a strategy.

REFERENCES

Arandarenko G., 1878. *Karategin*. Military collection, n. 5.

Arandarenko G., 1883. *Darvaz and Karategin.* Military collection, n. 11.

Jopha L.E., 1938. *Economic-geographical characteristic of the Upper Surkhob bassin.*

Kisliakov V.A., 1966-1970. *Tajiks of Karategin and Darvaz.* vol. 1-2.

Merzliakova I.A., 1966a. *Analysis of resource utilization in mountain region (Pamiro-Alay case study). GIS approach.* Ph.d. dissertation.

Merzliakova I.A., 1966b. *Monitoring system approach for mountain region development using GIS technologies (Pamiro-Alai case study).* Proceedings of the 4th International Symposium on High Mountain Remote Sensing Cartography, Karlstad, Sweden, August 19-21.

Mukhiddinov J. 1984. *Features of traditional agriculture of Pamir ethnic groups in XIX-beginning of XX century.*

Vasiliev, 1888. *Statistical records for Karategin.* Military collection, n. 10.

CHAPTER 9

Agricultural Landscapes in the Czech Republic:
Historic Changes and Future Development

(Vladimir Kremsa*)

1. INTRODUCTION

The Czech Republic is a country with a long and rich agricultural tradition. After World War II, agriculture and agricultural landscape in Czech lands and Moravia underwent a sea change. The transformation of the agricultural landscape and villages into United Agricultural Cooperatives during forced communist collectivization of private farming after 1948 was a dramatic process with many consequences for the society.

Recently, Czech agriculture is at a crossroad. We need sustainable agriculture that is economically viable, and meets the needs of society for safe and nutritious food, while conserving and enhancing the landscape, natural resources and the quality of the environment for future generations.

The transformation of Czech landscape results from complex interactions: 1) Socioeconomic and historical changes (land ownership and tenure, population growth, urbanization, industrialization, technology development, transportation, communications, etc.); 2) Political decisions (wars, agricultural policy, confiscation, subsidies,

*Research Center for Applied Science and Advanced Technology (CICATA-IPN), Legaria 694, Col. Irrigation, Mexico City, 11500, Mexico.

taxes, etc.); and 3) Environmental conditions (climate, soils, pollution, etc).

2. HISTORIC CHANGES OF CZECH AGRICULTURAL LANDSCAPES

2.1 Historical, Political and Economical Overview

The age old prehistory of the settlement and agricultural use of the territory and landscape of our-day Czech Republic is rich. A concise overview of the most important historical, political and economical issues in agricultural landscape development in the ancient times, middle ages and the twentieth century is given.

2.1.1 Ancient times

4th Century: Settlement of Slavonic tribes, clan villages, fertile soils, annex-farming system, population growth, *10th Century*: New villages, land reclamation, new farming techniques, crop rotation, fallowing system, individual farming, ownership: joint (woods, meadows, pastures) and private (arable land and gardens).

2.1.2 The middle ages

13th Century: Colonization of the Czech crown lands (mainly by Germans), better legal status of colonists (Emphyteutic law—hereditary ownership), growth of rural population, rising demand for farm products, extension of the area under cultivation, deforestation, amelioration, settlement (farmsteads, villages, strongholds), *17th Century*: Thirty year War (1618-48): loss of 1/3 of population, impoverishment of the country side, decrease of agricultural production, exhausted soil, ruined towns, great damages, *1701*: Abolishment of serfdom by the Emperor Joseph II, end of permanent bondage of land and landlords; leasing of land and farms to tenant farmers; higher productivity; improved crop rotation and crop alteration systems; fruit, wine and hops, *19th Century*: Crop alteration system, new technology and production methods (crusher, threshing machine, steam engine, etc.), changes in the crop structure, land reclamation, intensive cultivation. 1848: Freeing of peasants, parceling of farms, long and narrow strip fields, increasing yields.

2.1.3 The twentieth century

1918: Foundation of Czechoslovakia; 1919: Land Reform Act; 1920: Allocation Act; 1945-48: Displacement of the German population; 1948: Communist coup , Collectivization of agriculture; 1948-62: United

Agricultural Cooperatives (200-300 ha), State Farms; 1962-70: UAC (500-600 ha), specialization; 1970-89: UAC (6000 ha), cooperation, integration, specialization, concentration, 1989: "Velvet" revolution, 1991: Regulation of property relations and property in Cooperative Farms, Land Register, The Agrarian Chamber Restitution, Privatization, State Environment Fund, Environmental Inspection, 1992: Cadastral Act, Protection of Agricultural Land Fund, Protection of Nature and Landscape, Act on the Environment, River Systems Revitalization Program, 1993: Czech Republic, Agricultural and Forestry Support and Guarantee Fund; 1994: "Caring about our countryside", Territorial Systems of Ecological Stability, 1995: State Fund of Market Regulation, Forest Act, 1996: Land Property Relation, 1999: Landscape and Countryside Preservation, Non-production functions of forests.

2.2   Material (Historical Documents)

2.2.1   Statistical data on land use

There are altogether four provincial real-estate cadasters as a basic land use document: 1) The roll of assessment of agricultural land (1653-56), 2) The Teresian cadaster (1713-57), 3) The Josephinian cadaster (1785-89), 4) Stable cadaster (1817-43), and 5) The District Lexicon for Bohemia (census 31.12.1900).

2.2.2   Map documents

1) Mapa Geographica Regni Bohemiae (1723); 2) Military mapping (1763-87, 1842-52, 1874-80), 3) Topographic maps (1:10,000) and 4) Cadastral maps (1:2880).

2.2.3   Remote sensing

1) Black and white panchromatic aerial photographs (1:10,000 to 1:20,000, since thirties); 2) Multi-spectral color and infrared aerial photographs (since 1980); and 3) Satellite images: Landsat, SPOT (since 1970) (Kremsa, 1985, 1986a).

2.2.4   CORINE

The final product of the CORINE Land Cover Program (1993-96) consists of a geographic database in the scale 1:100,000 (1:50,000, selected areas) describing land cover forms in 44 (84) classes, which are grouped in three (four) level hierarchy and reflects both physical and physiognomic characteristics. The smallest area unit mapped is 25 (5) hectares in size. The methodology is based on the information from Landsat TM and SPOT Pan data (1990-92) in combination with ancillary information (aerial photos 1.20,000; topographic maps 1:50,000 and 1:100,000). Each level of nomenclature reflects different decision-making perspective (Tables 1 and 2).

2.3   Land Use Structure Development

Table 1   Land use development on the territory of the present day Czech Republic (%)

Land use/year	1848	1897	1948	1990
Arable land	48.2	51.6	49.9	41.0
Perm. cultures	1.1	1.5	1.9	2.9
Meadows	9.3	8.9	9.1	7.3
Pastures	8.3	5.3	3.8	3.2
Agr. land	66.9	67.5	64.7	54.4
Forest land	28.8	28.9	30.2	33.3
Water	0.9	0.5	0.6	0.6
Built-up land	0.6	0.7	1.1	1.6
Other	2.8	2.6	3.4	10.1
Total	100.00	100.00	100.00	100.00

Table 2   Forest land in the Czech lands and Czech Republic (1000 ha)

Year	1790	1839	1920	1930	1945	1950	1960	1970	1980	1990	1997
Area	1974	2267	2369	2354	2420	2479	2574	2606	2623	2629	2632

3.   PRESENT CZECH AGRICULTURAL LANDSCAPES

3.1   Common Agricultural Policy of the EU

After more than a year of debate and negotiation, in June 1992 the Council of Ministers formally adopted the radical form of European farming. The goal was to break out of the circle created by high prices and excessive production. There are five main aims: 1) to maintain EU's position as a major agricultural producer and exporter by making its farmers more competitive on home and export markets; 2) to bring production down to levels more in line with market demand; 3) to focus support for farmer's incomes where it is most needed; 4) to encourage farmers to remain on the land; and 5) to protect the environment and develop the natural potential of the landscape.

In the coming years, there will no doubt be a continuing decline in the number of EC farmers. The present structure, in some countries, where farming makes more than an average contribution to GNP is destined to change.

3.2   Landscape Typology

There are four basic functional types of present-day landscape developed and defined by the spatial structure of the land use: 1) man-made and urbanized landscapes, 2) agricultural landscapes, 3) agricultural-forest landscapes (forest-arable land; forest-grassland; forest-pond land), and 4) forest, meadow and rocky landscapes (Kremsa, 1987).

The functional types of agricultural landscapes involve: landscape with a distinct prevalence of arable land; landscape with arable land and a distinct share of grassland; landscape with arable land and a distinct share of vineyards and orchards; landscape with arable land and a distinct share of hop-gardens, landscape with arable land and a distinct share of fish-ponds; and landscape with a prevalence of grasslands (Tables 3 and 4).

3.3   Land Use Structure

3.3.1   Comparison with Central and Eastern Europe

Table 3   Land use structure (1995)

Country	Land area Thous. sq. km.	Rural popul. density No. per sq. km	Cropland % of land area	Perm pasture % of land area	Forest land Thous. sq. km
Hungary	92	75	54	12	17
Romania	230	107	43	21	62
Poland	304	99	48	13	87
Bulgaria	111	67	38	16	32
Slovakia	48	148	33	17	20
Lithuania	65	35	46	8	20
Latvia	62	40	28	13	29
Slovenia	20	414	14	25	11
Estonia	42	36	27	7	20
Czech R.	77	114	44	12	26

Table 4   Agricultural land (%) in Central and Eastern Europe (1996)

Country	Agr. land %	Country	Agr. land %
Hungary	66.5	Lithuania	48.5
Romania	62.0	Latvia	39.0
Poland	59.1	Slovenia	38.7
Bulgaria	55.5	Estonia	32.1
Czech Republic	54.3	CEC-10	55.9
Slovakia	49.9	EU-15	41.8

3.3.2 Comparison with EU member states

Reflecting the diversity of European landscapes, land use varies greatly from one member state to another. In Belgium and the Netherlands, which are highly industrialized and urbanized, there is proportionally less farmland and woodland than elsewhere. In Greece, Luxembourg, Germany and Portugal much of the landscape is covered by forests. In Ireland and Denmark, which are mainly flat countries, the landscape is used for agricultural purposes wherever possible.

Tables 5–8 show the position of Czech Republic according to the area of utilized agricultural land (%) compared with the member states of the European Union.

Table 5   Land use structure (%) in European Union and CR (1990)

Memb. state	Agric. land	Forest. land	Other
Ireland	81	6	13
UK	76	9	15
Denmark	65	11	24
Italy	57	21	22
France	56	27	17
Czech R.	54.4	33.3	12.3
Spain	54	24	22
Luxembourg	49	34	17
Portugal	49	32	19
Netherlands	49	10	41
Germany	48	30	22
Belgium	45	20	35
Greece	44	43	13
European Countries	57	24	19

Table 6   Land use structure (1995)

Country	Land area Th. sq. km	Rural pop. density No./sq. km	Cropland % of land A.	Permanent pasture % of land A.	Forest land Th. sq. km
Ireland	69	115	19	45	6
UK	242	107	25	46	24
Denmark	42	33	55	7	4
Italy	294	236	37	16	65
France	550	80	35	19	150

contd.

contd.

Country	Land area Th. sq. km	Rural pop. density No./sq. km	Cropland % of land A.	Permanent pasture % of land A.	Forest land Th. sq. km
Spain	499	60	40	21	84
Portugal	92	278	33	10	29
Netherlands	34	193	27	31	3
Germany	349	93	35	15	107
Benelux	33	39	23	21	7
Greece	129	178	27	41	65
Czech Republic	77	114	44	12	26

Table 7 Current economical and political trends

Indicat./year	1989	1990	1991	1992	1993	1994	1995
Consumer price index		10	57.9	10.9	20.8	10.2	9.1
Produce price index		16.6	54.8	8.4	13.1	5.3	7.6
Growth of GDP (%)	4.5	−1.2	−14.2	−6.6	−0.9	2.6	4.8
GDP per capita (US$)		3050	2358	2713	3024	3489	3600
Agriculture in GDP (%)		6.5	4.9	5.0	5.3	4.5	
Nominal net income (index)		100	118.4	136.3	175.3	218.6	
Real income (index)		100	75.7	78.3	83.6	94.9	
Inflation (%)	1.4	9.7	56.6	11.1	20.8	10.2	9.1
Unemployment (%)		0.7	4.1	2.6	3.5	3.2	3.1
Working persons in agricult. (%)		11.8		8.6		6.9	
Employment in agric. (%)		10.3	8.9	7.5	6.4	5.1	

Table 8 Decrease in number of persons employed in agriculture

Sector/Year	1991	1992	1993	1994	1995	1996
Civil—total	5,058,633	4,927,136	4,848,285	4,884,753	5,011,645	5,044,416
Agriculture, forestry, hunting	507,767	425,437	331,247	338,309	311,780	301,084
Fishing	2160	2020	2089	2039	2065	2149

4. FUTURE OF CZECH AGRICULTURAL LANDSCAPES

4.1 EU Scenarios

Four contrasting policy philosophies have been devised on the basis of the main movements in the debate on agriculture. These are extreme philosophies, in which the ideas which have been put forward in the debate are taken to their logical conclusions.

4.1.1 Free market and free trade

Under this scenario, agriculture is treated just as every other economic activity. Production is as low-cost as possible. A free international market for agricultural products has been assumed, with a minimum of restrictions in the interests of social provisions and environment. The philosophy which dominates this scenario is similar to the American approach in the negotiations on the GATT.

4.1.2 Regional development

This scenario accords priority to regional development of employment within the EU, which creates income in the agricultural sector. The predominant philosophy can be regarded as a continuation and extension of EU policy.

4.1.3 Nature and landscape

Under this scenario the greatest possible effort is made to conserve natural habitats, creating zones which divide them from agricultural areas. Besides protected nature reserves, areas would also be set aside for human activity. Nature conservation groups are exponents of this philosophy.

4.1.4 Environmental protection

The primary policy aim under this scenario is to keep alien substances from entering the environment. The main aim is to protect the soil, water and air. Natural and agricultural areas are integrated. Farming may take place anywhere, but subject to strict environmental requirements. The philosophy behind this is in line with the concept of 'integrated agriculture'.

4.2 Future vision of Czech agriculture

Our vision for the future, based on landscape-ecological holistic approach to the management of our landscape and natural resources is as follows: 1) A secure and well-managed resource base of agricultural landscape and soil to support the long-term productivity and competitiveness of the Czech agri-food system; 2) Agriculture that contributes to improved environmental quality through the use of environmentally sustainable production and processing practices; 3) Agriculture that has adapted itself to, and manages landscape resources available to it on a sustainable basis; 4) Czech agriculture and landscape to be managed for sustainability and long-term mutual benefits, 5) Agriculture that is able to respond to air and climatic changes, and which does not itself contribute to air and climatic problems; 6) Agriculture that is more efficient, less polluting and less dependent on non-renewable energy sources; 7) A major reduction in the impact of pollution on landscape resources (air, soil, water, etc.) used by the agriculture and food sector; and 8) Czech republic to have an accessible and sufficiently diversified genetic resource base that can be effectively utilized to assure the sustainability of agriculture for future generations.

4.3   Future Land Use and Landscape Patterns

An investigation of future land use and landscape patterns which examine possible strategies for future sustainable development, involves the following considerations: 1) Time perspective (long enough to foresee interactions between environmental transformations and socioeconomic development), 2) Spatial scale (sufficiently broad to incorporate large-scale transformations in the environment; enabling a linkage between causes, consequences and management of human development at the local, provincial scale), 3) Flexibility and resilience (options should be kept open for long-time alternative development and for adaptation to environmental changes), 4) Significant change (incorporated since the use of land cannot be sustained under static conditions), 5) Technological innovation (focused on how it would modify the environmental conditions as a consequence of socio-economic development), and 6) Allocation and renewability of resources.

Large areas of European agricultural landscape are likely to be taken out of production over the next few decades. The present agricultural surplus in the EU corresponds to an area of some 9 million hectares.

4.4   Scenarios for Agriculture and Landscape Development

According to the present situation and possible future development forecast, we can elaborate the following basic alternative scenarios for agricultural landscape.

4.4.1   Productive agricultural landscape

Agriculture finances production on its own by exploiting opportunities offered in terms of natural and economic conditions (climate, soils, location, infrastructure, etc.). The market decides the future of farmers, crops and farmland. Only the most efficient farmers survive in the long run.

Measures and instruments: Simulation of international competition and a liberal price and market policy, introduction of temporary set-aside programs whenever overproduction occurs; expansion of arable land during periods of strong increase in demand; expansion of the main infrastructure facilities (efficient transport via road, rail, water, air), protection of areas of specific environmental and historical value by means of the acquisition of land or by direct subvention to farmers (Kremsa, 1990).

In 1998, arable land occupied 40%, meadows 8%, pastures 3%, forest land 33%, water 2% and built-up and other land 14% of the soil fund of the Czech Republic.

4.4.2 Typical agricultural landscape

A typical agricultural landscape is the maintenance of a hierarchy of local and regional infrastructure networks. The autonomy of the region with its specific geographical and landscape conditions, its history and the image associated with it, and the existence of special high quality products, offers opportunities in the market.

Measures and instruments: Landscape amenity is part of the regional image, it is advertised and promoted in order to attract clients and tourists. Cooperation between authorities, chambers of commerce, tourist associations, etc. is essential. Joint funding of advertising and promotional campaigns, strict government control over original brand names, protection of 'copyright', facilitating the use of the landscape for various purposes (a mixture of housing, recreation, production and natural processes), protective measures against depletion of natural resources (water control, emission standards, recycling, etc), improved accessibility and communication (local and regional infrastructure networks).

Ponds and small reservoirs historically form a typical landscape element in many areas on the CR territory. They affect their vicinity in terms of water management, ecology and amenity value. The total water surface area of ponds on the CR territory is about 52,000 ha. These water bodies help in fish farming—one of the branches of agricultural production, especially in Southern Bohemia.

4.5 The Program for Renewal of Rural Areas

The program is concerned with participation of the rural population in the renewal of villages utilizing local traditions with active participation of civic societies and associations. Emphasis is placed on the development of economics of municipalities, construction renewal, construction of civic and technical infrastructure and also care for the landscape, as well as on preparing a suitable strategy (preparation of territorial plans or urban studies and local renewal programs) to precede the actual implementation of the local programs (Table 9).

The program for renewal of villages is a joint program of the Ministry of Local Development, the Ministry of Agriculture, the Ministry of Environment and the Ministry of Culture (Table 9).

Table 9 Renewal of rural area—distribution of finances (thousands CZK), 1994-96

Finances/year	1994	1995	1996
Total	100,000	220,000	202,000
Complex work	10,576	46,176	46,555

4.5.1 Protected agricultural landscape

Landscape is public property which must not be allowed to fall into neglect as a result of agriculture production and other damaging land use forms.

Measures and instruments: Implementation of regulations and budgets to delineate and manage nature reserves, protected landscapes; financial support to farmers who have the task of maintaining the landscape and must therefore lower production standards; extensification of production in intensively used areas; creation or preservation of a local mixture of agriculture, natural elements, outdoor recreation and housing (simultaneous use); creation of buffer zones between the rural and the urban, between the natural and the cultivated landscapes.

On the territory of the Czech Republic, there are 3 national parks with the area 110,304 ha, which represents 1.40% of total area of the CR, with a forest coverage of 77.6%. There are also 24 Protected Landscape Regions with the area 1,041,565 ha (13.21% of the total area of CR) with a forest coverage of 51.1%. Apart from this, Special Protected Areas were delimited: 42 in national parks, 507 in protected landscape areas, and 1,271 in other areas.

4.5.2 Protected landscape areas

A total of 24 protected landscape areas (10,415.7 km^2, 13.21% of area of CR) have been declared in the Czech Republic. These consist of extensive territories with a harmonic landscape, characteristically developed relief, a significant portion of natural ecosystems of forest and permanent grassland, with abundant tree species or with preserved monuments of historical settlements. In 1996, a strategy for the development of PLA was prepared, in which detailed features are defined and described, specifying the characteristics of these protected territories and setting forth the difference between PLA and national parks (Table 10).

Table 10   Specially protected territories in the Czech Republic (Dec. 1996)

Category	Number	Area (ha)	% of area of CR
National parks	3	110,304	1.40
Protect. landscape A.	24	1,041,565	13.21
Natl. nature reserves	118	26,434.89	0.34
Natl. natural memorials	100	2656.11	0.03
Nature reserves	572	25,675.19	0.33
Natural memorials	967	27,584.37	0.35

4.5.3 Landscape preservation program

The program is targeted towards maintenance or renewal of the cultural condition of the landscape and its ecological stability through individual subsidy programs: 1) Protection of the landscape against erosion (remediation of significant manifestation of surface and rill erosion and measures to ensure the stability of endangered features of nonliving nature; creation of individual biological anti-erosion measures through the establishment of linear and areal elements for ecological stability, care for tree stands along water courses, river bank tree stabilization stands, permanent grasslands); 2) Maintenance of the cultural condition of the landscape (elimination of Giant Hogweed (*Heracleum mantegazzianum*) and Japanese Knotweed (*Reynoutria japonica*); suppression of epidemic spread of diseases on tree species outside forests; removal of obstruction on water courses and linear structures for wild fauna); 3) Protection and renewal of the basic functions of the landscape (preservation of significant biotopes, support of target species composition, support of renewal of decreasing populations of native plant and animal species and their natural communities) (Table 11).

Table 11   Landscape preservation in 1996—implemented projects

Applicant	Number of projects	Finances (thousands CZK)
Cooperatives	82	44,983,901
Stakeholders	9	4,683,795
State organizations	51	43,472,110
Juristic and natural persons	108	18,933,497
Municipalities	45	31,834,132
Total	295	143,907,435

4.6   Sustainable Agricultural Landscape

The maintenance of environmental quality and ecological processes are fast becoming limiting factors for production. The task is to control the use of natural resources and to actively reconstruct landscapes in order to help balance the various land-use requirements (Kremsa, 1993, 1994).

Measures and Instruments: Application of the latest innovation in technological know-how; replacement of the use of pesticides by biological control; recycling of waste products, manure, polluted water, etc.; integrated quantitative and qualitative water control; effective implementation of legislation; subsidizing anti-pollution devices and measures; monitoring the system for early warning of pollution, erosion, etc.; stimulation of scientific research (landscape ecology, bioecology, bioengineering, etc.); and implementation of landscape plans establishing new frameworks connecting elements and zones of high stability and productive areas.

The following principles of sustainable agriculture and food production could be identified: 1) integration of the farming system with natural processes and landscape, 2) reduction of risk input that might harm the environment, 3) use of the biological and genetic potential of plants and animals, 4) improving the match between cropping patterns and landscape resources, 5) efficient production (improvement of farm management and conservation of soil, water, air, energy, biological resources, etc.), 6) development of food processing, packaging, distribution and consumption practices consistent with sound environmental management, 7) guidelines for reducing environmental degradation, conserving resources, providing an adequate farm income.

The forests in the Czech Republic are managed in accordance with the principles of sustainable forest management (Helsinki criteria). The Table 12 gives the long-term development of forest land area (1000 ha) in the CR.

4.7   Territorial Systems of Ecological Stability

Territorial Systems of Ecological Stability are the chief instrument employed in the creation and protection of the landscape in the sense of its permanent utilization. The preparation of territorial technical documents (TTD) continues for all levels of TSES (local, regional, super-regional), including the national network (which will become part of the currently established European Ecological network—EECONET). Practically the whole country is covered by general plans of local

Table 12   River systems revitaliation—number of implemented projects (1992-96)

Project/year	1992	1993	1994	1995	1996
Water reservoirs	14				
-renewal, revitalization		—	30	41	56
-new construction		—	10	18	15
-dredged	—	—	—	—	7
Water courses					
-overall revitalization	8	—	38	70	52
-individual	—	—	7	5	1
Spring Areas, Marshes	—	—	2	15	11
Biocentres, Greenery	—	—	20	14	13

TSES. Special attention is paid to the provision for protecting super-regional biocentres.

5. RIVER SYSTEMS REVITALIZATION

This program contributed significantly to the improvement of the devastated water regime of the landscape. Attention was paid to renewal and revitalization of water reservoirs, connected with the possibility of obtaining subsidies for dredging and maintenance, and also for renewal and improvement of the condition of water courses. There is a decrease in the number of isolated projects on water courses and an increase of more complex modifications of biocentres, especially wetlands and spring areas (Table 12).

6. ENVIRONMENT FRIENDLY AGRICULTURE

Environment friendly agriculture includes: 1) circumspect use of natural resources with limited or prohibited use of substances and procedures burdening the environment, 2) the breeding of domestic animals in accordance with their ethological requirements and a natural manner of breeding with limited use of veterinary pharmaceuticals, and 3) circumspect processing procedures (Table 13).

Table 13   Environmental friendly agriculture, 1990-96

EFA/year	1990	1991	1992	1993	1994	1995	1996
Units no	3	132	135	141	187	181	182
Area ha	480	17,507	15,371	15,667	15,818	14,982	17,022
Area %	0.0	0.41	0.36	0.37	0.37	0.35	0.40

The legislation of environment friendly agriculture is governed by an internal regulation of the Ministry of Agriculture of the Czech Republic, methodical instructions for Environmentally Friendly Agriculture of June 22, 1993 with subsequent amendments. The agricultural management of entities that wish to designate their products as environmentally friendly products, with the guarantee trademark BIO, is subject to independent controls (Table 14).

Table 14   Subsidy for activities with beneficial environmental impact (mil CZK)

Subject of subsidy	1994	1995	1996
Grass seeding	201	53	0
Afforestation	13	26	27
Grassland maintenance	438	1174	1452
Agriculture	35	75	64
Genetic reserve preservation	21	23	1
Biological protection	4	4	5
Water areas preserv.	27	35	0

7. ABANDONED AGRICULTURAL LANDSCAPE

Farming subsidies was taken away, leaving the upland farmers to compete with better farmers in the lowlands. This led to much land being abandoned.

The area of forest land on the territory of present Czech Republic has been growing since 1790 (the Joseph's Register). Over two hundred years it has enlarged by 658,000 ha and forest land coverage increased from 25 to 33.4%. During the last 50 years, the increase of forest land area has been 212,000 ha. Currently, forest area per capita is 0.25 ha (Table 15).

Table 15   Forest land in the Czech Republic (1,000 ha), 1990-97

Year	1990	1991	1992	1993	1994	1995	1996	1997
Area	2629	2630	2629	2629	2630	2630	2631	2632

Table 16 shows the current development of afforestation (ha) of agricultural land in Czech Republic (Table 17).

Table 16   Afforestation of agricultural land (ha)

Ownership	1994	1995	1996	1997
Private	287	507	519	306
Municipal	12	57	107	88
Other	0	3	24	39
Total	299	567	650	433

Table 17   Forest categories (%) in the Czech Republic

Year	Economic forests	Protective forests	Special-purpose forests
1980	78.2	4.0	17.8
1985	68.2	3.1	28.7
1990	58.4	2.5	39.1
1995	57.2	2.7	40.1
1996	61.3	2.9	35.8

8. POLICY FRAMEWORK FOR DECISION MAKING

Realization of the vision of sustainable agriculture and agricultural landscape requires a policy framework based on the following elements: scientific and technological advancement that promote innovative farming systems; elimination of policies that hinder sustainable agricultural practices, new policies that promote and reward good environmental management; policy decisions based on objective data, education of farmers, consumers and authorities; integration of environmental implications of farming practices and food preferences; integration of environmental considerations into policies on international trade; protection of landscape and natural resources; flexible institutional arrangements to meet emerging environmental needs and market demands; comprehensive development policies for Czech agriculture and agricultural landscape conservation, that integrate agriculture with alternative economic opportunities.

REFERENCES

Kremsa, V. 1985. Development of Remote Sensing Methods for Geoecological Evaluation of Structure and Dynamics of Landscape Systems. Research Report, Landscape Ecology Institute, Czechoslovak Academy of Sciences Ceske Budejovice (in Czech).

Kremsa, V. 1986a. Detection and Evaluation of Geoecological Functions of Agricultural Land Use. Research Report, Landscape Ecology Institute, Czechoslovak Academy of Sciences, Ceske Budejovice (in Czech).

Kremsa, V. 1986a. Remote Sensing Information for Management of Ecological Activities in Agricultural Landscape on Local and Regional Level. Research Report, Landscape Ecology Institute, Czechoslovak Academy of Sciences, Ceske Budejovice (in Czech).

Kremsa, V. 1987. Theoretical and Methodological Basis for Detection and Evaluation of Geoecological Functions of Agricultural Land Use. Research Report, Landscape Ecology Institute, Czechoslovak Academy of Sciences, Ceske Budejovice (in Czech).

Kremsa, V. 1990a. The natural conditions and distribution of agricultural production in Czechoslovakia. In: *Agricultural Applications of Remote Sensing*. Proceedings of the International Training Course FAO/UN, University of Agriculture, The Prague.

Kremsa, V. 1990a. Ecological Monitoring and Evaluation of Agricultural Land(scape)-Use Changes using Satellite Images. Research Report, Landscape Ecology Institute, Czechoslovak Academy of Sciences, Ceske Budejovice (in Czech).

Kremsa, V. 1993. Perspectives of Ecologically Sustainable Development of Agriculture and Agricultural Landscape in Czech Republic in European Context. Report for Czech Parliament, Inter-university Futures Studies Program (in Czech).

Kremsa, V. 1994. Landscape and Agriculture in the Czech Republic. In: *Landscape Research Application in Environmental Management*. Proceedings of 1st Conference of "Landscape Synthesis" Working Group of the International Association of Landscape Ecology, Warsaw University, Faculty of Geography and Regional Studies & Polish Association for Landscape Ecology, 6-9 October, 1993, 137-142.

CHAPTER 10

Driving Forces of Land Use Changes in Czechia over the Last 50 Years

(Ivan Bičík and Vít Štěpánek[*])

1. INTRODUCTION

General tendencies of land use changes observed in Czechia over the last fifty years are similar to changes in economically developed countries. It includes decrease of agricultural land, increase in forests and an intensive increase of built-up areas and 'other' areas (industry, transport lines, dumps, wasteland, etc.).

These land use changes have been initiated more than a century ago. It was in the 1880s that agriculture underwent sound intensification and market conditions were fully implemented as it was necessary to cover the dramatically rising consumption.

World War II and especially the post-war period brought about acceleration of land use changes. These changes, however, were to a great extent influenced by the centrally planned economy implemented immediately after Communists took power (1948) and were also influenced by the political climate in the former Czechoslovakia. That is why the post-war period is of special importance for land use studies, too.

Our land use research examines eight basic land use categories: arable land, permanent cultures (gardens, orchards, hopyards and vineyards combined), meadows, pastures, forests, built-up land, water areas, and 'other' areas. Analyses are based on a detailed knowledge of land use conditions in rather small areas called *cadastral areas* (Czech Republic consists of ca. 13,000 such small units). The arial extent of all land use

[*]Department of Social Geography and Regional Development, Faculty of Science, Universzita Karlova, 128 43 Albertov 6, Praha-2, Czech Republic

categories in each cadastral area is examined and changes over the time are observed. Such land use data are available for 1845, 1948, 1990, and 1995 (i.e. $4 \times 13,000 \times 8$ data). For the sake of historical comparison some cadastral units must be amalgamated in order to obtain statistical areas with no or only minor change of size over the years; such amalgamated units (called *basic territorial units*) number ca. 10,000.

Such land use information, of course, may not be thoroughly accurate in certain places and there may be differences between statistical data and the real situation. The reliability of data is regularly tested by fieldwork in a number of small test areas.

2. INFORMATION SOURCES

The initial purpose for gathering land use information in the eighteenth and nineteenth centuries was different taxation for different land use types. Until the 1970s, all land use information was obtained from fieldwork; data were kept in primitive files and the information of land use changes in bigger units (districts, provinces) could only be received by grouping the initial data.

Information technology brought new prospects into land use studies too. The use of GIS allows one to conveniently and quickly analyse and adjust large files containing millions of basic land use data. Thus, information on land use structure or land use changes in different cadastral units (13,000), municipal areas (5000), districts (76), etc. are readily available.

Of great importance are also land use maps. Rather detailed maps (scale 1:2880-1:2000) are available from the end of the eighteenth century, from the period 1825-43 onwards. These maps showing the land use structure of the same area in different periods allows one to trace the historic land use changes in detail and also look into what the nature-society interaction was like over the past few decades.

Land use changes are viewed as a very good indicator of such interaction, which is examined by a number of other scientific branches. The existence of land use data from early nineteenth century thus enables one to trace the nature-society interactions over more than 150 years.

Long-term land use changes have been intensively researched at the Faculty of Science, Charles University over a long period of time. The research team headed by Professor I. Bičík, partly backed by the Czech Grant Agency, has obtained original and unique results that allow wide interpretations of land use changes even beyond the boundaries of geography as a science.

3.   LAND USE CHANGES DURING WORLD WAR II

During World War II, Czechoslovakia was *de facto* occupied by Nazi Germany. In land use terms, the chief intention of German administration was to produce a sufficient amount of food with a limited workforce. The territory of today's Czech Republic was divided into *Sudetenland* (inhabited mostly by ethnic Germans) and *Protektorát Čechy a Morava* (inhabited mostly by ethnic Czechs). As German citizens were subject to conscription, there was a permanent lack of labour force, especially in the Sudetenland. Land use structure in the war period was much influenced by the permanent interest in foodstuff. Part of the foodstuff produced in the occupied Czechia was delivered directly to the German Army, some agricultural products were sold on the domestic market (partly illegally). This situation stabilized the land use structure and in some cases even led to an increase of arable (agricultural) land. Agricultural land was used in a relatively intensive way.

4.   THE GERMAN EXODUS

The period 1945-48 was dominated by large-scale population transfers in the whole Central/Eastern Europe. The former Czechoslovakia was not an exception: most of the ethnic Germans were expelled to post-war Germany. More than 3 million people were forcibly transferred (most in 1945 and 1946) and a number of people lost their lives in this process (estimates vary between 19,000 and 30,000). Practically all property of expelled Germans was confiscated by the Czechoslovak State on the base of collective guilt. This was also the case in Sudetenland where 3 million hectares of formerly German land became state property (and mostly remain state property even now).

This huge population transfer was followed by in-migration of ethnic Czechs and other nationalities from the East to the depopulated Sudetenland. About 1.9 million newcomers partly resettled in the border regions of former Czechoslovakia and though the Czechoslovak government encouraged the resettlement process, the pre-war population numbers have never been achieved (the population of former Sudetenland in the 1990s amounts only ca. 65% of the 1930 number). Most of the newcomers tended to concentrate in towns and large villages; on the other hand, many rural regions with dispersed settlements became totally depopulated (especially in mountainous areas and highlands).

These dramatic demographic changes in Sudetenland have also influenced the economic performance of the border regions.

Agricultural and forest management faced problems so far unknown, especially a total lack of labour force. As regards the land use structure, however, changes in the early post-war period were slow. The land use survey conducted in 1948 reflects the structure of land *de facto* before the German exodus, i.e. under conditions of intensive use of agricultural land. Data collected in this survey are of crucial importance for land use studies in Czechia: they can be compared with earlier data from the period 1825-43 as well as with more recent data.

5. LAND USE CHANGES AFTER 1948

Land use changes after 1948 were influenced by two major factors. First, there were *general economic tendencies* that led to a decrease of arable land in mountainous regions, decrease of meadows and pastures in fertile regions, increase of urban land, etc. Even more important, however, were *specific conditions* in the post-war Czechoslovakia that included the exodus of ethnic Germans in the border regions (resulting in an unusual decrease of agriculture and arable land in the 1950s), intensive processes of 'socialist' industrialization and urbanization, large scale open-pit mining, installation of the 'iron curtain', etc. In different periods of the long Communist rule (1948-89), however, different driving forces of land use changes were in effect.

5.1 Period 1948-60

The Communist coup-d'etat in February 1948 also had a crucial influence on the land use structure. The most important consequences of the Communist rule were:

— *de facto nationalization* of most of the land that were managed by the so-called state farms or Soviet-type cooperatives; these organiza-tions were soon responsible for some 90% of agricultural land (later this share reached 99%);

— general neglect of agricultural land in the border areas and its gradual decrease;

— shift from arable land to meadows and pastures, mostly in the border land and in mountainous regions;

— *rise of specially designated area* (military grounds, nature reserves, etc.

— large-scale *industrial and housing projects* that required a lot of land, usually partly a farmland. This was the case of open-pit mines, power plants, water reservoirs, new investments into 'socialist' agriculture (mechanization centres, large stables, stores), etc.

— installation of the *iron curtain* along the western border which effectively made large tracts of land close to the border inaccessible.

The combined German exodus plus the iron curtain effect had devastating consequences on general conditions in this area. More than 1,000 settlements ceased to exist here and the economic functions of such areas collapsed. The intensity of agricultural land use decreased to a large extent.

In statistical terms, the area of agricultural land and especially arable land acreage was quite reduced. Arable land was partly converted into meadows and pastures, in many cases (sloping land, mountains) were afforested former fields (mostly in a natural way). However, there were great regional inequalities in this process. The most intensive arable land losses were recorded in the mountainous western frontier. This was the 'iron curtain country': the wide space between the barbed-wire fence and the border itself was virtually inaccessible and the land use changes were consequently drastic. The adjoining areas were managed by less effective state farms.

5.2 Period 1960–80

The 1960s were a period of relative political liberalization that resulted in a failed attempt to reform the Communist regime in 1968. The following decade was dominated by re-installation of a rigid Soviet-style dictatorship.

Land use changes in this period were mostly influenced by the following factors:

— the process of 'agricultural socialization' continued. A lot of investments were allocated to rural area (fertilizers, upgrading wetlands, cowsheds, technical background in cooperatives).

— State farms and cooperatives were subject to a *special taxation system*: agricultural companies located in fertile areas had to pay a special tax and the money thus collected was transferred to cooperatives and state farms in poor natural conditions. This system helped retain arable land in regions where farming conditions were not economically viable (especially in mountains and highlands). The state hoped to become self-sufficient as far as food was concerned and this aim was achieved; the whole scheme, however, was a great waste of money, investment and labour force. It also balanced the regional differences of land use structure.

— As a response to great demand for housing, extensive prefab-
ricated housing estates were built mostly on the margins of
existing towns. Thus, large areas of high-quality agricultural land
were lost.

— The intensive exploitation of coal deposits and other raw
materials (uranium ore) completely changed the landscape in
vast regions especially in Northwestern Bohemia and Northern Moravia. In land use terms, it also meant great reduction
of high-quality agricultural land. Such land transformed to
open pits was statistically recorded as 'temporarily unused
agricultural land'; only a few such areas, however, were later
reclaimed and their current agricultural use is negligible.

— The sixties and seventies were periods of a great second housing boom. Second housing under Communism was indirectly
supported by a number of factors including availability of
abandoned farmhouses and plots in rural areas, low costs,
general housing shortage and poor quality of permanent housing, and abundance of free time as a number of activities (private enterprising, travelling abroad) were under Communism
restricted or banned. Second housing has contributed to a
special life style which was characterized by periodic weekend
commuting to second homes and also much influenced the use
of land especially in suburban areas (the southern environs of
Prague is the best example), in the vicinity of newly built ar-
tificially lakes and in the frontier, too (where abandoned German farmhouses were often converted into second homes).
The second housing boom resulted in an increases of built-up
land and a number of settlements in attractive, yet remote
areas survived only thanks to second housing.

5.3 Period 1980-90

At the end of the Communist period, land use structure remained
relatively stable as a number of legal protection schemes were enforced.
The Communist government was interested in food self-sufficiency and
the low-effective socialist farming system required large tracts of land.
The most important legal scheme was the Agricultural Land Protection
Act 1976. As a result, non-agricultural use of agricultural land was
strictly limited: the conversion of highest quality agricultural land
into other use (urban, forests) was legally forbidden and the
conversion of medium- and low-quality agricultural land had to be
paid for. Consequently, the spatial extension of cities and towns in
fertile regions was limited and the decrease of agricultural land
slowed down.

Second, a number of legally protected areas with high quality environment were proclaimed. This was the case of Protected Landscape Areas, Nature Reserves, etc. In such areas, the use of land was carefully controlled and the land use structure usually stabilized.

On the other hand, large-scale mining (partly in open pits) continued in Northwestern Bohemia and in Northern Moravia. The most intensive land use changes in the post-war period were recorded in these areas. For example, the index of change in the Karviná district (Northern Moravia) exceeded 20, i.e. on 20% of the territory there has been land use change.

Generally, the negative processes in the landscape reached its peak in the 1980s. This included landscape devastation in the coal mining regions, land degradation due to excessive use of fertilizers, environmental risks resulting from high concentraion of agricultural production (giant cowsheds) and increased erosion supported by amalgamation of plots. Waste management in agriculture was poor resulting from low individual responsibility in the decision-making process.

6. LAND USE CHANGES SINCE 1990

The events of 1989 brought fundamental changes into political, social and economic atmosphere in the Czech Republic. It was a key historical moment that terminated the long period of Communist dictatorship, which had started in February 1948.

The most important post-1990 processes that influenced land use changes were:

— restitution of private property nationalized under Communism (including agricultural land, farms, forests, etc.)
— partial privatization of state property
— increased environmental awareness
— transformation of Soviet-style agricultural cooperatives into cooperatives where legal rights of original landowners are respected
— removal of the 'iron curtain', accessibility of border regions to everyone
— existence of the land market accessible for Czech citizens only; state-owned land can be bought by individual persons and by private firms
The key tendencies of post-1990 land use changes are:
— decrease of agricultural and arable land continues;

— the extent of meadows and pastures remains stable, in some areas even increases;
— built-up land and 'other' land increase a lot; and
— forests continue to expand slightly.

However, the general tendencies often result from different or even contradictory trends in different regions. As the system of agricultural subsidies has fundamentally changed since 1990 (the 'better' cooperatives no longer pay for the 'worse' ones), an intensive decrease of arable land is observed in mountainous and hilly regions. These subsidies, however, are fairly low compared with EU-countries (about one-half) and almost all money is allocated into non-productive agricultural functions. As a result, natural conditions are a more important factor now.

Yet, the statistical differences between mountainous regions and fertile lowlands still remain relatively small. Land use changes are recorded with a certain delay and the most common shift (arable land towards meadows and pastures) takes time. But the process has already been started as field research repeatedly shows.

SELECTED READINGS

Bičík, I. 1995. Possibilities of long-term human nature interaction analysis: The case of land-use changes in the Czech Republic. In: The Changing Nature of the People-Environment Relationship: Evidence from a Variety of Archives I.G. Simmons and A.M. Mannion (Ed.). Proceedings of the IGU Commission on Historical Monitoring of Environmental Changes Meeting. Praha, 79-91.

Bičík, I. and A. Götz. 1996. Main Regional Changes in Agriculture of the Czech Republic after 1989. In: Transformation Process of Regional Systems in Slovak Republic and Czech Republic. Acta Facultatis Rerum Naturalium Universitas Comenianae, Geographica No. 37, s. 207-213.

Bičík, I., Götx, A., Jančák, V., Jeleček, L., Mejsmarová, L. and V. Štěpánek 1996. Land Use/Land Cover Changes in the Czech Republic 1845-1995. Geografie-Sbornik ČGS, 101, No. 2, 92-109.

Bičík, I. and V. Štěpánek 1994. Post-War Changes of the Land Use Structure in Bohemia and Moravia. GeoJournal 32,(3): pp. 253-259.

Bičík, I. and V. Štěpánek. 1994. Changing Land-Use Patterns in Liberec and Jablonec Districts. In: Territory, Society and Administration, Instituut voor Sociale Geografie, Amsterdam,   57-64.

Jančák, V. 1995. Dynamics of land-use in the southern outskirts of Prague—Case of Příbram District. In: The Changing Nature of the People-Environment Relationship: Evidence from a Variety of Archives, I.G. Simmons and A.M. Mannion (Eds), Dept. of Social Geography and Regional Development, Prague, s. 73-79.

Jeleček, L. 1994. Long term land use changes in the Czech Republic 1845-1990: some historical and environmental connections. IGU Regional Conference, Prague, 1994, Proceedings.

Jeleček, L. 1995. Changes in production and techniques in the agriculture of Bohemia, 1870-1945. In: Agriculture in the Industrial State, M.A. Havinden and E.J.T. Collins (Eds.), University of Reading, Rural History Centre, Reading, UK, 126-145.

CHAPTER 11

Land Use Changes in Gorenjsko

(Franci Petek[*])

1. INTRODUCTION

Discussed is the land use and its changes in Gorenjsko in the last century. The region lies in the northwestern part of Slovenia, in the corner between Austria in the north and Italy in the west. The entire area of Gorenjsko, occupying 14% of Slovenian territory is extremely diverse in landscape features and lies in the Alpine world. Typical of Slovenian Alpine world are high mountains on the one hand, and deeply cut glacial and fluvial valleys and broader flat basins on the other. Gorenjsko in particular shows its typical double characteristics. The central part consists of the Sava plain making the bottom of the Ljubljana basin which is surrounded by hilly and mountainous areas. Landforms exert the strongest impact on land use. Altitude above sea level, inclination and exposure of the surface place restrictions on agriculture. Lands with the following characteristics are the most suitable for agriculture (Vrišer, 1997):

- altitude up to 600 m;
- inclination up to 10° (machine cultivation allows up to 13°);
- good insulation (SE-SW position; exposures between 112.5° and 247.5°).

[*]Anton Melik Geographical Institute, Scientific Research Center of Slovenian Academy of Sciences and Arts, Gosposka 13, Si-1000 Ljubljana, Slovenia

1.1 Altitude Belts in Gorenjsko

The lowest altitude in the region of Gorenjsko is found at the bottom section of the Kamniškobistriška Ravan plain (Perko in *Krajevni leksikon Slovenije 1995*) which even drops below 300 meters. On the other hand, Mt Triglav in the Julian Alps with its 2864 meters is the highest peak. To put it in a generalized form, the altitude drops from the west, north-west and north, where the highest Slovenian high-mountain ranges lie (the Julian Alps, the Karavanke and the Kamniško-Savinjske Alps), toward the NW-SE axis (which coincides with the dropping direction of the Sava plain).

The data on altitude, inclination and exposure were calculated by means of a 100-meter digital model relief (DMR 100) of Slovenia. The DMR consists of 100-by-100-meter cells the corners of which provide data on altitudes. Although the precision is slightly diminished, it is nevertheless quite satisfactory for the analysis of data on large areas.

A greater difficulty occurs with settlement centroids where the number of inhabitants is also included. It is methodologically problematic to determine the centroids for large settlements (dispersed settlements) or settlements consisting of isolated farms (Kokra), and big settlements (Jesenice, Kranj). The indicators resulting from the distribution of settlements and population by altitude and inclination should only be taken as assessments. However, owing to a large number of input data they nevertheless show certain regularities (Perko, 1994).

It was calculated that the average altitude of Gorenjsko amounts to 848 meters which is almost 300 meters more than the average of Slovenia. The area percentage of 100-meter altitude belts declines parallel to altitude growth. The belt between 300 and 400 meters occupies the largest percentage, i.e. 15%. More than a tenth of Gorenjsko belongs to the next two higher 100-meter belts. Altitudes of up to 600 meters (areas still favourable for farming) in all represent 40% of the area of Gorenjsko (Table 1).

Besides, most of 374, 527 inhabitants, which is almost 18% of the entire Slovenian population, live in the lower altitude belts. Most outstanding is the belt between 300 and 400 meters in the lower wider section of the Sava plain, with almost 60% of the people of Gorenjsko. In the entire area of up to 600 meters live as much as 93.5% of the population! These data also show how important a factor is the altitude for the settling of people and therefore, also for their daily activities. Similar is the situation with the percentages of settlements by altitude belts. Nevertheless, the percentages of settlements decline more evenly with altitude growth. However, above 600 meters there are still 221 settlements (almost 28%) of the total 578 settlements in Gorenjsko.

Table 1   Altitudes above sea level; areas, population and settlements by altitude belts

Altitude belt in meters	Area		Population		Settlements	
	Ha	%	number	%	number	%
201-300	2675	0.9	6048	1.7	11	1.4
301-400	40,601	14.4	204,541	58.9	226	28.3
401-500	36,285	12.9	57,071	16.4	189	23.7
501-600	30,929	11.0	56,971	16.4	152	19.0
601-700	25,035	8.9	10,655	3.1	100	12.5
701-800	20,787	7.4	5313	1.5	63	7.9
801-900	17,464	6.2	5331	1.5	34	4.3
901-1000	15,204	5.4	1280	0.4	14	1.8
1001-1100	14,788	5.2	256	0.1	6	0.8
1101-1200	14,655	5.2	3	0.0	1	0.1
1201-1300	14,776	5.2	0	0.0	1	0.1
1301-1400	11,642	4.1	0	0.0	0	0.0
1401-1500	8976	3.2	0	0.0	0	0.0
1501-1600	7395	2.6	2	0.0	1	0.1
1601-1700	5636	2.0	56	0.0	1	0.1
1701 and more	15,126	5.4	0	0.0	0	0.0
Total	281,974	100	347,527	100	799	100

Source: Statistical Office of the Republic of Slovenia, 1991
          Surveying and Mapping Authority of the Republic of Slovenia, 1992.

1.2   Surface Inclinations in Gorenjsko

Land use is also influenced by surface inclination. The average inclination in Gorenjsko is 18.9°, and in Slovenia, 13°. For a clearer presentation, inclinations were grouped into 7 classes (Perko, 1998).

CLASS	INCLINATION
1	0.0°-1.9°
2	2.0°-5.9°
3	6.0°-11.9°
4	12.0°-19.9°
5	20.0°-29.9°
6	30.0°-44.9°
7	45°.0 and more

Class 1 can be considered as entirely flat (Perko, 1992). Classes 2 and 3, too represent the lands which are still favourable for agriculture. However, with the increased inclination conditions for agricultural land use rapidly impair and lands are only suitable for pasturing, forestry and hand mowing of grass.

Classes 1, 2 and 3 represent one-third of Gorenjsko. Beside the fact that the surface inclination increases with the altitude, steep slopes also occur in the lower sections of the region. These are the slopes of terraces, isolated elevations, and foothill sections above the narrow valleys in the mountains. Neither the high altitudes nor the steep slopes are attractive for permanent settling. Most of the people, which is as much as 65%, live in the areas of inclination between 2° and 5°. In the areas of inclination greater than 11° live a mean 12% of the entire population of Gorenjsko. Parallel to the increase in inclination the percentage of settlements declines.

It is interesting to compare hectare percentages between individual inclination classes and altitude belts, i.e. the two factors for which it has been confirmed that they strongly influenced the settling pattern, land use and general human activity in space. Discussed in the paper are only the inclinations and the altitudes which are still favourable for agricultural land use (up to 11° and up to 600 meters), and those which already represent the aggravated conditions. The former occupy a quarter, and the latter the remaining three quarters of the territory of Gorenjsko. When the two factors of suitability for agricultural land use are taken into consideration it becomes evident that the percentage of favourable lands diminishes. When only the altitude was taken into account, 40% of the territory ranked within this category, 33% when only the inclination was considered, and even less, 25%, when both these criteria were taken into account. Within the category of favourable farming lands, 18.5% lie on the entirely flat territory (0.0°-1.9°), as much as 52.5% on gentle inclinations (2.0°-5.9°), and 29% on inclinations between 6.0° and 11.9° (Table 2).

Table 2   Surface inclinations; areas, population and settlements by inclination classes

Inclination class	Area		Population		Settlements	
in degrees	ha	%	number	%	number	%
0,0° do 1,9°	13,106	4.6	26,610	7.7	41	5.1
2,0° do 5,9°	42,559	15.1	228,499	65.7	283	35.4
6,0° do 11,9°	38,283	13.6	46,593	13.4	229	28.7
12,0° do 19,9°	60,225	21.4	36,833	10.6	183	22.9
20,0° do 29,9°	66,639	23.6	8573	2.5	54	6.8
30,0° do 44,9°	51,232	18.2	419	0.1	9	1.1
45,0° and more	9930	3.5	0	0.0	0	0.0
Total	281,974	100	347,527	100	799	100

Source: Perko, D. 1992. Inclines in Slovenia and Digital Terrain Model.

1.3 Exposures

Land use and general activities in space are also influenced by exposure to the sun or orientation of the surface (Perko, 1994). However, inclinations play an important role in surface exposures. With the increasing inclination the explicitness of land forms exposure increases, as well as its influence on the remaining landscape components (Perko, 1994), and indirectly also on land use. Thus, in making calculations of theoretically favourable areas for agriculture, all the areas of up to 11.9° inclination that are oriented westwards, northwards, northwards, and eastwards were also excluded. Namely, an explicit influence of exposure is only felt at the inclinations greater than 11.9°.

2. LAND USE

Numerous problems occur during land use studies and particularly in those related to methodology. There is a constant problem on how to coordinate data of different periods, sources and territorial units when making an analysis or a graphic presentation of land use.

To establish land use it is necessary to proceed from the occurrence and distribution of land categories. A basic source for studying land use were the data from a cadaster which is managed by *Geodetska uprava Republike Slovenije* (Surveying and Mapping Authority of the Republic of Slovenia). The data from the cadaster are supposed to present the actual conditions by cadastral communes; yet, owing to a slow recording of changes the cadaster constantly lags behind the actual state (Gabrovec and Kladnik, 1998).

Trying to establish the actual state of land use, we have made use of data from an agro-map (Agrokarta, 1992). The latter was made for the needs of farmers, therefore, it was adjusted to them. It differs from the cadaster in land use categorization which was made for the agro-map on the basis of aerial photographs taken between 1987 and 1991 (*Navodila za izdelavo agrokarte*/Instructions for making agro-map/1987). The lag between the origin of data on the agro-map and their analysis which was made in 1999 resulted again in a certain deviation from the present landscape. New buildings, motorways, grassing fields and overgrown lands undoubtedly changed the ratio in percentages of individual land use categories in the last eight years.

The following five categories were selected for analysis and graphic illustration:

- fields;

- grasslands;
- lands being overgrown;
- forests; and
- infertile areas.

Forest areas are not marked on the agro-map because they are not considered farming lands. Therefore, the data on forests being an important land category were taken from the cadaster. Owing to the above-mentioned difference in the accuracy of the agro-map and the cadaster, and owing to the fact that data on farming categories were taken from the agro-map and data on forests and infertile areas from the cadaster, either a surplus or a deficit occurred in the sum of areas in certain cadastral communes. Besides, the cadaster discerns two different grassland categories, meadows and pastures, which were merged into a single category for the needs of the current study.

Orchards and vineyards, too, are registered as two different categories in the cadaster. There are no vineyards in Gorenjsko, while orchards represent but a small percentage. Therefore, this category was not included into the analysis.

Lands being overgrown are not registered as a category in the cadaster, yet, they have become an ever more important spatial element in Slovenia, in Gorenjsko in particular. The data on infertile areas were taken from the agro-map.

Used as a basic spatial unit in the first phase of the analysis and presentation of land use was a cadastral commune which has been a rather unchanged territorial unit since the introduction of Emperor Francis' cadaster two hundred years ago. In the cartographic presentation of prevailing land categories by cadastral communes a seeming nonsense may occur because of the percentage of an individual land category which shows but the average value. Thus, it is possible that fields, for example, stretch far above the altitude of their actual occurrence, all up to the border of the respective cadastral commune. In fact, this land category is mainly concentrated on the lands suitable for it (in the valley bottoms, etc.). Presented on the land use map is only the prevailing category of respective cadastral commune (Gabrovec and Kladnik, 1997).

2.1 Basic Characteristics of Land Use in Gorenjsko

The territory of Slovenia was originally covered with forests. Non-forest islands only occurred in the forms of moors, some flood areas along the rivers, and the areas higher than the natural forest line. Later on, humans with their settlements and other activities in space cleared lands and made glades, fields, meadows and pastures which especially formed on greater plains, the continuous areas or the so-called cultural steppes. It is evident from historical development that space, at the beginning, was subordinated to primary activities (farming, foestry, ore exploitation), but later, the socioeconomic development gave an ever greater importance to other activities, too, which occupied space (manufacturing industry, urbanization, transport, etc.) (Stritar, 1990). This process eventually resulted in the depopulation of rural areas and the abandoning of agrarian activities. Production specialization, market oriented farming, modernization of cultivation techniques and mass introduction of farming mechanization resulted in extensive abandoning of lands that had well been cultivated in the time of prevailing subsistence farming, on which the use of machines was impossible, or non-profitable at least (Gabrovec and Kladnik, 1998).

It is possible to conclude on the basic of landscape features of Gorenjsko that land use is most versatile in its lower and flatter central section. In the higher, mountainous and high-mountainous areas forests prevail with smaller meadow and pasture areas, and only rare fields surround villages and hamlets.

It is interesting that, on an average, 28% of the territory of Gorenjsko are farming lands (fields, grasslands, orchards, lands being overgrown), which almost equals the percentage of agriculturally favourable (suitable) lands following the criteria of altitude (up to 600 meters) and inclination (up to 11.9°). Yet, a gross third of theoretically suitable lands are covered with forests.

Moreover, almost 57% of the area of Gorenjsko is covered with forests which is approximately 5 per cent points more than the average of Slovenia (*Podatki o zemljiških kategorijah po katastrskih občinah*/Data on land categories by cadastral communes/1994). The areas above the natural forest line, lying approximately at 1700 meters in Gorenjsko (Lovrenčak, 1976, 1986; Gams, 1961), occupy a gross 5%, which is quite a lot in comparison with the whole of Slovenia. Prevailing above the upper forest line are rocky surface, *Pinus mugo*, and high-mountainous pastures (also registered as farming lands) which are up to 2200 meters suitable only for goats and sheep (Kladnik, 1981).

2.2 Changes in Land Use from the Beginning of the Twentieth Century Until Today

Already in the past, land use was more or less regularly registered in the cadaster. Thus, it was possible to monitor the capacities of subsistence farming.

Fran Orožen (1901), for example, wrote: "Trade between mountainous districts and fertile lowlands along the Sava river, which also served as the waterway, brought a certain level of welfare to Carniola. But, from the construction of railroad onwards, the economic conditions have impaired. Field crops do not satisfy the needs of the province any more." He also wrote: "In certain parts of the province, in Gorenjsko for eample, only small farms exist, often having dispersed land parcels, 20 in number or even more. As to the size of a farm in Gorenjsko, it measures about 18 to 20 hectares, of which more than a half is covered with forest."

A vast percentage of the territory is covered with forests which is due to natural conditions. Besides, it is also the result of changes in the economic policy that stimulated the production of wood as early as the beginning of the century (Grafenauer, 1970). At that time, forests were already managed more economically, and forestation was also started (Orožen, 1901). It is estimated that there was 19 to 23% of the so-called relative forest in central Slovenia in the middle of the century. Relative forests are the areas covered with forests although they would be suitable by natural conditions for farming activities; yet, owing to various causes based on social conditions of the time, these forests were not cleared (Melik, 1960).

Changes in land use categories that took place from the beginning of the century until 1991, are clearly evident from the comparison of area percentages by individual categories. Compared were the situations of the years 1901, 1938, 1961 and 1994. The following categories were taken into consideration: fields, grasslands (meadows and pastures merged), forests and infertile areas. Percentages of areas being overgrown were not recorded in the past since this phenomenon was not in such a spread as nowadays, although it was already mentioned that some rare, sporadic, pastures had been overgrown with forest (Melik, 1936). It is interesting to compare percentages of fields, grasslands and total farming lands as registered in the cadaster of 1994 with the situation of 1991, as presented on the agro-map.

Table 3 shows a constant decline in percentages of farming lands in the mean hundred years. On the other hand, percentages of forests and infertile areas have increased. At the beginning of the century, there were 14% of fields, 26.9% of grasslands, 49% of forests, and 10% of infertile areas in Gorenjsko. On the entire territory of Slovenia, infertile areas occupied but 5.5% at that time (Melik, 1936). The cause of their almost doubled percentage in Gorenjsko can be found in the fact that the majority of Slovenian high-mountain infertile areas lie precisely in Gorenjsko.

Table 3   Changes in land use in Gorenjsko between 1901 and 1994

Year	Fields %	Grasslands %	Farming lands %	Forest %	Infertile %
1901	14.6	26.9	41.5	49.0	9.8
1938	12.4	26.6	40.1	51.5	9.4
1961	10.6	24.5	36.4	53.0	10.6
1994	8.1	21.7	31.2	56.7	12.1
1991	6.0	13.4	28.2	/	/

Source:
— 1901, *Gemeinde Lexikon für Krain, Alfred Hödler*
— 1938, *Poljoprivredna godišnja stštistika,* and *Statistika šuma i šumske privrede*, Ministarstvo poljoprivrede kraljevine SHS.
— 1961 and 1994, Surveying and Mapping Authority of the Republic of Slovenia.
— 1991, Agrokarta, 1992.

Almost 40 years later, these ratios changed a bit. Lands occupied with fields were smaller by 2 per cent points. Such was also the situation with the percentage of total farming lands. The percentage of grasslands remained almost equal. A conclusion can be drawn that the missing percentage of fields was transformed into grasslands. A similar percentage of grasslands was overgrown by forests which increased their area by gross 2 per cent points. The percentage of infertile areas remained almost unchanged or even declined a bit according to the statistics. Yet, it needs to be taken into account that in the year 1938, the area included in the comparison did not comprise the area of the administrative unit of Ljubljana-Šiška.

In the period from 1938 to 1961, the percentages of all farming categories declined: fields and grasslands by 2 per cent points and total farming lands by 2.5 per cent points. In contrast to this process, the percentages of forests and infertile areas increased. The former by 1.5 per cent points and the latter slightly less. Fifteen years after World War II, the results of the changed farming policy which was accompanied with the process of depopulation and abandoning agrarian activities were already well manifested. Numerous constructions were built anew. Thus, on the one hand, settlements, big plants and main transport routes were constructed on more or less flat lands which were suitable for farming, and on the other, farming lands were abandoned.

The results became clearly evident in the following 30 years when the picture changed again. Farming lands further diminished in extent when compared with the situation of 1961; fields declined by 2.5 per cent points, grasslands by almost 3 per cent points, and total farming lands by more than 5 per cent points. Correspondingly, from the year 1961 forests increased by almost 4 per cent points, i.e. to 56.7% of the entire territory of Gorenjsko, and infertile areas by 1.5 per cent point.

In the period from the beginning of the century till today, it is possible to notice a continuing trend of decline in percentage of farming lands on the one hand, and the increase in percentages of forests and infertile areas on the other. A comparison of land categories according to the cadaster data of 1901 and 1994 shows that the percentages of farming lands declined: fields from 14.6 to 8.1%, grasslands by less than one-fifth, and total farming lands by one quarter. A percentage of forests increased from 49% in the year 1901 to 56.7% in 1994. In that same period the percentage of forests on the entire territory of Slovenia increased from 42 (Melik, 1936) to a gross 52%, or as much as by one-fifth. Moreover, according to the latest estimates of foresters, forests in Slovenia already occupy about 60% of the entire territory! (*Projekt Corine Land Cover v Sloven*iji/ Corine Land Cover Project in Slovenia/1999). This difference between the official data of the cadaster and the estimates of foresters results from the lagging behind of the cadaster from the actual situation in nature.

At the beginning of the century, infertile areas spread over 9.8% of Gorenjsko, and within a century this percentage increased to 12.1% or by one-fifth. A conclusion can be drawn that this land category spread exclusively on account of built-up areas. If this fifth is transformed into hectares it becomes evident that as much as 6475 hectares of the territory of Gorenjsko were built up in the past century.

On this occasion, it is suitable to include the above-mentioned data from the agro-map which is closer to the actual state. There are but 6% of fields or by a half less than in 1901. The greatest discrepancy between the data of the cadaster and those from the agro-map occurs in grasslands. The latter shows but 13.4% of grasslands or 50% less than 90 years ago. This discrepancy is due to lands being overgrown which are registered as a special land category on the agro-map. On average, there were 7.8% of lands being overgrown in Gorenjsko in 1991. The sum of percentages of fields, grasslands and lands being overgrown makes the percentage of total farming lands which, according to the agro-map, amounts to a gross 28% or one-third less than at the beginning of the century. For a better spatial presentation: according to the agro-map amounts to a gross 28% or one-third less than at the beginning of the century. For a better spatial presentation: according to the agro-map, 38,002 hectares of farming lands were somehow 'lost' in the last 90 years.

However, the agro-map too does not correspond entirely to the actual state. Problematic is the category of lands being overgrown. The agro-map discerns the lands being moderately overgrown and the lands being intensely overgrown. To a certain extent, the latter already equals the real forest. On the one hand, this category includes pastures which were determined as farming lands at the introduction of the cadaster although they already resembled thin forests at that time. On the other hand, numerous lands have hitherto been completely overgrown so that they are forests nowadays (Cunder, 1999). Thus, it can be presumed that the actual lands being overgrown represent a slightly smaller percentage.

2.3 Survey of Prevailing Land Use in Administrative Units by Cadastral Communes

A map on prevailing land use clearly shows a distribution of individual prevailing land categories. Shown for each cadastral commune is the prevailing land use which is separated from the other by using a different colour. Thus, for example, dark grey colour represents fields. This, by all means, does not mean that fields occupy the entire area of respective cadastral commune; they only represent the greatest percentage of lands on the specified territory.

Two different maps were made. The first one (Map 1) shows only the farming land categories:

1. fields
2. grasslands
3. lands being intensely overgrown
4. lands being moderately overgrown

Shown on the second map (Map 2) are all the categories of land use which occupy the greatest percentage of the territory in an individually cadastral commune:

1. fields
2. grasslands
3. forests
4. infertile areas

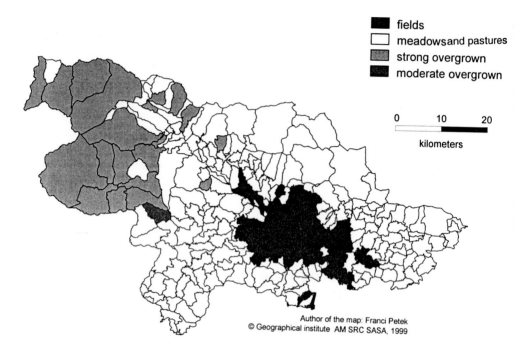

Map 1   Prevailing agricultural land categories.

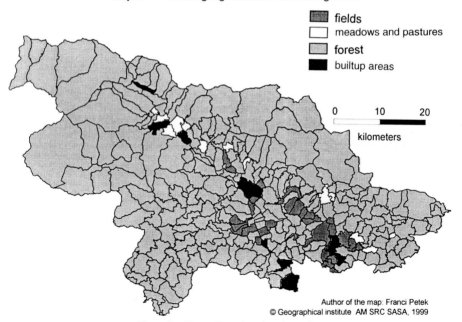

Map 2   Prevailing land categories.

A comparison of both maps shows a great difference. The first map reveals grasslands as the prevailing land use category in a cadastral commune occurring in all the administrative units. Fields prevail in the central and the lower sections of the Sava plain.

The second map shows that forests in Gorenjsko prevail by far most frequently. The first map shows grasslands as the prevailing category, but it becomes evident on the second map that they were preserved as such in individual cadastral communes only.

Fields as the prevailing land use category were better preserved, particularly in the cadastral communes with continuous smaller plains (the Kranjsko Polje, the Sorško Polje, the Ljubljansko Polje, and the Kamniškobistriška Ravan) within the largest plain along the Sava.

The category of lands being overgrown disappears and infertile areas occur instead. This category as the prevailing category in a cadastral commune occurs, on the one hand, in the high-mountainous world where barren rocky areas prevail, and on the other, in the areas of concentrated settlements. These are mainly the cadastral communes encircling the town cores of Jesenice, Radovljica, Bled, Kranj, Medvode, Ljubljana and Domžale.

3. CONCLUSION

The socioeconomic factors strongly influenced the changes in land use and, consequently, the changes in landscape appearance of Gorenjsko in the last century. Abandoning of crop production and overgrowing of farming lands belong to the most evident indicators of the partial disintegration of cultural landscape. At the cost of constantly declining fields and grasslands the percentage of lands being overgrown increased, and in the next stage, also of forests. Particularly worrying is an ever stronger pressure on fertile lands that are suitable for cultivation. Therefore, it will be necessary to plan the spread of settlements, construction of transport routes and industrial zones very carefully, and also concurrently consider the consistent development and the sustainable use of space.

REFERENCES

Agrokarta, 1992. The Agricultural Institute of Slovenia, Ljubljana.

Corine Land Cover in Slovenia, 1999. Institute of Forestry of Slovenia. Ljubljana.

Cunder, T. 1998. *Živinoreja* (Livestock production). *Geografski atlas Slovenije,* (Geographical Atlas of Slovenia), DZS Ljubljana, 202-208.

Cunder, T. 1999. *Zaraščanje kmetijskih zemljišč v slovenskem Alpskem svetu* (Abandoning of agricultural land in Slovenian Alps). Ljubljana. Paper in print.

Gabrovec, M. 1996, *Sončno obsevanje v reliefno razgibani Sloveniji* (Solar Radiation and the Diverse Relief of Slovenia). *Geografski zbornik* (Acta Geographica). Ljubljana.

Gabrovec, M. and D. Kladnik, 1997. *Nekaj novih vidikov rabe tal v Sloveniji* (Some new aspects of land use in Slovenia), *Geografski zbornik* (Acta Geographica), Ljubljana.

Gabrovec, M. and D. Kladnik, 1998. *Raba tal* (Land Use). *Geografski atlas Slovenije* (Geographical Atlas of Slovenia), DZS, Ljubljana, 180-191.

Gams, I. 1960. *O višinski meji naseljenosti, ozimine, gozda in snega v slovenskih gorah* (On the extreme Upper Limit of Rural Settlements, Winter, Wheat, Forest and Snow Line in Slovenia). Geografski vestnik (Bulletin de la societe de geographie de Ljubljana) Ljubljana. 32.

Grafenauer, B. 1970. Urbanizacija zemljišča, Gospodarska in družbena zgodovina Slovencev, DZS, Ljubljana.

Ilešič, S. 1979. Pogledi na geografijo, Ljubljana.

Kladnik, D. 1981. Izraba tal na Gorenjskem, Gorenjska (Zbornik 12. zborovanja geografov), Ljubljana.

Lovrenčak, F. 1976. *Zgornja gozdna meja v Kamniških Alpah v geografski luči* (The Upper Timberline in the Kamnik Alps), *Geografski zbornik* (Acta Geographica) Ljubljana 16.

Lovrenčak, F. 1986. *Zgornja gozdna meja v Julijskih Alpah in na visokih kraških planotah Slovenije* (The Upper Forest Line in the Julian Alps and in High Karst Plateaus of Slovenia), *Geografski zbornik* (Acta Geographica) 26, Ljubljana.

Melik, A. 1936. Slovenija 1, Ljubljana.

Melik, A. 1960. Slovenija 1, Ljubljana.

Navodila za izdelavo agrokarte, 1987. Republiški komite za kmetijstvo, gozdarstvo in prehrano. Ljubljana.

Orožen, F. 1901. Vojvodina Kranjska, Prirodoznaski, politični in kulturni opis, Ljubljana.

Perko, D. 1992. *Nakloni v Sloveniji in digitalni model reliefa* (Inclines in Slovenia and Digital Terrain Model). Geodetski vestnik 2, letnik 36, Ljubljana.

Perko, D. 1994. *Ekspozicije površja v Sloveniji* (Surface exposures in Slovenia). *Geografski zbornik* (Acta Geographica) 34 Ljubljana.

Perko, D. 1995. Razporeditevin sestava prebivalstva naselij. Krajevni leksikon Slovenije, DZS Ljubljana, str. 8-13.

Perko, D. 1998. *Nakloni površja* (Surface inclination). *Geografski atlas Slovenije* (Geographical Atlas of Slovenia), DZS, Ljubljana, 86-87.

Piry, I. and M. Orožen Adamič. 1998. *Upravna razdelitev* (Administrative division). *Geografski atlas Slovenije* (Geographical Atlas of Slovenia). DZS, Ljubljana.

Pratnekar, J. 1993. Pašno košna raba travnatega sveta. Viharnik, Glasilo delovne organizacije Gozdno gospodarstvo Slovenj Gradec. Slovenj Gradec.

Slovenija pokrajine in ljudje, 1998. Mladinska knjiga, Ljubljana.

Stritar, A. 1990. Krajina, Krajinski sistms; Raba in Varstva tal v Sloveniji. Ljubljana.

Valenčič, V. 1970. Vrste zemljišč, Gospodarska in družbena zgodovina Slovencev, DZS, Ljubljana.

Vrišer, I. 1997. Metodologija ekonomske geografije, Filožofka fakulteta. Ljubljana.

CHAPTER 12

Large-scale Dams as Drivers of Land Use/Cover Change in the Tropical Deciduous Forests — A Case-study of Sardar Sarovar Project (SSP), India

(R.B. Singh and Anjana Mathur[*])

1. INTRODUCTION

Building of dams over rivers in order to divert water for irrigation purposes goes back to ancient times. Small indigenous methods of making dams in rivers by laying big boulders in a river course have been mentioned even in ancient literature. Such dams were small in size and posed no major threat to the local forest cover, agricultural lands and habitation through submergence under mega-sized reservoirs. Since then, dams of continuously increasing size are being built over Indian rivers. Since the UN Stockholm Conference in 1972, increasing concern has been voiced over the adverse environmental impact of water resources projects in general and creation of man-made reservoirs by building dams in particular (Hafez and Shenouda, 1978). One cannot deny significant environmental repercussions of large-scale dams through a disappearance of the land use and land cover under water. The environment vs. development dilemma has recently appeared in India through the controversy surrounding the Narmada Valley Projects. These projects, including the Sardar Sarovar Project (SSP), will submerge around 56,000 hectares of forests (Narmada Control Authority,

*Department of Geography, Delhi School of Economics, University of Delhi, Delhi-110007, India.

1991), including the best deciduous teak forests in central India. More crucially, it would mean losing the vital ecological functions of a forest such as soil preservation, soil replenishment, microclimatic stabilization and storage of gene pools.

The main components of a multi-purpose project usually are the dam itself, the canal, dykes and the reservoir. Construction of canals as well as reservoir usually leads to the displacement of agriculturists as well as tribals living in the area. It is the height of the dam which usually determines the size of the reservoir. In the case of Sardar Sarovar Project, the height of the dam is now fixed at 260.64 m. This shall require the partial or full submergence of 234 villages under the rising reservoir waters. It is the height of the dam along with the size of the reservoir which has been attracting international attention. The water from the constructed reservoir is planned to be carried through a network of canals, measuring more than 750 km in length, to the cites of Vadodara, Surat, Bharuch, etc. more than 200 km away from the dam site. Around the reservoir site, virgin tropical deciduous forests cover the landscape with no urban settlement but a dominance of tribal villages and tribals whose lives are intrinsically woven with the forests.

The forest cover in the Narmada valley contribute a large proportion of productive forests to the country. *Sal, Anjon,* and *Kanji* grow widely in the forests and near the streams. In the Sardar Sarovar Project catchment area, Southern dry, deciduous forests can be found. Chamjoion has categorized the vegetation of this region as Tropical Decidous (Spate and Learmouth, 1967).

As seen from Table 1, Sardar Sarovar dam alone will submerge nearly 14,000 ha of rich deciduous forests. The magnitude of all the dams can be estimated from the number of total affected villages (nearly 600) and the amount of forests to be submerged (approx. 57,000 ha).

Table 1   Area to be submerged by Narmada Valley Projects

Project	Total submergence (hectares)	Forest (hectares)	Agricultural land (hectares)	No. of villages affected
Sardar Sarovar	39,134	13,744	11,318	234
Narmada Sagar Omkareshwar Maheshwar	105,597	42,803	44,363	337
Total	144,731	56,681	55,681	573

Source: Alvares and Billorey, 1988

1.1 Research Methodology

The main aim of undertaking a study of this nature was to understand the consequences of dam construction on forest cover and land use, and the subsequent impact on people. For this purpose 6 villages located upstream of the Sardar Sarovar dam were chosen for primary survey. A 5% survey of households was done on the basis of a pre-structured questionnaire.

Both primary and secondary sources were used during the study. Primary data included a structured questionnaire about life style, incomes and social composition. Secondary data sources included data from Narmada Bachao Andolan, Town and village directory, Bharuch district, Gujarat-Census of India, 1991, Civil Writ Petition, Original Jurisdiction (319) of 1990 in the Supreme Court of India; and various books on the topic by different authors.

1.2 Forest Cover in the SSP Area

According to a report by Mr Rajendra Sharma, the Principal of the Forest Range College at Rajpipla, "between 1970 and 1990, forests which extended west of Rajpipla had been decimated systematically, not only with the full knowledge but with the active participation of the member of the legislative assembly of Rajpipla and the series of ministers in charge of the forest department of the Government of Gujarat. This systematic and original forest felling had led to a recession of the forest area by about 60 km to the east of Rajpipla". In the Rajpipla division, the efforts made by the social forestry department had not made any dent in the rate of forest depletion (Patel, 1995).

Tropical dry forests are extremely rich in animal and plant species. They are now being altered or cleared more rapidly than at any time in the past. Deforestation rates during the 1980s were higher than the earlier published accounts. Comparison of the estimates of forest loss is difficult due to inconsistent use of definition of forest cover type and of deforestation. Even allowing for this, some recent assessments have shown accelerated deforestation rates in 1980s for many individual countries.

The total number of species in a tropical moist forest is unknown. The pattern of likely species extinction depends on the amount and spatial arrangement of the forest altered or destroyed. A better understanding of the process of deforestation and their implication for species extinction is essential in order to set priorities for conservation. Loss of genetic diversity within species is even less easy to detect than species extinction but is undoubtedly very prevalent and is an issue of major concern for conservation.

2. THE DAM: MAJOR CONCERNS

"Dams have caused the drawing of thousands of acres of forests. It is estimated that between 1950-1975, India lost, 4,79,000 hectares of forest land to various river valley projects. For the promoters of large scale dams, that loss of forests is generally seen in terms of economic loss only, that is the market value of timber submerged" (Goldsmith and Hildyard, 1984). But the benefits of forests are unquantifiable and their social and cultural values are unravelled as well.

The deforestation of tropical lands can have both local and global consequences. Locally, the climate may become extreme, soils may suffer physical and chemical deterioration, and hydrological balances may be disturbed. Massive deforestation, altering albedo and regional atmospheric water balance, could affect weather patterns, and there is particular concern of atmosphere warming due to the release of carbon dioxide into the atmosphere from the burning or decomposition of the biomass. Perhaps the single greatest cause for concern over the loss of tropical forests is that there is considerable body of evidence to suggest that it is leading to unprecedented loss of the biological diversity that the forests contain.

The Sardar Sarovar alone shall submerge 234 villages along its banks and displace thousands of inhabitants occupying its banks. Besides submerging the habitat, the reservoir of SSP would drown about 13,744 ha of tropical deciduous forests besides 11,318 ha of rich agricultural land. With the forest shall be lost a whole section of ecology and endangered species. A whole belt of precious forest trees such as *Sal* and *Mahua* will be submerged (Alvares and Billorey, 1988).

Destruction of forests for the dam mean a loss of one of the best deciduous teak forests in India. It would lead to a loss of vital ecological functions such as water replenishment, storage of genetic pools, etc. This shall also result in the death of thousands of wild animals, many of which are endangered. Canals in the black soil region would bring along with it the problems of water-logging, salinity and erosion. Not only would the flora and fauna be affected, it is the tribals living in the basin who would be affected the most. These people, whose lives are intrinsically woven with forests, shall have to bear the agony of being uprooted from their homeland, which not only provides them with everyday needs, but has given them an identity and sense of belonging to the land and forests. Although this is the story of every dam built, the speciality of SSP is the sheer nonnecessity of a project of this magnitude catering to an area, more than 100 km away, which is not in due need of water.

Submergence of such large forest tracts is also bound to create pressure on remaining forest areas in adjoining places. Similar demands on the remaining forests will come from the displaced people. Their fuel and other timber needs will have to be somehow met. The reservoir will forever swamp areas supplying some 300,000 quintals of nistar grass (fodder): this at a time when the State is already groaning under a fodder crisis.

2.1 The Study Area

The study area consists of the 234 villages to be submerged under water by the SSP in Gujarat, Maharashtra and Madhya Pradesh (Alvares and Billorey, 1988). All the 234 villages shall be fully or partially submerged. In order to fully understand the environmental and land use/cover, six villages—Vadgam, Surpan, Mokhadi, Gadher, Kathkadi and Makadkheda—were chosen, which are located on the border of Gujarat and Maharashtra states, close to the dam site of Sardar Sarovar (Fig. 1). All these six villages are in the list of submerging villages. A large part of the population of these villages have been moved to the rehabilitation sites (Table 2).

Table 2   Forest cover in the study area

Villages	Area (in ha)	% of forests to total area of village
Makadkheda	1642.66	71.74
Gadher	3347.36	68.76
Kathkadi	924.90	69.91
Mokhadi	2118.87	77.12
Vadgam	1911.81	53.08
Surpan	1792.55	89.08

Source: Town and Village Directory, District Bharuch (Gujarat), Census of India, 1991.

The total area of these six villages is 10,734.25 ha. Approximately 6500 people consisting of 7700 families reside in these six selected villages. Nearly 7700 ha of the village land consists of forests while nearly 1,000 ha is agriculture (Census of India, 1991). As they are tribal villages, the dependence on forest products is quite a bit and it forces the tribals to protect the forest for their own well-being. This is one of the main reasons for the percentage of forests to the total village land being so large. Also, larger the population size,

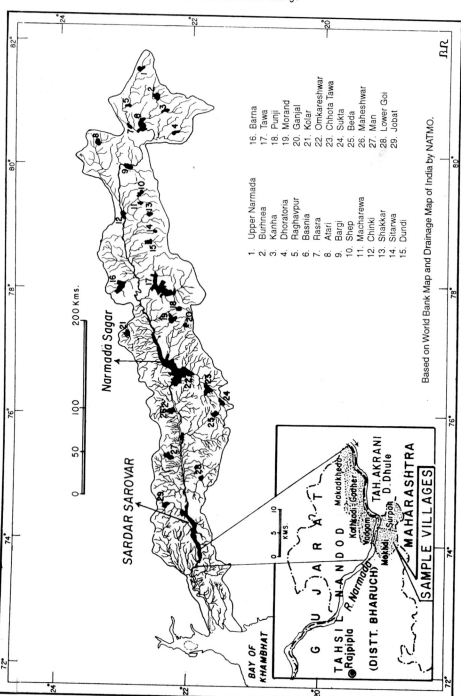

Fig. 1 Narmada catchment: Major projects and study area

Based on World Bank Map and Drainage Map of India by NATMO.

1. Upper Narmada	16. Barna
2. Burhnea	17. Tawa
3. Kanha	18. Punji
4. Dhoratoria	19. Morand
5. Raghavpur	20. Ganjal
6. Basnia	21. Kolar
7. Rasra	22. Omkareshwar
8. Atari	23. Chhota Tawa
9. Bargi	24. Sukta
10. Shep	25. Beda
11. Macharewa	26. Maheshwar
12. Chinki	27. Man
13. Shakkar	28. Lower Goi
14. Sitarwa	29. Jobat
15. Dundi	

and closer a village is to road or an urban site lesser becomes its ratio of forest to total land. Thus, Vadgam, an important village near the Gujarat-Maharashtra border has a ratio of forests much less than the rest of the studied villages.

2.2   Tree Cover in SSP Submergence Zone

Most of the villages which will be submerged are covered by dry tropical deciduous forests, endowed with numerous varieties of trees, shrubs, herbs and climbers along with a rich undergrowth of grasses and fodder plants. The forests are dominated by multiple layers in terms of height with exceptionally high trees, medium height trees and low trees. Shrubs, herbs are found at the ground level while climbers grow on high trees so as to catch the direct sunlight. Two main aboreal species of trees have been identified in the study area which are teak and sal forests (Joshi, 1987; Paranjpye, 1990).

2.2.1   Teak forests

The teak forests in Narmada basin are found in three layers. The teak forests form the topmost layer. The teak species found here are Saja (*Terminalia tomentosa*), Kairn (*Mitraquna pariflora*), Sonta, Salia, Jendia, Adnia and Cordifoli. The second layer is constituted by Ghor, bamboo, *Neacia catechowild*, Amathas and Dhaman. The third on the ground layer is formed by grasses such as *Apluda varia* Hach, *Indigo ferci*, impatiesns and Casia. The most common shrub is *Nyctanthes abontristic* Linn. Some of the climbers are Palasbel, Malkanjin and Dhimarbel.

2.2.2   Sal forests

The tops of the hill villages bordering Madhya Pradesh are covered by Sal forests (*Shorea robusti*). The lower slopes are a habitat of Kanji and Ajnan, which grow near the streams. *Butea monosperma* Taub variety of Sal is found on the areas where there has been a deposition of a thin layer of soil.

The economic value of the trees to be felled and submerged cannot be undermined at any point. Just one full grown tree of Teak costs more than Rs 40,000 (US$1000). And a full grown tree of Sal costs approx. Rs 20,000 (US$500). Thus, a hectare of forest cover with sal and teak trees numbering 100 is estimated to cost around Rs 300,000 (US$7500).

2.3 Forest Produce and Subsistence Farming—Lifeline of Tribal Society

The tribal way of living is quite visible in the crops grown in the study area. The crops can be classified as solely subsistence, solely cash crops and dual purpose crops of which the excess quantity is sold off in the nearby markets (Table 3).

Table 3   Crops grown in the study area

Subsistence crops	Cash crops	Dual purpose crops
Millets	Cotton*	Pulses like arhar*,
Vegetables like brinjal, tomato, potato, chilli, ladysfinger,	Tendu leaves	Moong gram, Bamboo, Mahua
kantola, timru fruit, pumpkin	Groundnut	Googar

*Crops which can also be grown at relocation sites.

Source: Personal Survey, 1996.

According to the villagers, the crops which can be grown in the newly allotted fields at resettlement sites are only cotton and arhar. This brings in an added burden of buying vegetables, pulses, etc. from the market for the crops which were earlier free of cost. Thus it can be derived that there is vast difference in the quantity and quality of crops which were grown earlier, and which can be grown in the newly allotted fields. The main cause is the quality of soil of the fields allotted to the rehabilitated villagers. The lands were initially wastelands which were acquired by the government from the market for the purpose of rehabilitation. The soils in the original villages was fertile and did not require much fertilizers. But the newly allotted lands are very poor in quality.

Along with the wild fruits and vegetables, a vast variety of medicinal plants are also available in the forest. The local tribals, for whom doctors and hospitals are a lost dream, depend on these medicinal herbs for their daily ailments as well as the major ones (Table 4).

The medicinal plants found in the forests are used not just by the villagers but hold an immense economic value for the promoters of indigenous medicine like Ayruvedic doctors and *vaids*. (doctors practising indigenous medicine—from local herbs, leaves, plants, animal product). A gram of many medicinal products found in the forests cost more than Rs 5000.

Table 4 Medicinal plants available in the forests

S. No.	Family and name	Uses
1.	Liliaceae	
	a) *Gloriosa superba*	Fracture healer
	b) *Asparagus racemosus*	General tonic, Feminine disorders, Cough, Ulcers
2.	Lyhraceae	Alimentary canal disorder
3.	Malvaceae	Reproductive disorder
4.	Melliaceae (*Azadirachta indica*)	Skin infection
5.	Menispermaceae	Coolent tonic, infant disorders
6.	Mimoseae	Skin diseases
7.	Moraceae	Reproductive disorders
8.	Rutaceae	Lead extract—liver stimulant
		Unripe fruit—diarrhoea
		Ripe fruit—mild purgative
9.	Nyctaginaceae	Used as diuretic and general tonic
10.	Amaranthaceae	Appetite killer
11.	Papilionaceae	Sore throat, tonic, skin diseases, coolent in sun stroke, eyedrops, leucoderms, cardiac stimulant, cough and bronchial troubles
12.	Rhamnaceae	Skin diseases
13.	Rubiaceae	Respiratory diseases
14.	Tiliaceae	Skin diseases and fertility disorder
15.	Verbanaceae	Diuretic
16.	Vitaceae	Indigestion
17.	Anacardiaceae	Severe fractures, skin blisters
18.	Apoyaceae	Piles, skin diseases, alimentary canal disorders, reproductive disorders
19.	Araceae	Skin diseases
20.	Asdepieadaceae	Bronchial congestion, piles, reproductive disorders
21.	Asteraceae	Reproductive disorders, skin diseases
22.	Bombacaceae	Pimples, abscess
23.	Laesalpiniaceae	Skin diseases
24.	Combretaceae	Ulcers, bleeding, tonic
25.	Cucurbitaceae	Digestive disorders
26.	Vamina	Breathlessness in kids
27.	Masuri	Infections
28.	Garmaro, Madga Heeng	Cold
29.	Heever, Kadvi Nai	Fever

Source: Cost of submergence, A study of Sardar Sarovar Project, CSS, Surat, 1983; Personal Survey, 1996.

3. LAND USE PATTERN

The land use pattern of the tribal villages of SSP is quite unlike the normal village land use in an urban vicinity. It is dominated by forests with very little agricultural land (Table 5).

Table 5   Land use in the study area (in ha)

Villages	Total area	Land use in percentage of total villages			
		Forest	Agricultural areas	Cultivable wasteland	Areas not available for cultivation
Makadkheda	1642.66	71.74	2.29	3.82	22.15
Gadher	3347.36	68.76	7.77	7.7	15.70
Kathkadi	924.90	69.91	—	—	30.09
Mokhadi	2118.87	77.02	6.06	5.52	11.40
Vadgam	1911.81	53.08	—	—	46.91
Surpan	1792.55	89.08	3.44	0.34	7.14

Source: Town and Village Directory, District Bharuch (Gujarat), Census of India, 1991.

Table 5 shows how the land use in the villages is distributed. While forests dominate the landscape, agricultural areas occupy a com-paratively smaller proportion of area. This is because the tribal economy is basically a forest dependent economy, where most of the eatables are procured from the forests. The need to cultivate is only for basic cereals which do not grow wildly, including jowar, bajra, gram, arhar, etc. The cultivable wasteland includes the fallow land and grazing pastures for the village cattle. Cattle rearing is another main activity of the tribals who depend on it for milk, skin and meat. Even for the cattle a very small patch of land is made available so as to maintain the forest balance. Vadgam and Kathkadi are the villages in the study area which do not have either agricultural or pasture land. This is because these villages are located at the foothills, near the river bank which is a steep cliff. Thus, agricultural area is negligible due to non-availability of water for irrigation in the village.

One of the main features of the SSP is the attractive land compensation package it offers. For every adult (male) PAP (Project Affected Person) in the family, 2 hectares of land is allotted. This considerably reduces the per capita availability of land in the village, as every member of the family is using forest as well as agricultural land. Thus, the allotted land at relocation sites falls dearly short of the land dependency ratio in original village (Table 6).

Table 6 Per capita land availability (in hectares)

Villages	Original per capita land (including agriculture)	Original per capita to forest land	Allotted per capita land	Difference in per capita land earlier and now
Makadkheda	3.81	2.81	0.81	(–) 3.00
Gadher	1.40	0.96	0.81	(–) 0.59
Kathkadi	2.79	1.95	0.81	(–) 1.98
Mokhadi	1.58	0.73	0.81	(–) 0.77
Vadgam	1.11	0.57	0.81	(–) 0.03
Surpan	4.29	3.75	0.85	(–) 3.44

Source: Civil Writ Petition in the Supreme Court of India, Narmada Bachao Andolan (Petitioner) vs. Union of India and Others (Respondents), 1989, New Delhi.

From Table 6, it can be derived that while in their original villages the tribals enjoyed the use of more than 1 hectare of land per head, in the relocation sites, it has been reduced by more than 70 per cent in some cases. Only in Mokhadi is the per capita land allotted more than the original village. This is because the size and the population of the village is small and the awarded compensation package is better (Morse et al. 1992).

4. A MIRAGE OF REHABILITATION

Of the 3 involved states, Gujarat is getting maximum benefits and has promised land for land along with employment to all the project oustees. But the promises are many and the scale of rehabilitation too large.

According to the International Labour Organization Convention on Indigenous People, 1954 (to which India is a signatory), whenever the tribals have to be rehabilitated, the same group should be moved together so as to maintain their social ties, culture and traditions. But the same essential element seems to be missing in the affected villages of SSP. The number of relocation size for people of one village have gone even up to 20 (Table 7) as land has been bought by Gujarat Government from the market for the purpose of rehabilitation.

"Many of those who have been resettled are people who have lived all their lives deep in the forest with virtually with contact with money and the modern world. Suddenly they find themselves left with the option of starving to death or walking several kilometers to the nearest town, sitting in the marketplace (both men and women), offering themselves as wage labourer. Instead of a forest from which they gathered everything they needed—food,

Table 7   Village-wise resettlement of project affected persons (PAPs)

Villages	Number of resettlements sites
Makadkheda	5+
Gadher	32+
Kathkadi	6+
Vadgam	27+
Mokhadi	8+
Surpan	6+

Source: Bhatia, 1993; Personal Survey, 1996.

fuel, fodder, rope, gum, tobacco, tooth powder, medicinal herbs, housing material—they earn between ten and twenty rupees a day with which to feed and keep their families. Instead of a river, they have a hand pump. In their old villages, they had no money, but they were insured. If the rains failed, they had the forests to turn to. The river to fish in. Their livestock was their fixed deposit. Without all this, they're a heart beat away from destitution. For the people who've been resettled, everything has to be re-learnt. Every little thing, every big thing from buying a bus ticket, learning a new language, to understanding money. And worst of all, learning to be supplicants learning to take orders. Learning to have Masters. Learning to answer only when you're addressed." (Roy, 1999).

5.   COMPENSATORY AFFORESTATION

The Department of Environment and Forests has issued guidelines for the forest felling (forest lost) and its compensation. Originally, for every hectare of forest felled, an equal area of non-forest land had to be afforested. But this policy changed. The new guidelines permit the authorized agencies to replant the uprooted trees. Where there is a non-availability of forest lands, the degraded forest lands are to be planted, but in double the area felled.

For 40,000 hectares of forests being submerged by Narmada Sagar Projects, Narmada Valley Development Authority (NVDA), has promised to afforest 90,000 hectares of degraded forest land. But such forests are being categorized as plantations. These 'forests' lack the originality and gene pools of natural forests and can be labelled as substandard substitutes for the priceless forests. According to the guidelines, 200 hectares of area near the dam site is to be forests. The area to the Narmada main canal and its distributors which are to be afforested comes to be about 18,000 hectares.

The nation and its environment have suffered a net loss in such a transaction. First, it is the duty of the forest department to afforest lands anyway. Second, that much forest area which is submerged is lost forever. Third, the Department of Environment and Forests has not even examined whether afforestation can be carried out on degraded forest lands. Fourth, the infrastructure to raise plantations is sadly missing from the official machinery.

Moreover, even the reforestation of degraded forest lands will hardly replace the loss of natural forests. First and foremost, the man-made forests of the Forest Department are better categorized as plantations. Often, they do not harbour such species as one would find in natural forests, particularly wild plants valued now for their genes. Equally important, they are unable to support either tribals or wildlife. So there is further loss: the priceless is being replaced by substandard substitutes.

6. FINDINGS AND CONCLUSIONS

It is in the interest of the mankind that the route to development is identified and prioritized. Small-scale, environment-friendly mechanisms are the need of the hour to bring out qualitative development. A process which brings out a lot of change in natural processes are best avoided, such as the SSP. Although the process of SSP construction cannot be reversed, as it has reached an irreversible stage, the maximum we can do is to reduce the height of the dam so as to minimize the inundation being caused by the reservoir and also ensure that the affected tribals' socioeconomic conditions are in conformity to their earlier way of life.

Although the tribals do not own any land of their own, their rights on forests cannot be left unattended. Over time, tribals have become a part of the natural food chain of the forest and have contributed their bit to the upkeep of the forest. Relocating such people away from their lifeline is a gross violation of human morality.

Our knowledge of the numbers, distribution, status and ecology of tropical forest species is so poor that the true dimensions of this problem are only beginning to emerge. In the absence of knowledge that would enable us to manage forests in a deliberate way to conserve their species diversity, it must be prudent to retain as much forest as possible under a region of minimal human disturbance.

The rate of tropical forest loss is so rapid, and the concentration of the world's species in these ecosystems so great that the view has been expressed that a significant proportion of all species of plants and animals are likely to become extinct in the next few decades, perhaps as many as 25-30 per cent by 2000 AD. There is little documentary evidence of species extinction, that many species survived deforestation, and that the risk inherent in tropical deforestation have been exaggerated.

For any future project, whether small-scale or large-scale, should be preceded by a thorough analysis of all flora, fauna, land use, land cover, people and the possible impacts of development on these. The indirect ecological consequences of the dams are even more serious than the direct negative consequences, and the former had not even been considered in the cost-benefit ratios used to support the idea of the dams.

Thus, before undertaking any activity of any scale, the definition of sustainable development needs to be understood and implemented to the very core, so as to prevent the earth's precious vegetation cover from the perils of concrete jungles and dams.

7. RECOMMENDATIONS

It has become mandatory for the World Bank as well as all the responsible governmental and non-governmental institutions to ensure that the scale of environmental damage is minimum.

Other avenues which need a thorough investigation are: finding ways to reduce the submergence area; locating similar alternative sites for forest development and relocation so as to maintain ecological balance; and checking the natural forest plantation in field.

It is also necessary to ensure that place is found to relocate trees and people together, so as to maintain the ecological balance and gene pools which shall be lost with the loss of either of the components.

REFERENCES

Alvares, C. and R. Billorey. 1988. *Damming the Narmada*, Natraj Publishers, Dehradun.

Bhatia, B. 1993. *Forced Eviction in Narmada Valley*, Report submitted in Gujarat High Court, Gandhinagar, July 15. 267-321.

Census of India. 1991. *Town and Village Directory*, District Bharuch (Gujarat), New Delhi.

Centre For Social Studies 1994. Surat, October 1993 to March 1994. Ministry of Environment and Forests, R & R Programme for Sardar Sarovar Project, Civil Writ Petition in The Supreme Court of India, (*No. 319 of 1994*) Annexure 69, page 67.

Goldsmith, E. and N. Hildyard. 1984. *The Social and Environmental Effects of Large Dams,* Wedgebridge Ecological Centre, Cornwall.

Hafez, M. and W.K. Shenouda. 1978. *The Environmental Impact of the Aswan High Dam, Water Development and Management,* Part 4, United Nations and Paragon Press, New York.

Joshi, V. 1987. *Submerging Villages,* Ajanta, New Delhi.

Morse, B., Berger, T., Gamble, D. and H. Brody. 1992. *Sardar Sarovar Project—Report of the Independent Review,* Resources Future International, Ottawa.

Narmada Control Authority. 1991. *Drinking Water from Narmada,* Pub. No. 3/91, Gandhinagar.

Narmada Control Authority. 1991. Submergence of Villages in Gujarat, Maharashtra and Madhya Pradesh with Construction of Sardar Sarovar Project, Pub. 1/91, Gandhinagar.

Paranjpye, V. 1990. *High Dams on the Narmada: A Holistic Analysis of the River Valley Project,* INTACH, New Delhi. 52-90, 177-300.

Patel, J. 1995. *The Myths Exploded: The Unscientific Ways of Big Dams and Narmada Project,* EDSA-TPA, Bombay, 1-23.

Roy, A. 1999. The Greater Common Good, *Frontline,* June 4, Chennai.

Spate, O.H.K. and A.T.A. Learmouth. 1967. *India and Pakistan: A General and Regional Geography,* Methuen and Co. Pvt. Ltd., U.K.

Thakkar, U. and M. Kulkarni 1992. Environment and Development: A Case of the Sardar Sarovar Project, South Asia Bulletin, Vol. XII, No. 2, Fall 1992.

CHAPTER 13

Diversification of Rural Agricultural Land due to Urban Intrusion — A Case-study of the Metropolitan Periphery of Delhi, India

(R.B. Singh and Jag Mohan*)

1. INTRODUCTION

Urbanization exemplifies a revolutionary change in the total pattern of socioeconomic and cultural life. It is a product of basic economy and technological developments and affects every aspect of human existence. Urbanization is one of the most striking phenomena of the developing countries. Towns and cities have been the focus of most developmental activities, through various stages of historical progression and continue to play a major role in the industrial and economic development of a region. India, one of the foremost developing nations among the Third World, has an urban infrastructure of gigantic magnitude. The rapid growth of metropolitan cities has also brought about horizontal spread of urban boundaries. Cities have expanded into the adjacent rural areas in a haphazard and unplanned manner (Sharma, 1985). The agricultural lands of the peripheral villages are converted for industrial, commercial, residential and recreational uses. The study of Indian urban landscape provides an intricate and complex inter-relationship between the biophysical and cultural dimensions and the people who live in these environments. The immediate and visible impact of urbanization in India is the change in

*Department of Geography, Delhi School of Economics, University of Delhi, Delhi-110007, India.

land use and economic conditions of the rural regions surrounding the city landscape (Desai and Sen Gupta, 1987; Chandhoke, 1994).

The perception of land by an Indian has changed drastically in recent decades from the status of mother land to a commodity status. The changing patterns of land ownership and tenure condition which developed through successive empires in India have made the possession and utilization of land a contentious issue (Amitabh, 1997). The people of the fringe villages have land which they are willing to sell for urban land uses at comparatively low prices. The process of urban expansion also results in what has been termed the *'impermanence syndrome'*, a sense of transition and instability among rural land owners making them more likely to sell to the developers (Lehman, 1995; Carter, 1981).

Urban land developers, industrialists looking for factory sites, businessmen and others who wish to invest black money and those people who want to take advantage of tax laws where agricultural incomes are exempted, are all attracted to the fringe villages. An offer higher than the current market rate is often sufficient to make people in the fringe villages part with their lands. As a result, haphazard residential and industrial development occurs in the fringe areas. The rural-urban fringe is often described as the garbage and sewage dump of the city. All obnoxious land uses, irrelevant to the normal life of urban areas, are pushed towards the city's outer limits and often into the fringe villages. The classic examples of such land uses are garbage dumps, water works, sewage disposal tanks and farms, burial and cremation grounds, airports, timber yards, brick kilns, etc. (Ramachandran, 1989; Nangia, 1976).

2. STUDY AREA

The land policy measures of the Indian government, and the pace of local urbanization processes, make the Indian environment a very attractive investment opportunity for big and small capital (India Today, 1990). Despite state interventions through various enactments and regulations, it is clear that some urban dwellers will see agricultural land mainly as a source of profit and investment. This motive is increasing especially in the case of the Delhi city. For an extensive study, two of the five developmental blocks in Delhi—Alipur and Najafgarh—have been chosen (Fig. 1). These blocks are still characterized as a region where farmers dominate the human landscape. But slowly the urban forces have started creeping into the rural life. Alipur block, over the last two decades, has been passing through a transition stage. Land use has changed from agriculture to non-agricultural uses like farm houses, godowns, dal (pulses) and flour mills, brick kilns, etc. Najafgarh block, on the other hand, still depends on its agricultural background although many illegal colonies have also mushroomed in few villages. Both Alipur and Najafgarh are Rural Development Blocks but the quality and subsequent land use transformation have set them apart.

The blocks were selected on the basis of their relative distance from the urban area. While Alipur is located in the north and north-west part of Delhi, Najafgarh is located in the south-western part (Fig. 1). The villages selected are located both near the urban areas as well as near the border, away from the city. This was done to understand the consequences of urban sprawl on rural society, which is intrinsically linked with land. Dhansa, Ujjwa and Dichau Kalan villages were selected from Najafgarh block and Hiranki, Bakoli and Sannoth villages were selected from Alipur Block. In total, 300 persons were interviewed on the basis of a pre-structured questionnaire.

3. SOCIO-ECONOMIC TRANSFORMATION AND RISING URBAN ASPIRATIONS

The most prominent feature of rural villages surrounding Delhi is the metalled roads which have greatly enhanced the accessibility of these remote areas. This increase in communication and the daily interaction with the city has brought about manifold change in the livelihood and land use of villages. Rural Delhi still tends to be characterized as a region where farmers dominate the cultural landscape and where farming remains the prominent occupation. But slowly the economic and social forces are remarking rural areas of the fringe, at times fundamentally so. Agriculture is being squeezed by non-agricultural pursuits, aspirations increasingly reflect the wish to avoid farming and the 'households' are being restructured as the compulsion and generations renegotiate their respective roles. The diversification of the household economy and the interpenetration of rural and urban have created multiple-hybrids where individuals and households shift between agricultural and industrial pursuits and cross between rural and urban areas. Farming is often considered subservient to non-farming and the industry is often dependent on rural labour. The present work focuses on these changes in rural life and livelihood, discusses their impact on agriculture and reflects their implications in rural

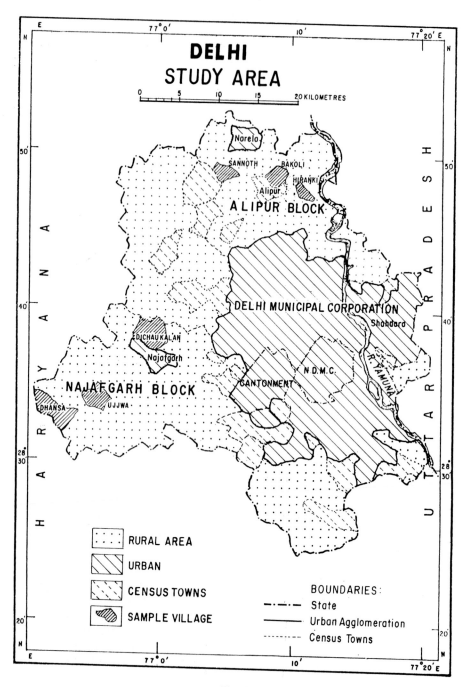

Fig. 1

development. Despite its essentially rural orientation, India is changing and the impact of urbanization is being frequently felt even at great distance from the cities. The evolving pattern of urban growth and development is driven by large profits to be made from converting agricultural land to non-farm uses in rural/urban fringe areas, by public subsidies, encouraging suburban development, and by various factions with place-specific concerns centered around issues of local geography, history, lifestyle, politics and economics (Lagon and Molotch, 1987; Pfeffer and Lapping, 1994; Pincetl, 1994). "Farmers in this areas do not want to be encroached upon, but if and when the path of development comes this way, they do not want to be blocked out of the process of selling their property" (Amitabh, 1997).

One of the most far reaching effects of urbanization has been on the structure of the family and rural resources. Traditionally, the family in India has been oriented towards agricultural occupations which encourages the joint or extended family structure, i.e. it is characterized by numerous members (many females to share household chores and many males to spread the burden of agricultural labour or other types of family support), with nucleation around an elder who is the head and is respected and revered. But with increase in land prices and agricultural input costs along with disinterest in agriculture, the very basis of the joint family system is upset and its economic stability thrown into disarray. Rural migration has created havoc in the rural areas of metropolitan cities. The main cause of this is the pull factor of urban areas which attracts population to it, who eventually settle down in its peripheral areas, putting an immense pressure on the already stretched rural resources like land and water. This process has continued since Independence and is reflected in the statistics of the rural population of Delhi (Table 1).

Table 1 Growth in rural population of the National Capital Territory

Year	Population
1951	306,938
1961	299,204
1971	418,675
1981	452,206
1991	949,019

Source: Census of India, 1951-91.

4. TRANSFORMATION OF THE FRINGE VILLAGES

The villages beyond the limits of a rapidly growing city undergo a process of change that ultimately results in their complete absorption within the physical limits. The changes taken place in the fringe villages have two fundamental aspects: (a) changes in the land use within the village and (b) changes in the social and economic life styles of the native inhabitants of the villages. The mechanism of changes in both cases involves interaction between the city and the villages. Another aspect, namely land use change, has more to do with decision and action of city dwellers. The nature and intensity of the interaction between the village and city can increase with time. Four stages of transformation of the fringe village have been identified. Each stage in the process of change corresponds to a household in terms of accessibility and interaction with the main city. The four stages are

a) the stage of rural-agricultural land use,
b) the stage of non-farming occupational change,
c) the stage of urban land use growth, and
d) the urban village.

5. SHRINKING VILLAGES AND CHANGING RURAL LAND USE IN THE METROPOLITAN FRINGE

Rural Delhi is passing through a transition period from the rural to the urban landscape. The concept of rural landscape/rural-urban fringe is multi-dimensional. In physical terms, it is reflected in what have been termed urban villages (UV); in human terms, in the increasing movement of people over a vital landscape of rural-urban interaction and in the diversity of livelihood and in economic terms, in the growing interdependency of agriculture and industry. The development landscape, in the very widest of terms, in being gradually remoulded by these forces of rural/urban change.

The changing nature of agrarian transition not only has an implication on the fate of the countryside, but also has a decisive influence upon the pace, manner, limits and the very possibility of capitalist industrialization. The rural landscape, both vulnerable and fragile, faces serious threats from the ongoing land use transformation. The scope and degree of land transformation depends on the character of the system in which the land is used by man. Under the impact of various land use systems, land and the whole environment changes (Mujtaba, 1994) positively or negatively. The impact of some land systems is limited to the area on which they are carried on, while that of others goes far beyond, transforming surrounding areas as well. Intrusion of urban landscape and population growth on the rural-urban areas and their impacts on land use systems are increasing; the resulting land transformation becomes more and more rapid, far reaching and often irreversible. Land use changes are playing an increasingly important role in determining patterns of wealth and poverty in rural Delhi. Many of the most striking changes in agricultural land use can be attributed to the evolving rural-urban interaction. These irreversible implications can be classified into two categories: social and economic; social changes are reflected in the status of women, lifestyles and the level of opulence of a household while economic changes can be gauged through the occupational structure, income levels and all sources of income. Land use theory suggests that, without public intervention the market will allocate land to the use that optimizes economic return. Thus in the process of urban growth, the owners are expected to convert agricultural land to non-agricultural use, since land suitable for development is more valuable (Sampson, 1979).

Delhi, the capital city of India, is not bereft of the dynamics of rural land use and the number of whose villages is declining steadily (Table 2). As the city grows, the villages are often absorbed in it with the village land being sold off for urban development. The villagers devoid of their lands, turn from cultivation to urban employment, although they have few skills to apply in the new environment. Villages situated near the cities are affected by an outflow of urban dwellers who flee the congestion of the city for the calm and quiet safety and lower living costs of the villages.

Table 2 Declining inhabited villages

Year	Villages	Year	Villages
1921	314	1961	276
1931	307	1971	243
1941	305	1981	214
1951	304	1991	199

Source: Census of India, 1921-91.

6. SOCIOECONOMIC BACKGROUND OF RESPONDENTS

Caste and place in the rural society plays a very important role in determining the occupational as well as the economic status of a family. Higher the caste, higher the social status like the Jat, the Rajput and the Brahmin castes. The Jat, besides being the numerically largest caste, are also the most powerful. They own and cultivate most of the land, and the villages have always been Jat dominated villages. Specially engaged in Zamindari system, Jats themselves were actively engaged in running the financial aspect of farming while agricultural labour is usually landless. Traditionally, Brahmins were the priest class or the learned class owning a lot of land but practising very little agriculture on their own, giving it away for contract. Lower classes as well as the higher traders/*vaishya* (*bania*) class owned negligible land. Lower class people have traditionally been landless, but today we find quite a few exceptions. In the last few decades, a lot of effort has been made on part of the government to raise the standard of living of the lower strata of society, usually the Scheduled Castes* who are also landless.

Table 3   Social composition of respondents

| Castes | Alipur | | | Najafgarh | | | |
	Bakoli	Sannoth	Hiranki	Dichau Kalan	Dhansa	Ujjwa	Total studied villages
Jat	7.69	33.76	64.51	61.29	62.56	48.15	44.67
Brahmin	3.85	31.17	12.90	3.22	7.55	7.41	12.67
Rajput	67.31	—	6.45	—	—	37.07	15.67
Bania	—	10.39	—	—	—	—	2.67
SC	13.46	22.07	16.13	22.58	24.53	7.41	19.33
OBC	7.69	1.3	—	9.67	5.66	—	4.67
Muslim	—	1.3	—	—	—	—	0.33
Total	100.00	100.00	100.00	100.00	100.00	100.00	100.00

Source: Personal Survey, 1998

About 33% reservation in government jobs and educational institutions have been made for these lower and economically weaker sections of the society. In rural areas, the SCs and the

---

*Lower and economically weaker sections have been divided into Scheduled Castes (SC), Scheduled Tribes (ST) and Other Backward Castes (OBC).

landless were given either a house plot or one acre of agricultural land, from the village common land in order to raise the standard of living of the people. Thus, today a large percentage of this population of rural areas is engaged in government jobs and their livelihood, which was earlier totally dependent on higher castes Zamindars, is now a diminishing phenomenon. The proximity to Delhi city, the capital of India has been a key factor in bringing about this change by providing a sea of job opportunities as well as free education to the rural poor. The higher castes on the other hand are also experiencing a transformation. The predominant agricultural land use has been changing to a more lucrative and easy to manage land use. In the study an effort was made to include all the sections of the society so as to get a better cross-sectional idea about rural society. The social structure of the villages is reflected in the sample population with Jats forming 44% of the total respondents, with Scheduled Castes forming the next largest group (Table 3). Although Rajputs are present in only two village—Bakoli and Ujjwa—their proportion was high and in case of Bakoli, they were even more than the Jats. Banias and Muslims were present only in the Sannoth village of the Alipur block.

7. SOCIAL SEGREGATION OF AGRICULTURAL LAND TRANSFER

On studying the social segregation of land sales (Table 4), it was found that the maximum sale (52.22%) has been made by the Jat community. This is due to the fact that Jats own maximum land.

Table 4 Social segregation of land transfer (in percentage of total acres of sold land)

| Castes | Alipur | | | Najafgarh | | | |
	Bakoli	Sannoth	Hiranki	Dichau Kalan	Dhansa	Ujjwa	Total studied villages
Jat	5.22	48.00	90.48	78.05	92.5	83.34	52.22
Brahmin	1.74	42.00	6.35	12.19	—	—	13.83
Rajput	93.04	—	—	—	—	12.50	28.72
Bania	—	10.00	—	—	—	—	2.61
S C	—	—	3.17	7.32	5.0	4.16	5.71
OBC	—	—	—	2.44	12.5	—	1.91
Muslim	—	—	—	—	—	—	—
Total	100.00	100.00	100.00	100.00	100.00	100.00	100.00

Source: Personal Survey, 1998.

Rajputs and Brahmins follow Jats in land sales with 28.72 per cent and 13.8 per cent respectively. This trend can be attributed to the status of land ownership in fringe villages, the curve of which is sharply skewed towards the upper caste. The Scheduled Caste community, which owns mainly allotted land from the village common land, have contributed very less to the total acreage of sold land.

During the fieldwork, it was generally observed that ownership of a large amount of land, a capital asset, provides the owner with a flexibility and risk manageability to change to another land use, the quality missing in the households owning less acreage of land. The urge to earn much more from the same piece of land in a very less span of time is one of the chief driving forces of land sale besides inability to continue with agriculture due to both human and environmental reasons. The land sales by Scheduled Castes include those lands, which are usually, non-productive (wastelands) and do not yield good crops, despite heavy investments to raise productive quality. It was also found that the Muslims neither owned land nor sold any, among the respondents of the fringe area. Baross (1983) included in his typology only the 'low income sub-division', as can be seen from the following description of a sub-division in Delhi. The development of residential colonies are in the form of regular plotted schemes, with the average plot size being 100 to 200 sq. yards. The plots are for sale. These settlements are usually generated through a nexus of property dealers, local politicians, and officials with a vested interest. The most successful property dealers happen to be retired politicians themselves who still maintain links with the power structure. Most of the times well-to-do owners of the plots let out the land and allow temporary construction to seasonal migrants. This way they can wait for the services in their areas (Jain, 1980, quoted in Baross, 1983).

From the tabulation of the temporal land sales (Table 5), it was found that the maximum sale transactions have taken place in between 1986-95. While in Alipur block villages, maximum land sales took place between 1990-95, in Najafgarh villages, maximum sales occurred between 1986-90.

On combining the data for two blocks, it was found that there is a continuous trend on land sales occurring between 1986-95. Thus, there is a slow rise of land sales till 1995 and then it drops off in 1996. This can be attributed to the continuous expansion of Delhi's urban residential limits since early 1980s, requiring large stretches of land for making construction material (bricks). Quarrying of agricultural land for soil rendered it less productive for further

Table 5   Temporal variation in land transfer (in percentage of total village land sold)

Castes	Before 1976	1976-80	1981-85	1986-90	1991-95	After 1995	Total (%)
Bakoli	—	7.82	6.09	22.60	51.30	14.79	100.00
Sannoth	10.00	5.00	20.00	32.00	25.00	8.00	100.00
Hiranki	3.17	11.11	20.63	46.03	17.46	1.58	100.00
Dichau Kalan	—	7.31	2.43	63.41	21.95	4.87	100.00
Dhansa	—	20.00	5.00	32.50	42.50	—	100.00
Ujjwa	83.33	4.17	—	—	—	12.50	100.00
Total studied villages	8.32	9.16	11.26	31.94	31.68	7.59	100.00

Source: Personal Survey, 1998.

cultivation, forcing the owner to part with it. Invasion of satellite television, increase in bus services and improvement of roads have played an important role in raising the land sales.

8.   DIVERSIFICATION OF AGRICULTURAL LAND

From the statistics showing the present use of sold land (Table 6), the actual transformation of land use from agriculture is visible. It was found that maximum transformation has been to farm houses (34 per cent) followed by residential uses (27.93 per cent) and commercial purpose (23.49 per cent). The figures clearly tell the story of the urban sprawl with surrounding areas developing into suburbs, residential and commercial land uses. Maximum farm houses have been constructed in Alipur block, while maximum residential colonies expansion has taken place in villages of Najafgarh block. But the main feature of land sales is the continuance of agriculture and related land uses. Very little land has been used for commercial or farm house purposes in the Najafgarh block. The main deterrent in the block's land use change is the lack of proper water supply and low ground water level, which prevents any land use change for fear of land and equipment degradation. Distance is another main factor affecting the land use transformation. While in Alipur block, good water supply, proximity to urban centre have promoted the land being used for farm houses, colonies and even commercial purposes, which gives much higher returns than mere agriculture.

The analysis clearly brings out the distance decay function operating in the rural-urban fringe of Delhi (Fig. 2). As compared to the two villages of Najafgarh block, the villages of Alipur block are closer to the urban centre and have experienced maximum land transformation, which coupled with good water availability has

Table 6   Diversification of sold agricultural land (in percentage of total agricultural
land sold)

Villages/Uses	Farm house	Residential	Agricultural or nursery	Commercial or warehouse	Industry	Total
Bakoli	61.30	3.91	2.60	27.82	4.34	100
Sannoth	13.50	39.00	-	47.50	-	100
Hiranki	69.04	28.57	-	2.38	-	100
Dichau Kalan	8.53	69.51	2.43	19.51	-	100
Dhansa	-	42.50	55.00	2.50	-	100
Ujjwa	-	-	100.00	-	-	100
Total studied villages	34.20	27.93	13.05	23.49	1.30	

Source: Personal Survey, 1998.

raised the proportion of land sales. In Najafgarh block, on the other
hand, poor water availability has proved to be a major stumbling
block in transformation of agricultural land to any other use. Even
in agriculture, crops grown are those requiring less water like wheat
and those giving fast returns like cauliflower, onions, etc.

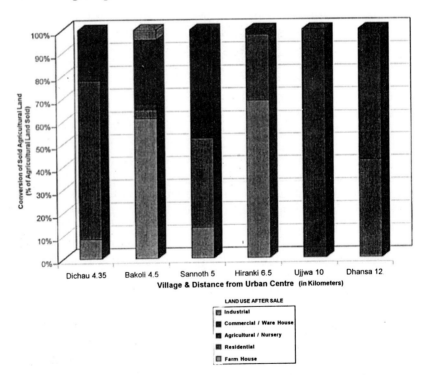

Fig. 2   Distance-Land Transfer Relationship in Rural-Urban Fringe of Delhi

9. CONCLUSION

It becomes clear that agricultural land in the proximity of an urban area is intensely subjected to the urban land use and the impact on agricultural land has a bearing on the socioeconomic status of the rural society. Although urban society imposes a developmental attitude in the rural people in terms of education, municipalities etc. as well as urban land use like industries, still the agricultural land is the one which suffers from the most negative impacts of urbanization. Agricultural land is the first point of attack of urban encroachment. Its transformation from a food granary (grain producers) to a totally non-productive permanent land use, in a way deprives the land from being reproductive and increases the pressure on the remaining agricultural land. A lure of cash crops and vegetables declines the remaining agricultural land's productive power, creating a shortage of food grains and a consequent upliftment of rural society. In such a situation, where urban impact is both beneficial as well as degradational, there is an urgent need to marginalize, categorize and prioritize rural and agricultural land use and plan for a sustainable development of rural-urban fringe of Delhi. Land use decision made by a large number of local governments fails to achieve results that protect our valuable agricultural resource, provide for adequate and reasonably priced housing, make urban habitats livable, reduce social inequality and provide for a sustainable economic base.

REFERENCES

Amitabh. 1997. *Urban Land Markets and Land Price Changes: A Study in the Third World Context*, Ashgate Publishing Ltd. England.

Baross, P. 1983. The Articulation of Land Supply for Popular Settlements in Third World Cities. In: Angel, S. et al. (Eds), *Land for Housing the Poor*, Select Books, Singapore.

Carter, H. 1981. *The Study of Urban Geography*, Edward Arnold, New Castle upon of Tyne, 316-326.

Census of India, 1991, New Delhi.

Chandhoke, S.K. 1994. "Neighbourhood and Lifestyles: Trends in an Exploding Metropolis". In: *Habitation and Environment, Interaction, Inter-relations and Adjustment*, S.K. Chandoke (Ed.), Har Anand Publication, New Delhi, 145-161.

Desai, A. and S. Sen Gupta, 1987. "Problems of Changing Land use Pattern in the Urban Fringe: The Case of Ahmedabad", In: *Perspective in Urban Geography* Vol. 12, C.S. Yadav (Ed.). Concept Publishing Company, New Delhi, 205-212.

India Today, 1990. 'Changes in the Indian Building Environment', India Today (A Monthly News Magazine), May 31, 1990, 49-51.

Lagon, J. and H. Molotch, 1987. *Urban Fortunes: The Political Economy of Place*, University of California Press, Berkeley, CA.

Lehman, T. 1995. *Public Values, Private Lands*, Chapel Hill NC and London, University of North Caroline Press, UK.

Mujtaba, S.M. 1994. *Land Use and Environmental Change Due to Urban Sprawl*, Daya Publishing House, New Delhi.

Nangia, S. 1976. *Delhi Metropolitan Region: A Study in Settlement Geography*, K.B. Publications, New Delhi.

Pfeffer, M.J. and M.B. Lapping 1994. Farmland preservation development rights and the theory of the growth machine. The view of planners. Journal of Rural Studies, Vol. 10, 233-248.

Pincetl, S. 1994. The regional management of growth in California. A history of failure. The Intenational Journal of Urban and Regional Research, Vol. 18, 256-274.

Ramachandran, R. 1989. *Urbanisation and Urban Systems in India*, Oxford University Press, New Delhi.

Sampson, R.N. 1979. *The ethical dimension of farmland protection*. In: *Farmland, Food and the Future*, M. Schnepf (Ed.) Soil Conservation Society of America, Ankency, 1A: 89-98.

Sharma, K.D. 1985. *Urban Development in the Metropolitan Shadow: A Case Study from Haryana*, Inter India Publication, New Delhi. 102-187.

CHAPTER 14

Processes and Causes of Land Use/ Cover Changes in Two Ecological Zones in Nigeria

(D.A. Oyeleye[*])

1. INTRODUCTION

Vegetation is the plant cover of the earth. This cover includes trees and grasses of different kinds. Some are natural whereas others are man-made. We refer to the trees that grow in the forest or the grasses that grow in the field which are not planted by man, as natural vegetation; the vegetation which man has deliberately planted like yams, maize, groundnuts, coconuts, ornamental trees and flowers are termed man-made vegetation.

Four factors work hand in hand to make the vegetation differ from place to place. These are climate, soil, relief and man. In Nigeria, the relevant climatic factors are humidity and rainfall, because these elements vary widely throughout the country. High relative humidity, heavy rainfall, little evaporation and a long wet season encourage the growth of vegetation.

Soil type and moisture content determine vegetation. Sometimes, the soil factor may be more important than the amount of rainfall, because what matters is not how much rain has fallen but how much of the rainfall has remained in the soil for plants.

Altitude also influences vegetation. In wet tropical countries, the lower slopes of the mountains are clad with luxuriant vegetation. Above 1,500 metres, the forest is replaced by thinner vegetation of

*Department of Geography, University of Lagos, Akoka-Yaba, Lagos, Nigeria.

a different type, made up of ferns, mosses and lichens which are better adapted to conditions at high altitude.

Human activities like clearing forests for cultivation or road cons-truction and overgrazing, have taken quite a toll of the vegetation. These activities have been going on over many centuries, with the result that in Nigeria the vegetation we see, especially in areas where the population and livestock are dense, bears little resemblance to the original plant cover.

2. TYPES OF VEGETATION

Two broad belts of plant groups can be found in Nigeria. Within each group, it is possible to distinguish three sub-types. Thus we have

(1) Forests   (a) Salt water swamps

(b) Fresh water swamps

(c) High forest

(2) Savanna

(a) Guinea Savanna

(b) Sudan Savanna

(c) Sahel Savanna

There is also a seventh sub-type—the Montane vegetation. Typical Montane vegetation is not strictly found in Nigeria, but signs of it can be traced in the Jos and Adamawa Plateaux. (Fig. 1)

Their belts run roughly parallel from east to west, emphasizing the dependence of vegetation on climate. It should be emphasized however that there is no precise boundary between one belt and the next; changeover from one belt to another is only a zone of transition where the characteristics of one gradually disappear as those of the next progressively take over.

Both the fresh and salt water swamps appear to show little modification by man for the following reasons:

(a) Sparse population and hence fewer trees are cut down or burnt except where mineral oil is being explored. In such areas, clear-ing has been undertaken for access roads, houses and oil well sites.

(b) It is difficult to reach the heart of these forest types because of the tangled nature of the vegetation and the absence of roads through the swamps.

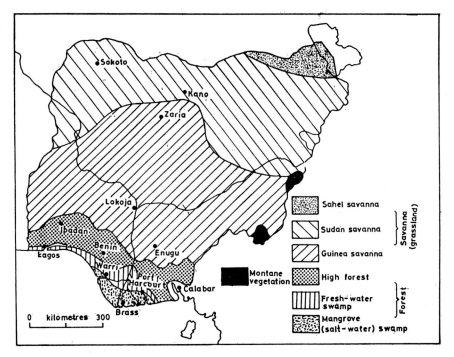

Fig. 1 Vegetation belts of Nigeria

(c) Even when the mangrove trees are cut down, they grow again rather quickly, nature being very generous in its supply for water and soil for plant growth.

Attention will now be focused on two contrasting vegetational belts in order to examine their distinguishing characteristics and how various physical and cultural factors have modified them. The two ecological zones are high forest and Sudan savanna.

2.1 The High Forest

The zone stretches from the western boundary of Nigeria south eastwards through Ibadan and Benin. Many big cities such as Ile-Ife, Ondo and Akure engaging in agriculture, lumbering and wood carving exist in this zone. The original characteristics of the high forest cover or rain forest belt are: perennial tree growth which is promoted by such factors as high rainfall (130 to 150 cm in the west and over 200 cm in the east), high humidity (generally over 80%) and the long wet season of about 8 to 10 months, all of which ensure an adequate supply of water and the continuous presence of moisture.

Vegetation shows a varied combination of different types of plant groups. The trees are arranged in three distinct layers or storeys. The ground storey is made up of herbs, shrubs and some grasses growing up to a height of 3 to 6 metres. They are most dense where the taller trees have been cleared and along the forest edges, where the sunlight succeeds in reaching them. The middle storey consists of tall trees, 18 to 24 metres high, possessing robust branches and heavy dark green foliage. The branches of one tree often intertwine with those of others, and this creates an almost continuous canopy of leaves which shuts off the sunlight from the shrubs and herbs below. This storey is made up of hundreds of plant species which are usually described as evergreen. In reality, however, they do shed their leaves but all the time new buds are opening out as the old leaves wither and die. The result is that the trees appear green all the time.

Standing out like islands in an ocean of densely packed vegetation are the third or top storey. They possess small crowns of pointed leaves resting on a few branches, which in turn are carried by tall straight stems towering up to a height of between 30 and 60 metres. Here are valuable trees such as mahogany, obeche and tropical cedar. Their roots are buttressed and the species so scattered that their economic exploitation is greatly retarded.

To the above three groups may be added a fourth, which differs from the rest in that its plants exist only by depending on their neighbours for food or for support or both. These include parasites, saprophytes, climbers and epiphytes.

2.2 The Sudan Savanna

This belt is found in the far north. It is separated from the high forest belt by a wide belt of Guinea Savanna. The latter is the broadest vegetational cover in Nigeria, occupying nearly half its area. Guinea Savanna is a byproduct of centuries of tree devastation by man and fire and a continuous attempt by the plants to adapt themselves to the climatic environment. Examples of trees found here are the locust bean tree. The trees grow in clusters, generally not more than 6 metres high, and are inter-spaced with elephant grass growing to a height of 3.0 to 3.6 metres.

Sudan Savanna is typical of places where the total annual rainfall is between 65 and 100 cm and relative humidity is constantly below 40%, except in the few wet months when it sometimes goes up to an average of 60%. The duration of the dry season is about 6-8 months. Sudan zone holds the greatest density of population in northern Nigeria. It produces important economic crops like groundnuts, cotton, millet and maize and has the highest concentration of cattle in the country. The Sudan Savanna has thus suffered great deprivation at the hands of man and livestock.

The landscape is less generously covered with plants than the Guinea Savanna or the high forest. In fact the actual vegetation is made up of short grasses 1.5 to 2 metres high and some stunted trees. The trees characteristic of the Guinea Savanna are absent. They are replaced by trees like acacia, the dum palm, the silk cotton and the baobab.

The Sahel is limited to a small triangular piece of land in the north-eastern corner of Nigeria, where the annual rainfall drops below 65 cm and the length of the dry season exceeds 8 months. The grasses in this area are short and tussocky 0.5 to 1 metre high. Acacia is the chief tree; though date palms have begun to appear. The land is not cultivated without irrigation.

3. HUMAN ACTIVITIES AS THEY AFFECT LAND COVER IN THE HIGH FOREST

Human activities have been the over-riding influence in the degradation of vegetation cover and soil in the high forest. Numerous people enter the forest area daily in search of timber, firewood and fodder. These people belong to the poorest segment of the rural population. Forest is also used by local residents in the forest settlements to provide firewood and fodder. Such local exploitation is carried out daily by hundreds of people whose livelihoods depend on forest products.

Timber collection involves cutting a carefully selected tree of good timber quality, usually in the diameter range between 40 and 60 cm dbh (diameter at breast height) and sawing the tree on the spot. Herbs and grasses are cut for fodder, and branches of palatable shrubs and trees are stripped. Timber production requires heavy labour, arduous travel throughout the forest area and stays of up to one week in the forest.

Fuel wood and fodder collection is carried out in relatively accessible areas near the forest boundary. In recent years, this exploitation has increased under the influence of the rapidly growing population. Many people from the north migrate regularly into the forest area to provide labour in the cocoa and oil palm producing areas.

Rapid population growth in the forest area has put pressure on land and created the problem of how to increase and sustain agricultural production while at the same time conserving natural resources. Apart from tree crops, most food crops such as maize and melon are cultivated twice in the year in tandem with the double rainfall peak. It has been documented that the removal of forest cover by land clearing results in immediate and drastic degradative changes in soil properties (Cunningham, 1963; Nye and Greenland, 1964; Lal and Cummings, 1979; Dumanski, 1994). Annual organic carbon additions are drastically reduced when former forests are brought under cultivation; crop residues usually provide only a small fraction of the dry matter previously supplied by forest litter and root decomposition.

The ideal high forest cover described above has been largely interfered with by man. For instance, in areas of intensive cultivation and selective tree cutting, the original tree species have been devastated giving rise to the growth of oil palm bush. These palm trees can be found spreading out their silvery fronds like umbrellas over the heads of the cultivated vegetation below. Such oilpalm bushes are more widespread in the eastern sector of the high forest than the west.

Moreover, on the northern fringes of the high forest belt, the vegetation is thinner and more deciduous in character as a result of low humidity and precipitation. The result is that when it is cleared, it is replaced by a type of parkland which represents an encroachment of the Guinea Savanna into the forest zone. It is made up of tall grasses and smaller trees which are diminutive survivors of the original plant species. It is variously called 'derived savanna' or 'forest-savanna mosaic'.

4. HUMAN ACTIVITIES AS THEY AFFECT LAND COVER IN THE SUDAN SAVANNA

Since the Sudan Savanna is an area covered with grassland, the rearing of cattle is very prominent and this leads to overgrazing in many areas. The Fulani cattle rearer practices pastoral nomadism. He moves northwards in the wet season but southwards in the dry season, when the grass in the far north has all died away. He also drives his cattle up the plateau in the wet season when the valleys are tsetsefly infested; but in the dry season when the valleys are free from this pest and when the plateaux are dry and patchy, he drives his cattle down. This is real trans-humance. Grazing and overgrazing of cattle across the plains of northern Nigeria also degrade the natural grasslands.

Moreover, elementary mixed farming whereby plants and livestock production are combined on a farm in such a way that they help each other is practised in the Sudan zone. For instance, grass and grains are used in feeding livestock, while the latter provide manure for the crops and means of transport; they as well pull the plough. The crops cultivated are quick maturing crops that mature between three and four months because the duration of rain is limited to about four months in the northern section of the belt and six months in the southern section. The main crops are groundnuts and cotton which are cultivated on a commercial scale but once a year in contrast to the forest area where double cultivation is possible. Because of the grassland nature of the cover, this vegetation type is more open and easier to cultivate than the high forest of dense vegetation. As a result farm sizes per farmer are larger in the Sudan Savanna in comparison to the high forest. The smaller farm sizes in the forest, a result of difficulty in forest clearance, do not lend themselves easily to the use of machines. By contrast, mechanization is practiced in Sudan and this encourages larger farm sizes and elementary scientific farming. Yield per ha per crop is also higher than in the high forest but total yield per unit area of mixed cropping in the forest area is higher than Sudan where mixed cropping is not feasible. In view of the large population concentration in Sudan, majority of whom are agriculturists, Sudan has experienced severe degradation of vegetation cover, soil and yield.

Rainfall in Nigeria, particularly in the north, is erratic; it varies widely in amount and often comes in thunderstorms. Such rainfall usually causes erosion and leaching and promotes diseases. It also contributes to the problem of environmental degradation.

Moreover, rapid population growth has put pressure on the land. For instance the Nigerian population has increased from about 65 million in 1965 to about 100 million in 1995. This has created the problem of how to increase and sustain agricultural production in both the forest and Sudan zones, while at the same time conserving natural resources.

Sustainable land management, improved technologies and improved economic performance are central to achieving the goals of sustainable agriculture. The objective of sustainable land management is to harmonize the complementary goals of providing environmental, economic and social opportunities for the benefit of present and future generations, while maintaining and enhancing the quality of land resources (Dumanski, 1997; Smyth and Dumanshi, 1993). There is an urgent need to combine the gains in productivity with stability over time. However, productivity and stability are often seen as irreconcilable goals, involving a conflict between short- and and long-term interests. Sustainable agriculture demands that consideration be given to achieving both goals simultaneously. Hence the need for planning for sustainable land management.

5. CONCLUSION

Natural resources can potentially be used in a sustainable way if appropriate land management technology, regional planning and the policy framework complement one another in a purposeful way in accordance with the principle and concepts of Sustainable Land Management (SLM). At the center of this thinking is the concept of 'ecosystem balance' and especially the questions of irreversibility of ecological processes, and resilience of ecosystems. A system of controlled forest exploitation which involves the preservation of forest reserves which can preserve climax vegetation in some areas together with their fauna is to be encouraged. Great importance should be attached to the few remaining areas of natural climax vegetation (forest reserves), not only because they provide tangible resource materials but also in order to create suitable sites for environmental research and education in resource management and conservation. Exploitation in such forest reserves should be limited to the hunting of games with official permit. Controlled lumbering could also be undertaken in like manner.

In the Sudan zone, fallow land planted with fine grass should be held in rotation with food crop land. Scientific method of cultivation which can discourage soil erosion, encourage the use of organic manure, modern techniques of farming and individualization of holding within both the forest and Sudan zones should also be encouraged. This will encourage individual farmers to develop his holding economically, while leaving each ecological environment less degraded.

REFERENCES

Cunningham, R.K. 1963. 'The effect of clearing a tropical forest soil'; J. Soil Science 14: 334-345.

Dumanski, J. (Ed.) 1994. Proceedings of the International Workshop on Sustainable Land Management for the 21st Century (Vol. 1) Agricultural Institute of Canada, Ottawa.

Dumanski, J. 1997. 'Planning for sustainability in agricultural development projects. Agriculture and Rural Development 4.

Lal, R. and D.J. Cummings. 1979. 'Clearing a Tropical Forest: Effects of Soil and Micro-climates' Field Crops Research 2, 91-107.

Nye, P.H. and D.J. Greenland, 1964. 'Changes in the Soil after Clearance in a Tropical Forest' Plant Soil 21: 101-112.

Smyth, A.J. and J. Dumanski. 1993. 'FESLM'—An international framework for evaluating sustainable land management. World Soil Rep. 73, FAO, Rome.

CHAPTER 15

Land Use Changes and Related Issues in the Suburban Environment in Colombo Metropolitan Region of Sri Lanka

(U.A. Chandrasena*)

1. INTRODUCTION

Suburbanization, which merges villages with towns is also described as a phenomenon associated with metropolitization, extending cities towards their hinterland, due to out-migration of people and decentralization of activities from the core areas. Unlike in the developed countries, the suburbs in the third world are populated mainly by cityward migrants from rural areas. The rural-urban fringe, which is explained as a transition zone contains most of the subrubs which are developed mainly as residential areas, and gradually acquire other urban functions. Amongst most visible processes of sub-urbanization, the conversion of land in the countryside into urban uses is predominant. It takes place often in a haphazard, uncontrolled and unplanned manner in the third world countries. Hence, there are many issues arising due to suburban development in these countries, which are major concerns of present-day urban planners. The main objective of the present paper is to discuss in detail the past and present trends in the suburban environs of Colombo Metropolitan Region (CMR) of Sri Lanka.

The Democratic Republic of Sri Lanka (Ceylon) is a tropical island situated at the southern tip of India and covers an area of 65,609 sq. km. Major physiographic features of the island are a central mass of

*Department of Geography, University of Kelaniya, Kelaniya, Sri Lanka.

highland, from where most of the rivers flow radially, and the surrounding lowland. The latitudinal location in the tropics and the insularity are major factors determining her climate. Perennially high temperature and seasonally derived rainfall are major elements of the climate and the island has been conventionally divided into a Dry Zone and a Wet Zone. Most of the southwestern and central parts of the island are in the wet zone. Sri Lanka has a rich culture and a continuous history which spans over a period of 2500 years. European invasions and their influence, mainly by Portuguese (1505-1658), Dutch (1658-1796) and British who finally ruled the entire island until independence in 1948, have significantly changed the history of the island. Sri Lanka is a developing country with a per capita GNP of US$ 837 and an economic growth rate of 4.7% at present and the economy is basically rural and agricultural. Also, she ranks high among developing countries accord-ing to welfare indices such as PQLI or HDI. The distribution of population, economic functions and infrastructure, etc. are highly skewed in the western part of the country, illustrating a core-periphery relationship. For adminis-trative purpose the island is divided into 9 provinces and 25 districts.

2. URBAN SYSTEM OF SRI LANKA

The urban settlements in the island have a history going back to the time of Sinhalese kings, but the present era of urban growth commenced during the European rule in Sri Lanka. Colombo, Galle and Trincomalee have been developed first as major ports and then as commercial and administrative centres. The towns inland have mostly developed as nodal points of major trunk roads, railways and local administrative and commercial centres. The urban local authorities were first established in Sri Lanka in 1865, recognizing Colombo and Kandy as Municipal Councils. Colombo continued her supremacy as the capital city of Sri Lanka, a major port as well as an administrative and commercial centre. Having locational advantages, connecting east-west sea routes, it has grown to a primate city in Asia, and presently it occupies a pivotal position in international commercial and investment fields. The census of population in 1946 reported 42 urban centres and at the last census taken in 1981, there were 134 urban centres. Majority of the urban settlements are small and medium size towns, with a population of less than 100,000.

The urban population in Sri Lanka has grown very slowly during the past 100 years or more. At the first census of population in 1871, there were 2.4 million people in the country and 10.8% were urban residents. In 1901, the percentage of urban population was 11.6% while in 1981 it increased to 21.5%.

In Sri Lanka, urban settlements were defined administratively without taking into consideration proper criteria and the urban system included Municipal Councils (MCs), Urban Councils (Ucs) and Town Councils (TCs) until the census in 1981. In 1987, reclassification of local government authorities as MCS, UCS, and Pradeshiya Sabha, excluded 84 town councils and incorporated them into rural settlements. Indrasiri (1997) based on a study of UDA, identified 337 urban centres, having considered their economic characteristics as well as the pattern of land use. These include 51 existing officially reorganized urban areas, 83 centres which lost urban status in 1987, and 203 emerging urban centres.

The past growth rates of towns show that the capital city reached its maximum growth rate by the middle of this century and has tended to decline during past three decades, but the growth rates of medium size and small towns have risen in the recent past. This trend is vividly presented in the demographic trends of the suburban areas of Colombo.

Colombo Metropolitan Region (CMR) which was first designated as a planning area in the Colombo Master Plan Project (1978) and the present Colombo Metropolitan Regional Structure Plan (CMRSP) (1998) of the Urban Development Authority of Sri Lanka consists of the three administrative districts of Colombo, Gampaha and Kalutara or the entire Western province. This region accommodates 68% of the total urban population in 52 cities and towns. It spans over 369,420 ha or 5.6% of the total extent of land in the country and accommodates a population of 4.6 million or 26% of the entire nation.

The CMR is significant in the national and international context due to the location of the port and international airport and the very high concentration of administrative, social and economic functions. It contributes about 44% of the GDP of Sri Lanka and about 77% in the non-agricultural sector. It accounts for 31% of total employment and 53% of industrial employment in the country. CMR accounts for nearly 40% of the area under paddy, rubber and coconut in the wet zone.

The CMR is a high population density area, with about 13 persons per ha (1996) or a residential population density of 35 persons per ha (1994). The built-up area of CMR is 5.5% (1996) and it varies from one district to another. The Colombo district has 15.4% of built-up land while Gampaha and Kalutara have 3.3% and 2.2% respectively.

The urban system of CMR comprised 23 TCs, 14 UCs and 3 MCs at 1981 census, but after the reclassification of towns in 1987 there were only 14 UCs and 3 MCs. The UDA study however revealed that there were about 58 UCs in the area considering the emerging service centres, etc. (Indrasiri, 1997). The CMR is the most dynamic and diversified socioeconomic region of the country, with a highly mixed land use and settlement pattern. Based on existing physical development there are three broad land use categories which can be identified as (a) highly urbanized area; (b) semi-urbanized area; and (c) rural area. The highly urbanized area covers about 18.7% of CMR and the built-up area is about 60% of that extent. Semi-urbanized areas and rural areas cover about 31.8% and 49.5% respectively. Based on the land use, and settlement characteristics, Wanasinghe (1984) has identified three broad regions of CMR as follows:

a. The Central City
b. Suburban Crescents
c. Urban-rural fringe

3. SUBURBAN ENVIRONS OF COLOMBO

The suburban environs of Colombo, on which the present paper mainly focuses consists of a broad area around the capital city of Colombo, and extends as crescents towards north-east and south into the rural hinterlands. This area, as the present paper considers, includes the rapidly changing landscape of the immediate hinterland of Colombo as well as the urban-rural fringe where most of the influences of urbanization are beginning to operate. The suburban areas and urban-rural fringe have been identified, measured and demarcated by various scholars in Sri Lanka during last two decades. Panditharatne (1961), based on the suburban commuting pattern, the circulation of news papers and various public services, identifies the intensive field of Colombo which covers a contiguous zone extending to Ragama, Kelaniya, Nugegoda and Moratuwa. The fringe zone, generating about 2% of commuting to Colombo extends upto Negombo, Minuwangoda, Gampaha, Veyangoda and Kalutara according to him.

Silva and Gunawardane (1970) studied the migration patterns, land use, transportation services, manufacturing, etc. and found that the urban centres in the fringe were beginning to exceed the growth rate of Colombo due to the influx of out-migrants from the city centre as well as the movement city-ward migrants from the periphery.

Wanasinghe (1984) who did a comprehensive survey of recent urbanization trends in CMR identified that 85% of the area falls within the rural-urban fringe, incorporating inner and outer crescents of suburbs and the urban settlements. The inner crescent of suburbs have emerged since the early decades of the present century mainly due to the diversion of migrants, the extension of transport network and service facilities. According to her study, a transformation took place in terms of expansion of residential land use, decline of primary sector employment and growth of commuter settlements. The major causes of suburbanization, as she explains, are the availability of cheap buildable land, low cost of transport and preference of people to live in calm environs, and deconcentration of industries, etc. (Wanasinghe, 1984). Between 1921-1963, further transformation took place in the fringe and a second suburban crescent evolved around the first crescent.

4. LAND USE CHANGES IN THE CMR

Land use change is the most significant aspect of suburbanization process and it indicates the intensity of transformation in the hinterlands of urban centres. The land use structures of the CMR as a whole are given in Table 1.

Table 1   Land use pattern of the CMR (1981-1996)

	Land use type	Percentage	
		1981	1996
01	Urban built-up area	3.3	4.7
02	Homesteads	32.4	34.9
03	Tree and other perennial crops	32.7	28.8
04	Cropland (mainly paddy)	21.4	21.6
05	Nature forest	5.2	5.3
06	Scrub and grass	0.8	0.8
07	Wetland	1.4	1.2
08	Water bodies	2.5	2.5
09	Barren land	0.3	0.2
	Total	100.00	100.00

Source: CMR Structure Plan, Vol II. 1998. Urban Development Authority.

According to the table, major land use categories include homesteads and tree crop sector, which include mostly rubber and coconut which are also primary export commodities of Sri Lanka. Comparing the land use pattern of 1981 with that of 1996, CMRSP report presents the major land use trends in the area.

Spatial patterns of urban expansion such as sprawling and ribbon development have significantly affected the land use pattern of the CMR. A recent study conducted by Malik Majid, on Urban Expansion of Greater Colombo Area since 1956 revealed the trends and patterns of expanding built-up area over the rural landscape (1996). In 1956, according to his estimate, the built up area of the region extended over 1911 ha and the figure was 15,635 ha in 1994. This increase was mainly through ribbon development in a northward direction up to Katunayake, Negombo and southwards to Kalutara. The urban core has expanded up to Wattala, Kotikawatte, Nawinna, Egoda Uyana in Northern, Southern and South-Eastern directions respectively. The proportion of core area relative to entire built-up area changed from 73.45% in 1956 to 56.5% in 1994, while the peripheral suburban built-up area accounted for 43.5% of the land.

5. GAMPAHA DISTRICT: A CHANGING SUBURBAN ENVIRON

Gampaha district, formally a part of the Colombo District was designated in 1978 as a separate administrative area. It covers 1378 sq. km and a land area about 2% of the total island. The land of the district gently slopes towards flat coastal belt in the west. Most of the area consists of undulating topography interrupted by valleys and alluvial plains while there are few hills and rock outcrops rising about 200 km which are found in the east. The unique feature of the district is the presence of vast low lying area in the western part consisting of flood plains, marshes, wetlands, etc. For administrative purposes Gampaha district is divided into 13 Divisional Secretary areas and subdivided into about 1800 Grama Niladhari (village level officers) areas comprised several villages in each.

Gampaha is the second most important district in terms of size and density of population. The Demographic Survey of 1994 estimated her population as 1,739,160 and population density as 1003 per sq. km. The Divisional Secretary areas of Kelaniya, Negombo and Wattala in the Western part of the district showed a high population density, while Weke, Divulapitiya, Mirigama, Attanagalla and Minuwangoda divisions were low density areas.

The population of Gampaha district increased at an average annual rate of 1.8% between 1971 and 1981. The data of the Demographic Survey 1994 showed an increase of 22% since 1981. The increase of population at the divisional level reveals that Katana, Negombo, Gampaha, Attanagalla and Mahara received more people during the period between 1981-1994. About 27.9% of the total population in the district were living in 16 urban areas in 1981. However, the number of officially accepted urban areas was reduced to seven in 1987. A UDA study identified that there are 27 centres with urban characteristics in the district. Most of the urban population lived in the western coastal belt (Fig. 1).

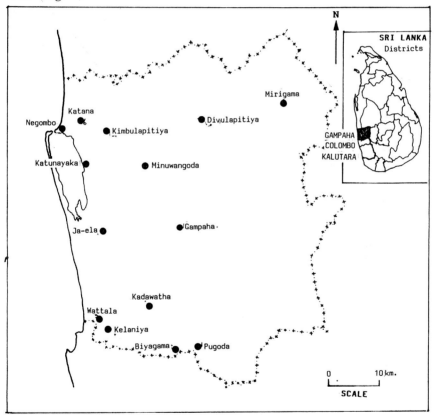

Fig. 1   Major Urban Centres in Gampaha District

Industrial composition of the employed population in Gampaha showed the service sector as the dominant source of employment and manufacturing as the next important sector in 1981. The percentage share of employment in manufacturing sector increased from 23.3% in 1981 to 34.1% in 1994.

5.1 Migration Pattern

Migration pattern is a demographic process closely associated with the land use changes in the Gampaha district. Gampaha is the second largest recipient of migrants in the island and the only district in Sri Lanka with net-inmigration in the wet zone, except Colombo district.

During the mature phase of suburban growth, the migrants to the inner-crescent suburbs were dominant according to Wanasinghe (1985). Due to low cost of buildable land and low rental value there has been a decentralization of manufacturing and service establishments into the suburbs, providing more employment. This process has gradually transformed the dormitory settlements into suburbs providing employment in the 1960s and 1970s.

The 1981 census reported that 15.6% of the total population in the Gampaha district were born in other districts. In the urban sector, share of migrants was greater with 26.8%. It was also revealed that some urban centres like Peliyagoda (31.5%), Dalugama (42.4%), Kelaniya (34.6%) and Welisara (33.1%) had more population born outside the area. According to the 'Previous Residence Method', the census of 1981 revealed that 12.8% of the population had their previous residence in other districts. The migration into Gampaha has been increasing rapidly since 1981 due to an expanding industrial sector and availability of buildable lands in the district.

The data of Demographic Survey, 1994, revealed that 29.7% of the population in Gampaha district had their previous residence in other districts. The divisional level data on place of birth and previous residence of population revealed that DSDs like Biyagama, Kelaniya, Mahara, Wattala and Katana had a high proportion of immigrants. About 14.3% of population who migrated within the district or into the district have moved to own houses and 11.1% for employment while others were due to displacement, education and other reasons. Those who moved to their present residence for employment showed a high proportion in Biyagama (19.2%), Katana (18.1%), Gampaha (10.8%) and Wattala (11.8%). The migration for employment is clearly evident in the division like Katana and Biyagama due to the employment opportunities in the industries in FTZs (Free Trade Zones). Those who moved for seeking residence were high in the divisions like Biyagama, Mahara, Negombo, Katana and Gampaha as well as in more rural divisions like Weke and Divulapitiya.

A survey conducted in 1989, on the boarders living around and working in Katunayaka EPZ revealed that only 27% of them were from the same district. Other districts from where workers had come for employments were Kurunegala, Kegalle, Matara, Kandy and Galle in a descending order. This means a large majority of population moved to the district seeking employment.

A census of public sector, semi-government sector and provincial government sector employees in 1994 showed the second highest percentage of employees in public sectors, were living in the Gampaha district. Thus 14.7% of semi-government sector employees, 12.4% of public sector employees and 8% of provincial sector employees were residents in Gampaha. The same survey also revealed that 65.9% of the public sector and 68.7% of semi-government sector employees working in Gampaha district were residents of the same region.

Industrial sector activities in the district commenced in the 1960s with the state sponsorship, by locating several industrial plants for manufacture of tyre (Kelaniya), petroleum and fertilizer (Sapugaskanda), textiles (Pugoda and Veyangoda), oils and fats (Seeduwa), hardware (Yakkala) in 1960s and 1970s. An industrial estate was established in 1960s at Ekala (Seeduwa) providing basic facilities for private entrepreneurs. These industrial activities encouraged residential development, extension of road network, electricity and telecommunication services in those areas. Some of the private sector industries were also established in Kelaniya, Dalugama, Wattala, Ja-Ela and Negombo areas due to the availability of these basic facilities. Availability of land for factory sites, accessibility by railways and highways, close proximity to water-sources such as Kelani Ganga river were some of the factors for locating the industries in these areas.

The government which came into power in 1977 followed an open economic policy, replacing hitherto existed, import substitution industries approach, by export oriented industrialization. In 1978, the government established the Greater Colombo Economic Commission (GCEC) the statutory areas of which covered most parts of the Gampaha District. The objective of the GCEC was to encourage direct foreign investment in export-oriented industries, providing more employment and more foreign exchange earning. Two Export Processing Zones (EPZs) were developed under GCEC, in Katunayake (1978) and Biyagama (1986). These industries provided employment for about 80,000 people and have made a significant impact on their surrounding areas.

The annual surveys of industries by the Ministry of Industries indicate that number of industrial units and their employment opportunities provided by them increased rapidly in the DSDs such as Ja-Ela, Wattala, Kelaniya, Katana and Biyagama between 1985-1993 (Table 2).

Table 2   Industrial units and employment in several DSDs in Gampaha district
(1985-1993)

Division	1985		1993	
	No. of units	No. of employment	No. of units	No. of employment
Ja-Ela	34	3776	136	22,672
Wattala	24	1646	121	13,531
Kelaniya	19	1763	104	13,997
Katana	18	1450	149	71,284
Biyagama	7	552	60	34,059

Source: CMRSP, Vol V.

A survey conducted in the Gampaha district (1994) reported that there were 10,341 industrial units, employing 113,272 persons in addition to two EPZs. Most of these industries were located in Biyagama, Kelaniya, Wattala and Ja-Ela areas. The largest number of industrial employees were found in five Divisional Secretary areas Divulapitiya and Ja-Ela, Katana, Kelaniya and Wattala. Further the Katunayaka and Biyagama EPZs provided 55,644 and 26,675 employment opportunities respectively. Since 1992, the GCEC renamed as Board of Investment (BOI), has extended its services to areas other than EPZs. Thus more industries which benefited from BOI concessions and incentives, developed within the district. Under the present industrial development programme the establishment of two industrial estates have commenced in Wathupitiwala and Mirigama. The rapid industrialization in the district, accompanied many other developments such as attracting more employees from other areas, increasing the demand for residential facilities, transportation and other services.

5.2 Urban Development

Urban development in the Gampaha district has taken place by extending the urban area into rural lands, redesignating town areas and the rapid development of built-up areas due to an increase in urban population, urban functions as well as expanding infrastructure facilities and amenities (Fig.1).

Between 1977-1981 urban population growth rates for individual towns showed that Hendala (TC), Seeduwa-Katunayake (UC), Welisara (TC), Ragama (TC) were growing at a rate of over 2% per year, while Negombo (MC), Kelaniya (TC), Peliyagoda (UC), Kochchikade (TC), Minuwangoda (TC) and Veyangoda (TC) showed growth rates less than 1%. Only Mirigama (TC) showed a higher growth rate of over 3% during that period. A study conducted in 1980 identified a hierarchy of about 160 growth centres including existing urban areas in the district. Most of the lower order centres were located in rural areas and were gradually gaining urban functions. Compared to the growth of population, land area or corporate limit of towns has not expanded in the recent past. For example Negombo (MC) had covered only an area of 10.4 sq. km since 1963 up to 1981. Peliyagoda (UC) expanded only from 3.3 sq. km to 4.5 sq. km during that period. With the new development in the industrial sector and infrastructure services, urban population in the officially recognized towns has increased faster. For instance, population of Negombo reached 101,099 at the Demographic Survey of 1994. Seeduwa-Katunayake, Ja-Ela and Gampaha also show faster growth rates. As a result of these urbanization trends, the urban influences have extended beyond their corporate limits. Malik Majeed (1995) showed Katana division had an 11.1% increase in built-up areas between 1981-1994 while Ja-Ela had an 8.4% increase. Other major areas which gained over 5% increase in built-up areas were Gampaha, Biyagama and Mahara according to the study.

The UDA identified 40 towns in 5 orders of hierarchy in the Gampaha district. Some of the urban areas which envolved in the recent past are Kadawatha, Miriswatta, Yakkala, Nittambuwa, Kiribathgoda, Ragama, Sapugaskanda, and Biyagama. Clustering eight emerging urban centres, the UDA proposed three urban growth centres for future development in the Gampaha distict. They are,

1. Negombo-Katunayake growth centre
2. Gampaha/Nittambuwa/Veyangoda growth centre
3. Biyagama/Sapugaskanda/Kadawatha growth centre

Besides, the UDA has already launched an urban development program for the Gampaha District in major towns like Gampaha, Veyangoda and Nittambuwa. There are proposals to develop several other urban centres including service centres like Pugoda and Ragama. These trends in urbanization will definitely bring about major changes in the land use pattern of the immediate environs of the towns in the district.

5.3 Housing Development

Housing development is a dominant sector which has changed the land use patterns in the Gampaha district. In 1981, the census of population and housing reported 265,951 occupying housing units. The estimated number of houses in 1994 was 363,262, which is an increase of 36.5%. Housing development in the district takes place through individual construction and state sponsored programmes. The National Housing Development Authority (NHDA) of Sri Lanka has implemented various housing projects such as electoral Housing Program, model villages, fisheries sector program, urban housing program, etc. Two major middle class housing projects were completed in 1980s at Katana (Raddoluwa Scheme) and (Ranpo-kunagama Scheme). Attanagalla DSD areas and another middle class housing scheme opened recently in Kelaniya (Polhena) division. These major projects converted agricultural land or low-lying areas (Kelaniya) into residential areas.

Individual housing construction has led to land use changes in three different ways as follows.

1. Converting low density residential areas into high density areas.
2. Converting low lying areas and abandoned agricultural lands into residential areas.
3. Fragmentation of larger coconut and rubber lands into small residential holdings.

The direction and concentration of housing development over a geographical space depends on various factors such as accessibility, amenities, price and availability of land. Our observations on the residential development in selected DSD areas will further elaborate these factors. According to the division level data, about 35% houses constructed in the district since 1980 are found in Gampaha, Ja-Ela, Katana, Negombo and Mahara DSD areas.

Along with industrial and housing development in the district the demand for infrastructure and amenities increased. With a view to facilitating industrial development zones, the government constructed a new bridge over the Kelani Ganga at Kaduwela and extended highways to Biyagama area, expanded other main roads and minor roads, while water, electricity and telecommunication services were provided to most suburban areas. These induced other activities such as boarding houses, stores, container transshipment and other services in the suburban areas.

Among other important activities that took place in the district were the establishment of Universities, a teaching Hospital, Teacher Training Colleges, Defence Training Centres in Kelaniya, Biyagama, Mahara and Gampaha divisions which attracted more people, demanding services from nearby areas leading to considerable impact on the land use pattern of the district. These spatial patterns of developmental activities indicate that large-scale physical developments took place along the highways from Colombo to Negombo, to Kurunegala via Minuwangoda and to Kandy as well as areas within the two EPZs.

5.4 Land Use Pattern

According to the land use maps of 1960s (1:63,360) the Gampaha district was a predominantly agricultural area with coconut, rubber, paddy and homestead gardens as major land use types. The estimated land use data of 1980s (District land use map 1:100,000, Survey Department) indicated that homesteads (69,670 ha) paddy (22,550 ha), coconut (25,000 ha), and rubber (5190 ha) accounted for the major land uses while a considerable area is covered with wetlands (4490 ha) and built-up areas (2220 ha). However the divisional level data provides some variation in the dominant land use types in different areas. The largest area under homesteads is found in the Mirigama division, but in terms of percentage share of total land, the highest value is at Minuwangoda. The major coconut areas are Divulapitiya, Mirigama, Attanagalla, Negombo and Weke, but in the Katana division 42.7% of the area was under coconut cultivation. Weke, Mirigama, Divulapitiya, Attanagalla, Minuwangoda and Gampaha divisions are major paddy producing areas. In Gampaha division 29.1% of the land was under paddy cultivation. Wetland, covers a major portion of the land in Negombo, Ja-Ela , and Wattala division. Urban land is a major land use in Negombo, Ja-Ela, and Wattala divisions. Urban land is a major land use in Negombo, Ja-Ela, and Wattala divisions. Urban land is a major land use in Negombo, Ja-Ela, and Wattala areas. This land use pattern has largely changed during the last two decades (Fig. 2).

A UDA study found major land use changes in the district as given in Table 3.

Table 3   Land use changes in Gampaha district (1981-1996)

Land use sector	% of Total land	
	1981	1996
Urban built-up area	1.6	2.3
Homesteads	49.8	52.9
Tree Crops	23.0	19.5
Marsh and mangrove	2.5	2.2
Barren land	0.4	0.5

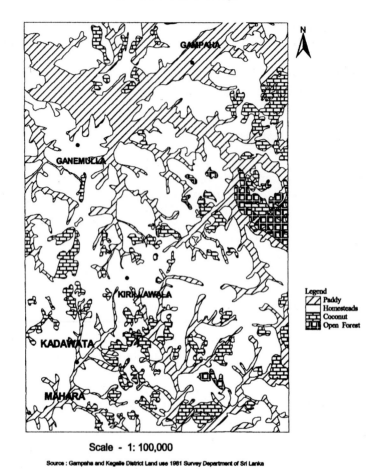

Scale - 1: 100,000

Source : Gampaha and Kegalle District Land use 1981 Survey Department of Sri Lanka

Fig. 2 Land Use Pattern: A Selected Suburban Area of Gampaha District

These changes imply that nearly 7.7% of the area in Gampaha district has been subject to some kind of change during this period such as,

1. Increase of residential lands
2. Decrease of coconut and rubber lands
3. Increase of abandoned paddy lands
4. Decrease of wetland
5. Expansion of urban land uses beyond their jurisdiction

Among the major land use changes, the increase of population migration pattern, industrial development and expansion of urban areas encroaching on rural lands are predominant. In order to meet the new demand for land, specially for residential purposes, major course of action that has been taken in the district are,

1. densification of existing low density residential areas,
2. fragmentation of land under coconut and rubber cultivation,
3. land filling of low-lying areas and abandoned paddy lands, and
4. encroachment of vulnerable and ecologically sensitive areas especially by poor families.

Market forces are very strong in accelerating the land use changes in the district. The rising value of land has been a recent phenomenon in the area, specially in the rural areas, near the urban centres. The price per perch of land changes depending on proximity to urban centres, main highways, availability of electricity, pipe borne water and telecommunication facilities in the areas. Even within the urban limits the dominant land use type (66%) has been the residential sector. However, due to the competition of commercial, industrial and service sector activities, residential areas have sprung up within suburban areas as well as along the main highways.

The intensity of land use change has been in a North-South direction along the coastal belt and towards the interior, due to the sprawling Colombo-Kandy highway. Developing contiguous built-up areas merging with existing urban land uses is visible adjacent to the major towns and industrial zones.

A major consequence of land use changes has been the loss of prime agricultural land and a reduction in agricultural production as well as farming sector employment in the middle part of the district. Unpublished data shows that between 1980-1990, coconut areas in Biyagama and Wattala and paddy areas in Kelaniya have reduced due to land being put to other uses. The paddy land area in the district has been reduced from 16,414 hectares in the 1992/93 main cultivation season (Maha) to 13,790 hectares in 1998/99 in the same seasons. During the same period, cultivated paddy land area was reduced to 31.5% of the total paddy land under major irrigation projects, 46.6% of the minor irrigation projects and 97.3% of rainfed lands. Unplanned and uncontrolled way of land filling and building construction on the low-lying area, not only caused poor drainage and loss of wetlands, but also made some areas vulnerable to storm water floods during the rainy season. Recent rainfall was an example of the flood hazards which displaced many people, damaged houses and inundated roads. Using marshes and abandoned paddy lands for garbage dumping has created an environmental problem in many areas near the urban centres. These lands are subsequently reclaimed and developed into buildable sites.

The official sources (land use planning office—Gampaha) revealed that abandonment of paddy land was greater in the DSDs like Gampaha (521.46 ha), Katana (454.92 ha) and Mahara (146.61 ha). Other divisions where the abandoned paddy lands are prominent are Weke, Biyagama, Divulapitiya, Minuwangoda and Attanagalla. The approval for reclaiming paddy lands for other uses is given in Table 4 as provided by the Agrarian Services Office, Gampaha.

Table 4   Approval of permits to reclaim paddy lands in the Gampaha district

	1995	1996	1997	1998-1999 May
Number of permits	9	9	17	7
Total area (hectare)	8.80	4.15	3.80	5.2
Major DSDs (% of the total area permitted)	Wattala (59%) Minuwangoda (36%)	Wattala (78%)	Ja-Ela (45.4%) Katana (21.2%) Biyagama (12%) Kelaniya (9.3%)	Wattala (98%)

Source: Agrarian Services Department, Gampaha.

Fragmentation of high land area into residential holdings is carried out by individuals or property developers. The property developers have a major role as broker/middlemen in the land market in the area. The available data of the number of auctions, area and number of blocks auctioned in some Pradeshiya Sabha areas are shown in Tables 5 and 6.

Table 5   Sub-division of lands: Biyagama PS areas

	1994	1995	1996	1997	1998-1999 June
Number of auctions	43	5	12	14	12
Total area (hectare)	29.8	4.40	9.09	8.56	7.75
Number of blocks	558	97	174	155	132

Table 6   Sub-division of lands: Gampaha PS areas
(Henarathgoda sub-office and UDA declared area only)

	1994	1995	1996	1997	1998-1999
Number of auctions	182	28	24	36	30
Total area (hectare)	91.74	22.06	21.9	20.13	27.20
Number of blocks	1678	409	466	354	449

Source: Biyagama and Gampaha Pradeshiya Sabhas.

Availability of land as well as land prices largely determine the expansion of residential areas into existing agricultural areas. During the past two decades the land value has risen rapidly in the district. Compared to other areas in the CMR, the land in the Gampaha district is relatively cheap. So the demand has been increasing for residential holdings. The studies revealed that there are greater variations in land value depending on the locations, available facilities and the nature of land. The average annual rate of increase in land value between 1978-1994 was estimated for some PS areas (Abeygunawardana) as given in Table 7.

Table 7   Average annual rate of increase in land value for some PS areas

PS area	Average annual increase of Land Value (%)
Mahara	19.3
Wattala	19.7
Kelaniya	23.0
Biyagama	27.2

Source: Economic Review, June/July, 1999.

According to another study, land value of the area along the main highways in the Gampaha district increase rapidly due to the demand created by commercial and industrial sectors. Our study revealed the variation of assessed value of land in different village areas in the same Pradeshiya Sabhas. In Gampaha PS area, value of land per perch varied between Rs 35,000 in Mudungoda to Rs 2000 in Oruthota in 1998. In the Biyagama PS area, the price of land per perch ranged from Rs 2500-5000 in Kanduboda, Gonawala to Rs 20,000 in Udupila, Meegahawatte, Delgoda and Siyambalape. In Biyagama Industrial Zone, the value of a perch was about Rs 40,000. The gradient of price change in different areas around town centres was assessed for the period 1980-1990, comparing the values published by property developers. In Gampaha the rate of increase was 150%, Yakkala 600%, Ragama 200% and Ganemulla 100%. Our observations of the major areas where land fragmentation has taken place by property developers during past two decades show that Ja-Ela, Gampaha, Kelaniya, Mahara and Attanagalle DSDs have been mainly affected by this process. The close proximity to highways and railways and the axial nature of sprawling urban landscape have influenced the selection of these areas by auctioneers.

A survey of building applications submitted to the PS found that construction activity is concentrated in certain (GN) village areas. In Gampaha PS area, Yakkala, Galahitiyawa, Ganemulla, Imbulgoda, Bollatha, Aluthgama and Weliveriya villages show the highest concentration of building activity. In Biyagama PS area, villages show more building construction in Biyagama, Gonawala, Heiyanthuduwa, Makola and Biyanwila. In Kelaniya PS area the major areas with more construction activities are along the Biyagama main road (Sinharamulla, Pethiyagoda) along Kandy road (Dalugama, Kiribathgoda, Wedamulla), Waragoda, Wanawasala and Hunupitiya. In Mahara DS area there are three major clusters of villages where building construction is increasing; they are Gonahena, Ranmutugala, Kirillawela, Udupila, Henegama, Pahala Karagahamune, Suriyapaluwa, Mahara-Nugegoda.

A closer inspection of these areas show that they are presently developing into high density settlements due to subdivision of land among family members, purchase by outsiders or sale by property developers. The land value is high in most of the village areas closer to railway stations, main highways and their feeder roads, and in areas with electricity and other amenities; so the tendency is for the residential areas to extend into interior villages. The next stage of residential land use change will be an increased use of low-lying areas for residential purposes and reclaiming and sale of lowland either by state authorities or private companies. In the areas along the main highways, especially in the Kelaniya, Wattala, Ja-Ela and Gampaha DSDs a common practice is filling lowlands by dumping garbage and with earth removed from other areas causing environment problems at both ends.

Land use changes in the suburban environment will continue due to the pressure of an increasing population on the land, concentration of industrial and commercial activities as well as infrastructure development. It is projected that Gampaha district will have a population of 2,335,000 and a workforce of 1,394,500 people by 2010. The population of major towns will nearly double by that time. The proposed highways to Kandy, Katunayake and Southern Province are planned to pass through some areas in the district. These areas will rapidly change in the near future attracting more urban activities. The growth centre strategy of UDA covers several urban centers as well as their hinterland. They will provide more land for industrial and commercial purposes. Therefore, it is important that the physical planning for overall development of the suburban areas forms a part of the development strategy. The CMRSP has proposed several strategies relative to the environment, welfare and economy of the areas for the period between 1999-2010. A mixed strategy which favours both concentration and dispersal has been suggested for CMR. Three growth centres and industrial townships are major components of the proposed strategy.

The environmentally sensitive areas have been taken into consideration in the management plan. Major issues that have to be addressed in the CMRSP are domestic water supply, transport development, sewerage, storm water drainage and solid waste management.

6.   CONCLUSION

Our discussion so far, continued on land use change in CMR, highlighted some unique characteristics of suburbanization process in Gampaha district. This region gained more industries, more people and exerted more pressures on land during the past four decades, than any other region in the island. As a result, the physical development in the suburban crescents of the CMR, covering most of the Gampaha district, took place in a rapid rate and unplanned manner. There are a number of issues arising due to the land use changes related with economic growth in the district. The destruction and degradation of environmental resources and increasing demand for amenities, infrastructure and services exceeding their capacities are visible symptoms of this unhealthy development in the district. However, due to expanding industrial and service sectors in the district it should be expected to continue suburbanization process at a more rapid rate in the near future. Most of the areas subject to these changes fall within the Pradeshiya Sabha limits which are not officially recognized as urban in Sri Lanka. Therefore, there is a need for some legal and institutional measures to integrate them into the overall urban development strategy.

REFERENCES

--- "Suburbanization around Colombo" Vidyodaya J. Arts. Sc. Vol. 13, No. 2, 1-31.

A Development Plan for Gampaha Distict. 1981 Marᵤa Institute, Colombo, 316-324.

Colombo Metropolitan Regional Structure Plan. 1998. Vol I, Vol II and Vol V, Urban Development Authority, Colombo.

Economic Review, 1995. Peoples Bank.

Economic Review, March 1996. Peoples Bank.

Indrasiri, L.H. 1997. Urbanization of Sri Lanka: A New Perspective (unpublished paper). Presented at the Workshop on Population and Urbanization, University of Ruhuna.

Majeed, Malic. 1996. Urbanization trends in the Greater Colombo Area from 1956 to 1995.

Panditharatne, B. 1961. "The Urban Field of Colombo" The Ceylon Geographer. 24-33.

Silva, W.P.T. and K. Gunawardane. 1969/70. "The Urban Fringe of Colombo. Some trends and problems concerning its land use" Ceylon Studies Seminar, University of Ceylon 1969/70 Series No. 3.

Wanasinghe, Y.A.D.S. 1984. "The Rural-Urban Fringe of Colombo—A Zone in Transition" Vidyodaya J. Arts Sc. Lett. Silver Jubilee, Vol 12, 152-170.

CHAPTER 16

Application of GIS in Measuring the Development Planning Potentialities: An Example from the Bhaktapur District, Nepal

(Krishna P. Poudel[*])

1. INTRODUCTION

Planning is a procedure whereby we try to achieve our goals with the limited resources at a minimum cost. It concerns with the rational where planning goals, analytical tools and ways of implementation are well defined or properly operated. Adequate knowledge about the resources available on certain spatial units and identification of needs for the inhabitants are the prime variables for the rational planning process which require to further readjust with the given environmental condition for sustainability. Spatial variation in the distribution of phenomena is the focal point of regional planning. Spatial information about the phenomena has been the part of planning procedures (Winata and Dias, 1991). The Spatial Decision Support System (SDSS) is considered an appropriate method for rational planning. Application of GIS as a means in the SDSS is gaining popularity even in developing countries like Nepal. GIS has myriad functions, which help the planners, decision-makers and even implementers (Demers, 1997). Over the last few years, the field of GIS application is growing rapidly.

Maps, animation through overlay of spatial data and simulated results could provide quick and eye-view examples to decision-

[*]Department of Geography, Tribhuvan University, Pokhra, Nepal.

makers about the spatial problems. Computerized GIS has a
capability of handling all those spatial as well as aspatial database
(Burrough, 1986). It cannot make decisions for people, however, it
is able to provide simulated results and recommendations by which
decision-makers can make easy and objective informed decisions
(EPA, 1992). The entire procedure is also much more transparent
and communicable to experts of diverse fields or people within the
government and the society. Input, storage, retrieval, manipulation,
analysis and output reproduction are some of the traditional functions of GIS. However, simulation of various logical expectations
and conceptualization for model building are advance operations of
the SDSS.

The computer assisted GIS tool can bridge the sets of information
within a rational framework of planning (Demers, 1997). Following this
approach GIS tool has been used to measure the existing scenario of the
distribution of resources and means of development and services as well
as to identify the potentialities of settlements in terms of development
planning of the Bhaktapur district. Specifically it attempts to identify
the spatial planning gaps through the existing development means and
supplies from sectors and agencies at VDCs; and measure the planning
potentialities of nodal settlements based on the existing resources and
the pattern of linkages.

2.   RESEARCH DESIGN AND METHODOLOGY

The study is designed to develop an operational procedure to integrate
the spatial data depicted from the available large-scale map (1:25,000
scaled topographic map prepared by HMG/FINNIDA, 1995/1996
based on the aerial photographs taken in 1992) and attribute data
collected by the District Development Committee (DDC) during 1995-
1996.

The study has been designed in two modules.

2.1   Village Development Committee (VDC) Module

The VDC module is entirely based on logical ranking procedure of
the variables selected. The ranking procedure is dependent on the
frequency and domination of the services and facilities over the
VDCs. In this module, VDC has been considered the spatial entity
of rural development as there was a lack of attribute database at the
micro scale of spatial units smaller than the VDC level. The objective
of the VDC module was to identify the existing flow of
infrastructure and service facilities over the VDCs of the district.

Nine parameters have been taken as major indicators of the function and services of a VDC under study and ranked them from 0 at minimum to 16 at maximum according to the nominal scale of measurement. (Table 1).

Table 1   Selection of variables and scores

Parameters	Variables		Score
1. Service facilities	a.	Medical shop	1
	b.	Tea/hotel/restaurant	1
	c.	Utensils	1
	d.	Cold storages	1
	e.	Co-operatives	1
	f.	Cloth/embroidery	1
	g.	Agro-services	1
	h.	Watch/radio	1
	i.	Electric goods	1
	j.	Petrol pumps	1
	k.	Stationery/newspaper shop	1
	l.	shoe/leather	1
	m.	Gold/silver	1
	n.	Furniture	1
	o.	Maintenance (vehicles, etc.)	1
2. Communication facilities	a.	Post-office	1
	b.	Wireless	1
	c.	Telephone	1
	d.	Fax/telex	1
	e.	Ex-del	1
3. Health facilities	a.	Hospital	1
	b.	Health centre	1
	c.	Health post	1
	d.	Sub-health post	1
	e.	Private clinic	1
	f.	Ayurvedic	1
4. Education Facilities	a.	Lower secondary	1
	b.	Secondary	1
	c.	Higher secondary	1
	d.	Campus/University	1
5. Banking facilities	a.	ADBN	1
	b.	RBB	1

contd.

Table 1   contd

Parameters	Variables	Score
	c. NBL	1
	d. SFDP	1
	e. RB	1
6. Drinking water facilities	a. > 75% of the facilitated settlement of the VDC receive water supply by pipes	4
	b. 50-75% of the facilitated settlement of the VDC	3
	c. 25-50% of the facilitated settlement of the VDC	2
	d. 0-25% of the facilitated settlement of the VDC	1
	e. no facility	0
7. Road network facilities*	a. > 75% of the coverage of the VDC area	4
	b. 50-75% of the coverage of the VDC area	3
	c. 25-50% of the coverage of the VDC area	2
	d. 0-25% of the coverage of the VDC area	1
	e. no facility	4
8. Industrial facilities	a. large-scale	3
	b. medium-scale	2
	c. small-scale	1
	d. cottage	
9. Electricity facilities	a. > 75% of the facilitated settlements of the VDC	4
	b. 50-75% of the facilitated settlements of the VDC	3
	c. 25-50% of the facilitated settlements of the VDC	2
	d. 0-25% of the facilitated settlements of the VDC	1
	e. no facility	0

*Road network coverage area has been identified through the buffering of road layers as of 2 km from the highway, 1 km from the paved feeder road, 500 m from the gravelled road and 250 m from the fair weather road.

A linear combination model was used to integrate these data layers. By this combination all the layers were integrated through the ranking score of the variables.

The linearly combined score was regrouped into five zones of intensity of the facilities as least development, medium development, high development and very high development respectively accordingly to the average value. The categorizing procedures were further verified from the standard deviation of the value.

2.2 Settlement Module

The settlement module is basically designed up to the point entity of the spatial location where the attribute data are directly linked.

Main purpose of the settlement module analysis was to measure development potentialities of particular settlement existing as a nodal point in a spatial entity. The degree of nodality was measured on the basis of three parameters.

2.2.1   Measurement of functional association

Five different types of functions which are service types (as of VDC module), banking facilities, health facilities, education facilities (in this case primary schools are considered), and communication facilities (in this case post office and telecom both are considered separate) have been taken as major indices for the nodal settlement points. The sum of the value based on the absence and the presence of each parameter was taken as; service index (SI), financial input index (FI), education index (EI), communication index (CI) and health index (HI). Symbolically

Functional Index of Settlement (FIS) = Σ(SI + FI + EI + CI + HI)

Following this procedure six different classes of range of function have been delineated as: no data, 1-10, 10-20, 20-30, 30-40 and above 40.

2.2.2   Measurement of accessibility

To measure the accessibility of the settlement, the layer of existing road network was used. From the base-map all four types of motorable roads were digitized. In that road data layer, different distance (2 km from highway, 1 km from paved feeder, 500 meter from gravel and 250 meter from fair weather) have been assumed as accessible zone. The roads of different types were buffered by taking the assumed distance. The buffered distance layers were overlaid and four different zones of accessibility were identified, namely the area of no access, access with gravel and fair weather, access with paved feeder, and access with highway and all other. Finally the settlements with larger than 10 number of functional agglomeration were overlaid on road accessibility layer and level of accessibility of those settlements identified.

In spite of this, the pattern of linkages among nodal settlements through motorable road network has been measured with the computation of index of centralization (Cox, 1972). In this procedure, the layer of nodal settlements was overlaid with the road network map and the connectivity of roads among the settlements was computed. Mean and variance of the connectivity was calculated to show the intensity of the linkages of motorable roads.

2.2.3 Population concentration

Population was considered as one of the most important criteria for the centrality of location. A total of 558 settlements were mapped in the Bhaktapur district. Those settlements consisted of about 1200 population in maximum and about 200 on an average. The settlements with above 200 population were considered as important settlements of the districts.

A 200-meter aerial distance might be covered in a 10-minute walk in a homogeneous terrain. Therefore, the minimum distance threshold of 200-meter aerial distance from each settlement has been taken for identification of the total locational point of the potential settlement units of the districts. Less than 10 functional associations in minimum could not pose importance of centrality. These criteria were further verified with the total number of population over that location. Some of the settlements which are closely associated with each other do not have individual importance, so the minimum distance threshold has been assumed.

To suggest the planning procedures the identified nodal points have been further analysed with due consideration to land use, slope, altitude, density and accessibility. These data layers were overlaid with nodal settlement cover and the potentiality of those units were analysed with due consideration to development planning perspectives.

3. THE STUDY AREA

Bhaktapur district is one of the smallest districts of the country. It covers only 12,737 ha of total area comprising 21 VDCs and one municipality until March 1997 (Fig. 1). Recently, the government has made some amendments, by adding the new municipality and reducing the VDCs number. According to the data collected from the DDC the total population was 120,171 (excluding Municipality) in 1995.

Physiography of the district is quite homogeneous. Elevation gradually lowers westward. The watershed divides with Bagmati system and Koshi system separate the eastern and south-eastern boundary of the district. On an average most of the area of the district falls on gentle to flat slope categories and only a small portion of the district has a steep slope. The average range of altitude between the valley and the summit is less than 700 meters. Because of its site and situation, Bhaktapur district is one of the most accessible districts in

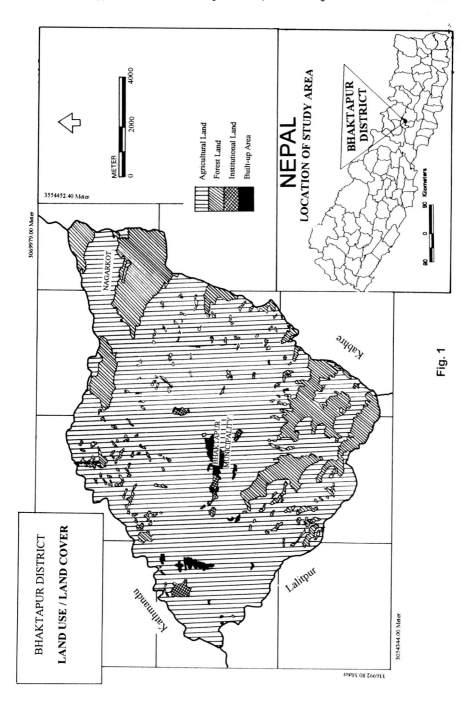

Fig. 1

the country in terms of modern means of development such as transportation and communication, school, health facilities, banking services, commercial establishments, electricity, drinking water, etc.

Out of the total (12,737 ha) area of the district, cultivated land covers more than 80 per cent (10,235.6 ha). The second largest cover is the forest, covers 16.68 per cent (2124 ha). The fallow or wasteland includes rivers banks, landslide and steep cliffs covers 1.26 per cent (160 ha) and built-up area covers 1.05 percent (134 ha) of the total area. The institutional field and artificial pond cover 76 ha (0.61 per cent) and 6.4 ha (0.05 per cent) respectively.

From the general land use distribution pattern, Bhaktapur seems the most ideal district in the country as it covers the largest cultivated area. The district has a great potential in productivity but a significant portion of the lowland is under built-up area. The pace of change of cultivated coverage to the built-up area is continuous.

4. MEASUREMENT AND DISCUSSION

4.1 Road Accessibility

The total road networks cover about 188.547 kilometers length in the district. Out of the total the only highway (Araniko Highway) covers 13.798 kilometers and paved feeder roads (both broad and narrow) cover 73.014 kilometers. The gravelled roads cover 88.496 kilometers. The fair weather roads shared only 13.239 kilometers. The distribution of road network over the VDCs is not even (Table 2). The analysis of accessibility was carried out on the basis of the existing road network. All the road networks marked in 1:25,000 scale (latest large-scale base-map) maps were digitized and transferred into vector database. Different types of roads were assumed as major systems for linkages and their zone of influence was assumed individually as mentioned above.

The assumed accessible distance of the road network was taken as buffered distance of the road layers and operation was carried out in the ARC/INFO GIS. Based on this operation four zones of accessibility were identified (Fig. 2). It seemed that no area of the district is 5 kilometres (straight-line distance) away from motorable road. However some of the pockets of hills are quite away from the regular means of transportation. The highly accessible area is confined along the Kodari Highway. The peripheries of the districts have less accessibility.

Table 2   Distribution of different types of roads in the VDCs of the district

(Road in kilometer length)

VDCs	Highway	Paved road	Gravel road	Fair weather	Total
1. Bageswori	0	3.961	4.719	2.696	11.376
2. Balkot	0	0.135	6.083	0	6.218
3. Balkumari	1.597	0.230	0	0	1.827
4. Bhaktapur Municipality	1.185	9.865	2.464	5.887	19.401
5. Bode	0.240	2.306	1.459	0	4.005
6. Changunarayan	0	1.584	1.176	0	2.760
7. Chapacho	0	1.563	0	0	1.563
8. Chhaling	0	5.197	5.572	1.998	12.767
9. Chitpol	1.009	0	6.777	0	7.786
10. Dadhikot	0	7.994	8.590	0	16.584
11. Duwakot	0	4.326	1.671	0	5.997
12. Gundu	0	1.678	8.320	0	9.998
13. Jhaukhel	0	4.386	1.412	0.518	6.316
14. Katunje	2.289	4.231	5.550	1.428	13.498
15. Lokanthali	2.573	1.770	4.834	0.289	9.466
16. Nagadesh	0	0.357	0.793	0	1.150
17. Nagarkot	0	12.295	0.638	0	12.933
18. Nankhel	3.876	0	0	0.394	4.270
19. Sipadol	1.029	0.773	12.253	0	14.055
20. Sirutar	0	3.598	0.270	0	3.868
21. Sudal	0	0.920	14.428	0	15.348
22. Tathali	0	5.845	1.487	0.026	7.358
Total	13.798	73.014	88.496	13.239	188.547

Source: Digital data digitized from the base-map (1:25,000 scale topographic sheets.)

4.2   Development Status of the VDCs

On the basis of above stated analytical procedures, development status of the VDCs of the district was measured as a composite result. Based on the linearly combined score of the total parameters, the status of the development was categorized as very high, high, medium and low. The range of the score was normalized with the standard deviation of the distribution. The VDCs of the districts have different pattern of development (Fig. 3). Only one VDC (Balkumari) out of 21 VDCs of the district falls under the highly developed class. Six VDCs, i.e. Duwakot, Gundu, Jhaukhel, Sipadol, Sirutar, Sudal and Tathali fall on less developed class. Balkot, Bode,

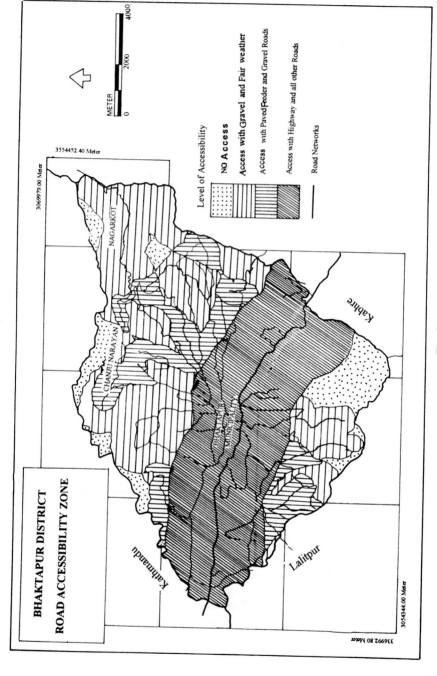

Fig. 2

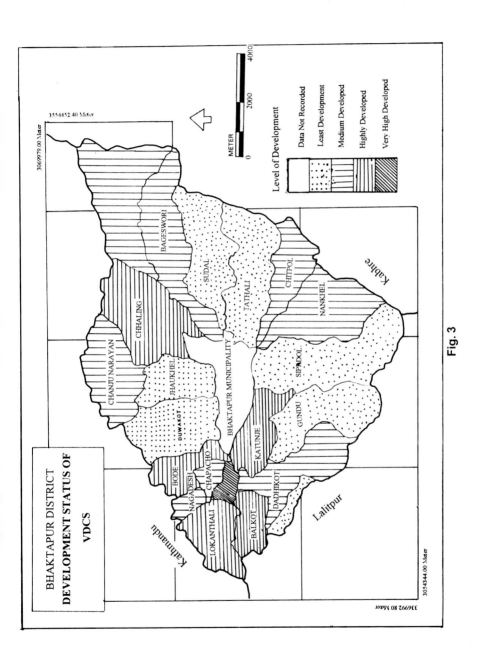

Fig. 3

Chhaling, Katunje and Lokanthali VDCs are towards the developed class and the remaining seven VDCs, i.e. Bageswori, Changunarayan, Chitapol, Dadhikot, Nagadesh, Nagarkot and Nankhel are just above the least developed class.

4.3   Potentiality of the Settlements

Settlements existing over space stands for the most strategic importance in terms of development. Settlements comprise various types of functional associations and those functions are directly related to the accessibility of those areas as well as the number of people residing over there. Therefore, some of the settlements bear the strategic location as nodal point and disseminate services and facilities to the peripheries whereas the peripheries support the nodal points through a flow of goods and services. From the planning perspective, the identification of nodal point and peripheries is highly important.

4.3.1   Functional agglomeration

Among 558 settlements recorded in the database, the range of functions above listed was from zero in minimum to 75 in maximum. The mean value was 7.5 and the standard deviation of the values was 10.4. Out of the total settlements, recorded of the districts, 101 settlements do not have any functional establishments. Only 10 settlements of the districts recorded as high as 40 number of functional associations. Basically high functional agglomeration are confined along the accessible locations either along the good road linkages areas or some of the traditionally established market centres.

4.3.2   Population concentration

The importance of the settlement was also measured on the basis of the total population concentrated over the space. The distribution of the population has been categorized under five classes. The distribution classes were defined from the average distribution of the total. Therefore, the classes were categorized accordingly as less than 200, 200 to 400 , 400 to 600, 600 to 800 and above 800.

4.3.3   Potential settlements

All those settlements, which have some sort of function, represents certain level of importance and present high population concentration. Out of 558 settlements, 450 settlements of the district have some level of functional association. But 101 settlements, out of the total of the district, have no functional association. Among 101 settlements with no functional establishment, majority have less than

200 population. Only two settlements within this group have above 300 population, which are Thapatole of Katunje VDC and Gusitar of Chhaling VDC, having 369 and 312 population respectively. Out of the highest functional agglomeration centres (only ten settlements of the district were recorded with a functional association as high as 40), two settlements Bahaka of Chapacho VDC and Gothatar of Lokanthali VDC have a population above 1000 in a single settlement.

For generalization purpose, only those settlements which have a functional agglomeration greater than 10 and a population larger than 200 persons are taken into consideration. Within this category, 69 settlements of the districts fell under the major potential class. From a planning perspective, the distance within settlement is important, because those settlements which have closer location do not necessarily have to give prioritization for both. Therefore, to identify the most potential locational points, a distance of 200 meter (straight line distance) is taken as a buffer distance from each location among 69 most potential locational points. After this operation, 42 locational points came out as an important location within the district (Fig. 4).

4.3.4 Centralization of potential centres

Centralization patterns of the potential settlement units of the district was measured through the connectivity index of centralization of different types of motorable roads of the district. Based on this procedure, the mean distribution of connectivity is 2.05 and the variance (as an index of centralization) is 2.7475 (Table 3). According to this measurement, Thimi was highly accessible in terms of road network connectivity. The Sundar Basti is the second most accessible centre. Lokanthali, Lukundol, Chitrapur and Thapatol are the third most accessible centres. Ten out of 42 centres have no direct connectivity to motorable road linkages.

Table 3   Connectivity index of centralization of potential settlements of the district

Settlement name	Connectivity	Mean-connectivity	(mean connectivity)^2
Khapala	4	1.95	3.8025
Kundol	0	−2.05	4.2025
Thimi	7	4.95	24.5025
Sano-thimi	3	0.95	0.9025
Jatigal	2	−0.05	0.0025
Lokanthali	4	1.95	3.8025
Kausal tar	3	0.95	0.9025
			contd.

Table 3   Contd

Settlement name	Connectivity	Mean-connectivity	(mean connectivity)^2
Gatthaghar	2	−0.05	0.0025
Budhathoki gaun	2	−0.05	0.0025
Balkot	3	0.95	0.9025
Khatritar	1	−0.95	0.9025
Lukundol	4	1.95	3.8025
Rawatgaun	2	−0.05	0.0025
Bistagaun	2	−0.05	0.0025
Chitrapur	4	1.95	3.8025
Chakrapani chowk	2	−0.05	0.0025
Thapatol	4	0.95	3.8025
Kiwachok	2	−0.05	0.0025
Tallokiwachowk	3	0.95	0.9025
Kisitol	0	−2.05	4.2025
Dhokathali	3	0.95	0.9025
Gundu	2	−0.05	0.0025
Suryabinayak	3	0.95	0.9025
Sunderbasti	6	3.95	15.6025
Chhatapukhutol	0	−2.05	4.2025
Mathlorauttol	0	−2.05	4.2025
Kharipati	0	−2.05	4.2025
Gairitol	2	−0.05	0.0025
Waspatol	2	−0.05	0.0025
Gairigaun	0	−2.05	4.2025
Bisitol	0	−2.05	4.2025
Gainda gaun	1	−0.95	0.9025
Gusitar	3	0.95	0.9025
Karkigaun	2	−0.05	0.0025
Rawatgaun	2	−0.05	0.0025
Chapagaun	2	−0.05	0.0025
Tatagol	0	−2.05	4.2025
Chapkhyal	3	0.95	0.9025
Kapahiti	1	−0.95	0.9025
Halchhap	0	−2.05	4.2025
Sangadaha	0	−2.05	4.2025
Narayantar	0	−2.05	4.2025
Total = 42	86	0.2	115.395
Mean = 86/42 = 2.05			Variance = 115/42 = 2.7475

Source: Computed from the base-map data.

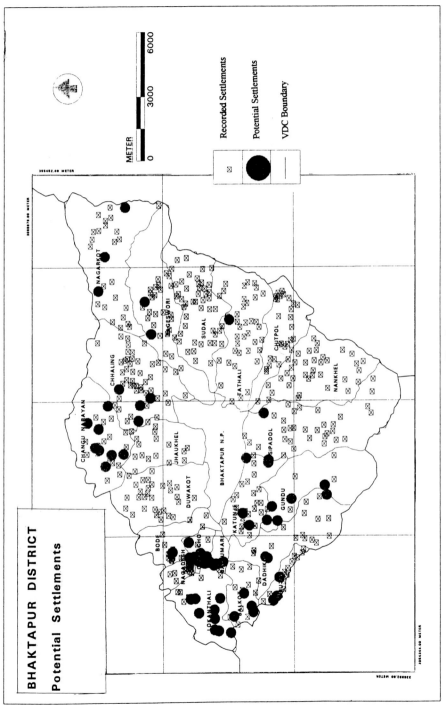

Fig. 4

From these discussions it is revealed that most of the potential settlements have motorable road linkages. Some of those are in good conditions. Most of the potential settlements are highly concentrated accessible locations either at physiographically better land or at the influence zone of road networks.

5. CONCLUSION

The distribution of the potential centres clearly follows two different patterns. The first concentration is along the highway and low lying valley-floor where the modern means of development is adequately distributed. Lokanthali, Balkumari, Balkot, Katunje and Sirutar VDCs are confined in this group. The second concentration is along the historical area of Changunarayan and Chhaling VDCs. Even though these VDCs do not have well-developed road network accessibility, due to their historical location many potential settlements are confined over there. Beside this, the Thimi area has quite a high concentration because of historical importance as well as accessibility of location.

The other rural areas have very few potential centres. Among them the influence zone of road along the Bhaktapur-Nagarkot have few centres. Therefore, most of the rural and inaccessible areas have very few potential centres.

From the VDC level analysis, Duwakot, Gundu, Jhaoukhel, Sipadol, Sudal and Tathali came as less developed VDCs of the district. Out of these VDCs Duwakot, Jhaoukhel and Sudal do not have a single potential centre. Beside these, Chitapole and Nankhel also do not have such settlements although those are categorized as above the less developed VDCs of the districts.

Suggested strategies for development planning:

1. Those settlements where population concentration is very high and also a high population density within the peripheries and less number of functional agglomeration priorities should be provided infrastructure improvements and service facilities. Basically these settlements are located at rural areas. Specifically Duwakot, Jhaoukhel, Sudal, Tathali, Chitapol and Nankhel VDCs should be focused.

2. Some other settlements, which have a high population with a large number of functional agglomeration and located at poorly accessible areas, require improvement of the linkage system. After the development of good road linkage system, those

centres can be developed as important nodal centres for the development of the region as a whole. Specifically Mathlo Rawt tole of Tathali, Gairigaun and Bisitole of Nagarkot and central part of Changunarayan VDCs fall in this group.

3. The distribution of the potential centres has a clear pattern over the district. Basically the steep slope and elevated parts have only few centres. Particularly those centres are confined in Nagarkot, Chhaling and Changunarayan VDCs. These VDCs have also weak linkage systems. Therefore linkage systems should be improved to these VDCs.

4. Population density is also high in Chitpol, Sudal, parts of Nankhel, Jhaoukhel and Duwakot VDCs, but there is no potential centres. However those VDCs have good linkage system of roads though there is no potential centres. Therefore priority should be given to those areas for the establishment of functions and services.

5. Most of the concentration of population and functional agglomeration is confined along the cultivated low-land of the district. This is because of the rapid increment of the urbanization process. Therefore Balkot, Lokanthali, Balkumari, Chapacho VDCs of the districts have a heavy concentration of functions and population. Those areas fall on growing built-up area. Therefore planning should be focused with due consideration to the development of fringe areas.

REFERENCES

Burrough, P.A. 1986. *Principles of Geographic Information Systems for Land Resources Assessment*, Clarendon Press, Oxford p. 7.

Cox, K.R. 1972. *Man, Location and Behavior: An Introduction to Human Geography*, John Wiley and Sons, Inc., New York and London, 152.

Demers, M.N. 1997. *Fundamentals of Geographic Information Systems*, John Wiley and Sons, Inc., New York, p. 6.

Environmental Protection Agency (EPA). 1992. *Geographic Information Systems (GIS). Guidelines Document*, (Washington D.C., Office of Information Resources Management, US Environmental Protection Agency) p. 1-2.

Winata, T. and H.D. Dias. 1991. *GIS for Locational Planning Framework: Part I, Conceptual Framework*, (Bangkok, Division of Human Settlements Development, AIT). p. 2.

CHAPTER 17

Application of Satellite Remote Sensing Information to Study on Landscape in Northeast China

(Zhang Bai[*])

1. INTRODUCTION

Northeast China which is more than 1.2 million sq. km including Liaoning, Jilin, Heilongjiang provinces and the four leagues of Inner Mongol Autonomous Region, accounts for some 12.5 per cent of the total land of China. It is surrounded by mountains except in its southern region. The small Xingan Mountains, Changbai mountains and others lie in the border of the great Northeast Plain, liking the shape of hoof, and Bobai Bay to the south. There are several large river systems in this region, such as the Heilongjiang river, Wusulijiang river, Songhuajiang river, Tumenjiang river, Yalujiang river and Liaohe river. It is a temperate monsoon climate zone, except the northern part of Xingan Mountains and Hulunbeior Plateau which are in frigid temperate zone, and Liaodong Penenla with warm temperate zone. The whole region is an integrated geographical unit, and has been studied as anti-independent unit by geographers both at home and abroad, because of its geographical position, natural and economical conditions and human and historical factors as well.

Satellite remote sensing information provides good techniques for studies on the distribution and dynamics of the varied and distinct landscape in Northeast China. Since the 1970s, many application

[*]Changchum Institute of Geography, Changchun, 130021, China.

studies of satellite remote sensing information have been carried out on the wetlands of Sanjiang Plain and the forest net of Northeast Plain. Yield estimation of main crops has made great progress. These studies were the foundation for further applications of satellite remote sensing information to carry out studies on landscape. This led to the application being systematized, diversified and practicalized to provide powerful scientific supports for ecosystem protection and tactics for production and management of agriculture. At the same time, it also provides support for studies on responses to the global environment change, by studying the landscape dynamics in Northeast China, which is based on strengthening the international cooperation and interchange.

2. STUDIES ON SURVEYING NATURAL AGRICULTURAL RESOURCES IN SANJIANG PLAIN

Sanjiang Plain lies in the northeast part of Heilongjiang Province, where there is the confluence of Heilongjiang river, Songhuajiang river and Wusulijiang river, and it is the biggest mire area. The concentrated rainfall, low evaporation and obstructed drainage lead to the development of mort, which accounts for about half of the plain. Among mires, the heavy mire is mainly distributed in the old river course, low flood land and in other low places, the soil is called low-mire, which has water all the year round, and its soil has heavy viscosity, therefore, it appears grey-black on images, while light-mire also called high-mire is mainly found on high flood land, terrace and other high places, where there is shallow water on the surface and is covered with grassy marshland, reeds and other exuberant plants, so it appears red on images. A part of the high-mire is fast becoming agricultural land. This is a result of the exploitation of land and the build-up of the drainage system. There are many large mechanized state farms whose area is 20-40 ha or more than 40 ha in general. The rectangular farms add to the regular drainage system and appear as lattice on images and is easy to identify. Agricultural land and light-mire appear red on Rseado-color composite satellite images during spring and summer, while heavy mire and marshland are dark grey or black. They are distributed alternatively with distinct lumpy structures which is an important character of the type of mire in Sanjiang Plain. This is an important basis for macro-study of the regional distribution and constitution structure of mire-types using RS.

2.1 Types of Mire

2.1.1 Carex lasiocarpa mire

It is distributed in the low-lying flood land on both sides of modern rivers, old river course, high flood land and the first-level terrace on the great plain, appearing dark-tone light black or black on images, and it seems like strip-chains circles and ellipses. But it is different from reservoirs, lakes and other water bodies in the shape on MSS 6 and MSS 7 images.

2.1.2 Carex Pseudocuraica mire

The strip-like mire is mainly along the modern river bed, old river course, where there is water all the year round with weak movement. It has ten centimeters of grass root, soil forms the distinct landscape "floating blankets". It appears grey, dark grey or light black. It is typically distributed in the middle and low branch of Nenjiang river, Yalujiang river and Bielahonghe river.

2.1.3 Phragmites australis mire

This kind of mire grows around the shallow basket in the lower branch of Qixing river and on low flood land in the lower branch of Raolihe river. The reed growth is different because of the different water conditions and artificial steps. For example: in Shuichenzi along Duluhe river, the reed appears light grey, while Changlingdao along the Qixinghe river is dark grey on image.

2.1.4 Carex meyeriama-carex schmidtii mire

It is mainly distributed in low-lying land at the foot of mountains, little valleys and the vacant place in the plain's forest. The northeast part of Bielahe river has a good prospect for development, due to its concentrated distribution and large area. On the verge of low-lying flood land or terrace (such as the two sides of Lianhuahe river, Rolihe river and the upper branch of QiLiqinhe river) and in old meados whose material on the surface is coarse (such as Yalujiang river, Duluhe river and Wutonghe river), where the terrain is high, and the drainage condition is good, so it appears grey or dark grey and like strips, concentric arcs, slumps and rasters.

2.1.5 Carex-Deyeuxia *angustifolia* mire

It spreads around the Plain's plate-shape low-lying land, on the verge of low places between rivers where there is little water and the groundwater level is low. It is widely distributed in the eastern side, while the western side concentrated distribution only in Duluhe river drainage area. Its shapes are arcs, chains and slumps with light grey color.

2.1.6 Marshy waste land

Its the transition zone from marshland to meadow. When there is accumulated water on the surface, it appears light grey, while it is grey-white or light grey, if there is no accumulated water. It is mostly irregular slump-shape, in which the dark grey or black light and is heavily mire inlaid. Marshy waste land area is an important farm area, due to its large area, strong potential and concentrate distribution.

2.2 Identification of Mire and Crop

According to the spectrum features of satellite image (July 25, 1975) and combining the farm records in farmland archives and the object's interpretation marks, we can identify mire and crop. The following are introductions of colorful composite image and density splitting image.

2.2.1 Interpretation of false-color composite image

The low-lying land which accumulates water and morass river (Bielahonghe river) is black whereas lasiocarpa mire is dark purplish red and carex-Deyeuxia *argustifolia* mire is pinkish red or tangrie, meanwhile it looks like concentric circles in the light of land forms and water conditions. Forest is scarlet, and is sometimes distributed in a tree-like valley extending to light yellow hills and mountains, so it can be recognized from other plants. The crap's color changed with the period on the image. Therefore, it makes up for the insufficient black-white image which improve the accuracy of interpretation for eyes.

2.2.2 Interpretation of pseud-color density splitting image

Through high-electric transformation, the image is divided into 12 revels, and different colors represent them, therefore it shows up in the image profile of some object, and make the mire more outstanding. On satellite image of Sanjiang Plain, the dark purple represents the most dense objects, such as the morass river (Bielahonghe river), accumulated water low-lying land (plate-like) and heavy mire. Purplish-pinkish red is light mire with concentric circles or chain-pinkish red is light mire with concentric circles or chain shape. Yellow is mire meadow. Light blue is mainly farmland and partly bush and shrub. Light or yellow green represent the least dense objects such as broad leaved forest. Hills in the northern side of Bielahonghe river are lump-like or strip-like, while long-tail forests are strip-like.

3. STUDIES ON SURVEYING THE FIELD FOREST NETS USING RS IN NORTHEAST PLAIN

Before liberation, peasants spontaneously built the forest for breaking wind, fixing sand in the central and west of the Northeast Plain, such as north part of Nongan county, Zhenshen in Fuya country and Dongling in Changling county. The scale is small and the effect limited, but it is recommended for they began to recognize its importance and took protective measures under their social and historical conditions. The large-scale forestation began after liberation under the leadership of the party and the People's Government. In 1950, former People's Government of Northeast China made the decision to build farmland-protected forests in the West of Northeast China, and the area extended to 52 countries or cities in 1954. After the 1960s, it has become an important task to build field-protected forests and tackle mountains, rivers, farmland, forests and roads in a comprehensive way, hence the shelter belt is increasing. In 1978, the PCC and state council decided to build the 'Three-North' shelter-forest system and the 'great green wall'. After lot of hard work, it reached a certain scale. The first project period has been completed well above the quota of 44 per cent among which field-protected forest accounts for 58.8 per cent. The forested land increased from 8.47 million mu in 1977 to 14.47 million mu, and the coverage degree of forest increased from 5.5 per cent to 11.5 per cent. All these played an obvious role in resisting natural disasters, preserving soil and fertility, improving the climate of farmland, assuring stable-high yield of agriculture, solving the problems of income. The field-protected forest system with rectangular paddy field, lined trees and forest network is basically complete.

Selecting the optimum temporary is the premise and key to increase the quality of interpretation, for the nature is a bit system. In surveying forest networks, mainly the new generation age—TM besides aerial-photography RBV and MSS are used. Due to its high spatial, spectrum, and radiation resolution, TM image can reflect the finer objects and improve the accuracy of object classification. When magnifying and composing an image, we use the contrast linear strengthening correlated analysis and gathering analysis of every TM band, according to the green plant's spectrum characters. Also we use TM-118-29 CCT digital tape to carry out multi-band linear grey strengthening, ratio stretching and computer classifying, printing grey-scale image and drawing the grey value curve of every band.

TM4 is an ideal band to identify black pine, deciduous pine and poplar, while it is easy to distinguish the poplar forest from sparse forests on TM5. The contrast between soil and vegetation is obvious on the image composed with TM4, TM5 and TM3. After stretching the composite image of TM4, TM5 and TM7, we can draw out the relationship between the grey scale, color character, soil and land form.

On the false-color composite (TM2, 3, 4 on September 21, 1984, and TM4, 5, 7 on June 26, 1987) the two neighbouring counties Qian and Changling, which are west of the Jiling Province, appears grey-white, blue, grey, light-red, green and yellow-white, yellow; yelow and green from northeast to southeast. While Lishu county and Gongzhuling city appears yellow, orange, green, orange, red, green, red and green from northwest to southeast on the false-color composite image (TM3, 4, 5, on June 26, 1987). These completely reflect the regional distribution trend of the natural environmental conditions and social activities.

At the background of the macro-changed color the west and central area are covered by many concentric circles, the complex distribution of alkali grass, off and on strip-like and sparse forests. There are favorable natural conditions with more cultivated land in the net-shaped forest area, while there is a small net in the sand and alkali land. The irregular sparse forests, which broke the wind and fixed sand distribution in the northeastern part where the forest network is less than that in the southeastern part. Wood forest is close to the settlements, while in the central area and on the mountains in the southeastern region, the forest is rich, which can preserve water and soil.

4. YIELD ESTIMATION OF MAIN CROPS

Corn is a worldwide crop, and its yield accounts for 25 per cent of the world total crop yield, only less than that of wheat and rice. China is the largest corn-producing country in the world, so corn-production and its yield estimation have great effect both on Chinese and the world grain production and estimation. Corn yield acounts for 18 per cent of the total grain yield. In China corn has a strong adaptation to the environment, so it can grow in wide areas: from Hainan to Helongjiang and from Taiwan to Xingjiang. But the main planting area accounting for more than 85 per cent of the total corn planting area in China is Northeast China, North China and the mountain area in Southwest China.

We must carry out dividing districts and set sample sites when monitoring corn change and estimating yield using RS. In the light of the large area used for yield estimation, we made out the corresponding index of the district based on the kinds of completed agriculture districts, agricultural climate, landform, soil, land use, crops, crop planting districts, historical yield, production, agricultural technique, disasters and socio economical conditions. In concrete dividing district, we must consider these consistent: the crop's growing conditions (climate, landform, soil, farming season); socioeconomic conditions with cultivation measures; and agricultural techniques. Most importantly, we take the distribution of crop yield as a leading factor. This explains the regional diversity of crop production and strict rules of the integrity of the district county and the regional diversity.

In order to obtain related survey parameters on ground surface for yield estimation using RS, we set a sampling frame which can provide basis for monitoring the crop planting area and growing situation, yield estimation model and accuracy examination. The number of sample sites can be determined by dividing into several levels according to the need of accuracy. Level one of the division reduces the non-cultivated land. Level two computes the area in proportion to the crop whose yield is to be estimated to the cultivated land, and selecting sample county according to the rule of the division's representative character is the third level.

The fourth level is combining the integrated natural division in the county, at the same time, considering the division character of the second level and selecting several samples according to the theory of weighted sampling with equal distance, then selecting sample fields from samples, calculating the real area on the country's land use map, and determining observation site in sample field which is the survey position of agronomical observation and yield data. Most important, the selection must be representative and stable in the growing period.

The main information sources in corn yield estimation are TM and information obtained by NOAA moteyological satellite, which are used for abstracting planting area and monitoring growing situation, and modeling respectively. Corn experiences three stages during its life time: seedling, heading and pollening. The growing period of corn starts from the day seedling matures. It is about 70-150 days in China. It can be divided into three classes: early-maturing, middle-maturing and late-maturing. The growing period of early spring corn is 70-100 days, which needs 2000-2200 accumulated temperature; middle spring corn is 100-120 days and 2300-2500 accumulated temperature, while the late spring corn is 120-150 days and 2500-2800. Owing to its different growing period, the growing process of corn is discrepant, so we should take its difference into account when selecting remotely sensed images.

TM(1, 2, 3, 4 bands) image serve as the main information source to obtain the basic data in yield estimation area such as corn planting area and environmental background data. As to the data related to a large area, such as a growing situation of NDVI, we use the data obtained by meteorological satellites (CH1 and CH2 as the main bands, while others as auxiliary data). During corn's seeding, jointing, heading, blooming and maturing, the growing situation information can easily be got, as also the planting area during heading and pollination.

In general, we use sample area as basic and TM image as basic data sources, meanwhile, USE NOAA AVHRR, landsat image and other remotely sensed data, consult land use map, spectral data on ground-surface agronomical observation data and its investigation and examination in field, integrate point with plane, multi-level remotely sensed data sources and many kinds of non-remote sensing data, so that it can get the planting area accurately, quickly, efficiently and economically.

RS is capable of global observation, due to its multi-bands, multi-temporary and all-weather characters. It cannot be replaced by any other methods or techniques in the global environment change research. The emergence of the environmental problem on a global scale such as the land degradation , global warming, rising of sea level, the deduction of living beings' diversity, and global resources crisis make the human observe the earth from a global angle and a different level, study the mechanism of material and energy circulation and interaction between both sub-systems and circles of the earth, even between earth and interplanetary space. All these promote the development of space sciences (especially RS). The development of RS technique, both its platform and sensor techniques, mainly aims at observing the earth, continuously improving spectrum resolution, spatial resolution, temporal resolution of RS platform. For example: to compete on work in aerial space technology with America, Japan, ESA, etc. enormous funding is being put in on new EOS plan. From TIROS satellite to NOAA, landsat MSS to landsat TM, SPOT to new generation ADEDS and Radarsat, and so on, all these are to improve their spatial and temporal resolution so that it can get a global or a large-scale earth resource and a dynamic environment data. RS plays a very important role in monitoring and surveying resources and environment dynamic in the northeast China. Northeast, with its complex natural environment, ecosystem structure, distinct regional diversity of natural additions, lies in the monsoon climate zone. In order to know the resources and environment situation of northeast China, we have carried out, in the past 30 years, monitoring of the environment, surveying the resources using RS, collected a large number of dynamic data on land cover, forest and grassland, and farmland. Now we are in the process of constructing the regional pattern of system of global environment change and the sustainable use of resources and environment.

➢ **18**

Influence of Intensive Land Use on Groundwater Resources in the Hebei Plain, China

(Kuninori Otsubo[1], Zhaoji Zhang[2] and Takemasa Ishii[2])

1. INTRODUCTION

The Hebei Plain is located in the eastern part of China and it belongs to the littoral and semiarid climatic zone. This is one of the very large agricultural areas of China at present, but clear changes in land use began in the 1970s. The rapid development of agriculture and industry resulted in the increase of water for industry and agriculture, and thus the resulting shortage of water resources has become a serious restraining factor for the economic development of the area. Furthermore, pumping of groundwater is beginning to affect the environment adversely such as the fall of groundwater level and land subsidence.

Agriculture and industry are expected to be developed here in the future, increasing the pumping of groundwater, and the environment will most probably deteriorate further. Thus this area is one of the regions in China where the deterioration of environment by change of land use is feared to be most serious in the future.

In this work, first we acquired as much data as possible regarding the climate, geology, hydrogeology, and land use of the Hebei Plain. Then the changes of land use and hydrogeological conditions were clarified,

[1]National Institute for Environmental Studies, 16-2, Onogawa, Tsukuba City, Japan
[2]Geological Survey of Japan ; 1-1-3, Higashi, Tsukuba City, Japan

and the characteristics of groundwater behavior and the groundwater budget were analyzed. Next, groundwater flow differential model based on quasi three-dimensional alternating direction implicit method was developed and the secular changes of the unconfined and confined groundwater distribution during the 11 years from 1985 to 1995 was simulated. For the simulation, physical parameters obtained by field surveys and data on the amounts of pumped groundwater, irrigated water, and weather data, were adopted.

2. OUTLINE OF GEOLOGY AND HYDROGEOLOGY

Studies show that the quaternary formation are deep in the Hebei Plain, generally reaching 400-600 m in depth, being divided into four aquifers (Zhu Y., Jia Y., Yan J., Zhang C., Ma B., Ji T., Qi Z., LI M., Li J., Ye H., Xu J., Zhang Z., and Liu J. 1992; Yan J 1991). The depths of the boundaries of each aquifer and the underlying layer are 40-60 m, 120-170 m, 250-350 m, and 400-600 m respectively. All aquifers consist of sand and gravel, fine sand, and silt. The constituents of the first and third aquifers are large grained and homogeneous. Their sand layers are thick, and their groundwater resources are large. The first aquifer contains unconfined groundwater, while the second, the third, and the fourth aquifers contain confined groundwater. Thus the groundwater within the quaternary formations are pumped as agricultural and industrial waters. The first and the third aquifers, particularly, are the major sources of water and a large amount of water has been pumped.

The water resources of the Hebei Plain are not abundant; the amount of unconfined fresh groundwater resources (including fresh water, slightly saline water, and saline water) is 12.63 billion m^3/y. Of this, the amount of fresh groundwater resources is 9.045 billion m^3/y. Evaporation, discharge to sea, and other factors, which cannot be controlled by present technology, lose parts of these water resources. Thus the total amount of groundwater resources, which can be used continually, is 8.971 billion m^3/y, and the amount of usable unconfined and that of confined groundwater resources are 7.986 billion m^3/y and 985 million m^3/y, respectively (Zhu Y., Wenren X., Zhang F., Liao J., He W., Ma Z., Sun J., Cheng D., Liu S., Li B., Li J., and Zhang Z. 1990). The amount of surface water varies widely, being directly affected by annual precipitation, thus, the surface water is not a stable source of water supply. For example, the average surface water resource of the Hebei Plain is 6.987 billion m^3/y, but in 1997 the available amount was low at only 2.152 billion m^3/y.

3. LAND USE AND WATER RESOURCES DEVELOPMENT

The changes of water resources development are closely related to the changes in land use. The amount of usable water resources is limited. Intensive use of land and urbanization, however, increase the demand for water. When the water resources are used beyond limit, the groundwater level falls and eventually the groundwater will dry up. This will be a serious environmental deterioration.

The Hebei Province has the fourth largest agricultural area of all the provinces in China and thus agriculture is the major economic activity of this province. Therefore, a major use of water resources here is agriculture. The use of water for agriculture in the Hebei Plain in 1997 was 12.109 billion m^3/y, and it occupied 78% of the total use of water (15.760 billion m^3/y) of that year. The water use for agriculture is not only affected by annual precipitation, irrigation technology and irrigation methods, but also by land use. In recent years, in the Hebei Plain, the average amount of water use for irrigation is 0.39 m^3/m^2, and the groundwater use has increased by 2.7% with the increase of arable land by 1.1% (Fig. 1).

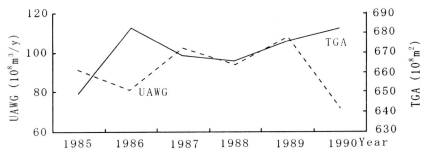

Fig. 1   Related chart of used agricultural water (UAWG) and total grain area (TGA)

Industrial water occupies 11% of the total water use, but it has been pumped intensively from specific wells, which has been deteriorating the environment. The amount of industrial water is determined by economic conditions (for example, GDP). Presently the intensity of industrial water used per GDP is 560 $m^3/10^4$ yuan, and during 1985-1995, GDP increased 10.6-14.3% and industrial water use increased 6.3% (Fig. 2).

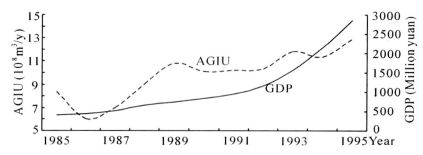

Fig. 2 Related chart of GDP and amount of groundwater for industrial use
(AGIU)

Domestic water constitutes 8% of the total water use. In recent
years, the water used for daily life per person is 216 liters/day in the
urban areas, and 55 liters/day in the farming areas. The increase of
population is about 0.8% per year, whereas the water for daily life
pumped from the groundwater increased rapidly at 8.5% per year.
This increase is believed to accompany a gradual rise of living
standard (Fig. 3). The water for daily life per person in the urban
areas was 130 liters/day in the late 1970s and rose to 216 liters/day
in 1990, and in the farming areas it was 30 liters/day in the late 1970s
and rose to the present 55 liters/day.

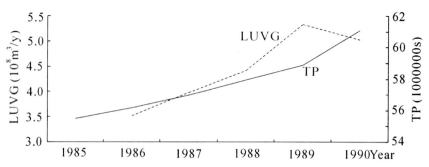

Fig. 3 Related chart of life use volume of groundwater (LUVG) and total
population (TP)

4.   GROUNDWATER AND ITS EFFECT ON
THE ENVIRONMENT

Before the 1970s, pumping of groundwater was low, and neither the
unconfined nor confined groundwater was affected by human activities.
Thus, the groundwater level kept fluctuating within a specific range

in accordance with the annual precipitation. After the 1970s, the increase in pumping groundwater began to result in the fall of the groundwater level, land subsidence and other environmental problems.

The fall of the unconfined groundwater level during the past 30 years in the Hebei Plain, was greater near the mountains and the average reached 12-25 m, and it was smaller in the central part and near the coast with average values of 2-10 m. For example, the falling rates at Shijiazhuang, Hengshui, and Cangzhou were 0.67 m/ y, 0.17 m/y, and 0.11 m/y, respectively (Fig. 4). The flow of unconfined groundwater has changed, flowing naturally in the SEE direction, but it now joins nearby cities.

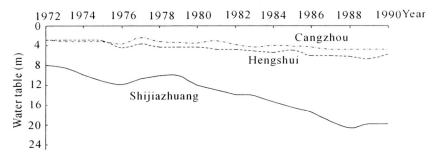

Fig. 4   The change of water table of unconfined aquifer

The rise and fall of the unconfined groundwater level is closely related to the salinization of soil. During the past 50 years, the source of irrigated water has changed many times from groundwater to surface water, and again from surface water to groundwater. The area of salinized soil has fluctuated with these changes (Jia Y., Lai Q., Wang J., Chen J., and Xin J. 1990). For example, in a certain county, water was irrigated from shallow wells 50 years ago and the salinized area was stable. But in the 1960s, water was irrigated from the Yellow River, without clearly thoughtout plans, and this resulted in the rise of groundwater level, increase of salinized land, and decrease of food production. Later, channels were dug and groundwater was drained, and shallow well irrigation was revived. The result was the fall of the groundwater level, gradual decrease of salinized land, and the gradual increase of food production (Zhang, T. 1990) (Fig. 5).

The storage coefficient of confined groundwater is low and thus the fall of the water level is faster than that of unconfined groundwater. The rate of this fall is larger near the coastal part of

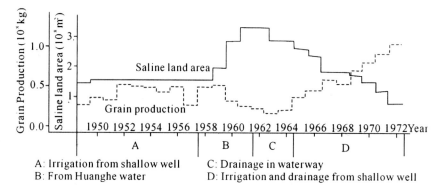

A: Irrigation from shallow well   C: Drainage in waterway
B: From Huanghe water   D: Irrigation and drainage from shallow well

Fig. 5 Related chart of saline soil and grain production of
each phase in a certain prefecture

the plain, and in 60 to 70% of area the groundwater level fell 20-60
m below sea level. The rate of the fall of the groundwater level is
1.44 m/y at Shijiazhuang near the mountains, 2.28 m/y at Hengshui
in the central part of the plain, and 3.33 m/y at Cangzhou near the
coast. Area of land subsidence expanded near the coast caused by
the drastic fall of the groundwater level. The accumulative
subsidence is 253 mm in average and the maximum 113 mm (Guo Y.,
Shen Z., Zhong Z., and Wang D. 1995) (Fig. 6).

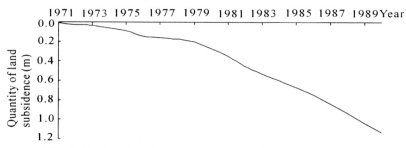

Fig. 6 Diachronic diagram of ground subsidence in
Cangzhuo city

5. QUASI THREE-DIMENSIONAL GROUNDWATER FLOW DIFFERENTIAL EQUATION

Quasi three-dimensional differential equations for unconfined and
confined groundwater flow are developed in order to consider the
behavior of groundwater. The simulation of groundwater level in the
Hebei Plain is conducted, based on the data of usage of groundwater
mentioned in the preceding sections.

5.1   Darcy's Law for Groundwater Flow

Darcy's law assumes that there is a direct proportional relation (linear) between the flow (Q) of water through a fixed section at right angles and the hydraulic gradient (I), and it is expressed by the following equation

$$Q = KIF \tag{1}$$

Q: Amount of water flow through the section at right angles

K: Permeability of porous media

I: Hydraulic gradient

F: Area of the section

5.2   Basic Equation for Groundwater Flow

When we assume a minute volume dv of aquifer, the changes of groundwater flow within dv is expressed as follows by Darycy's law.

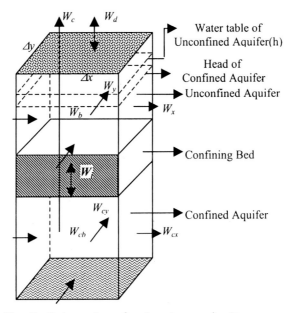

Fig. 7   Balance law of water at groundwater

(1) Unconfined water

Groundwater flow W_x in x direction within Δt time:

$$W_x = \Delta y \Delta t \frac{\partial Q}{\partial x} = \Delta x \Delta y \Delta t \frac{\partial}{\partial x} \left(Kh \frac{\partial h}{\partial x} \right) \tag{2}$$

Groundwater flow W_y in y direction within Δt time:

$$W_y = \Delta x \Delta t \frac{\partial Q}{\partial y} = \Delta x \Delta y \Delta t \frac{\partial}{\partial y}\left(Kh\frac{\partial h}{\partial y}\right) \qquad (3)$$

Change of stored water in aquifer W_b within Δt time:

$$W_b = \mu \, \Delta x \, \Delta y \, \Delta t \frac{\partial h}{\partial t} \qquad (4)$$

Budget W_d of recharge and discharge from the surface within Δt time:

$W_d =$ (Recharge amount from surface-discharge amount through surface) $\Delta x \Delta y \Delta t$ $\qquad (5)$

Amount of groundwater W_j passing through confined bed within time Δt:

$$W_j = (h_c - h) \, K_z \, \Delta x \, \Delta y \, \Delta t \qquad (6)$$

The groundwater budget will be expressed by the following equation

$$W_x + W_y + W_d + W_j = W_b \qquad (7)$$

When equations (2)–(6) are substituted in Equation (7), we have a differential equation for unconfined groundwater flow which will be expressed as follows:

$$\frac{\partial}{\partial x}\left(Kh\frac{\partial h}{\partial x}\right) + \frac{\partial}{\partial y}\left(Kh\frac{\partial h}{\partial y}\right) = \mu \frac{\partial h}{\partial t} - W_d(x, y, t) - (h - h_c)K_z. \qquad (8)$$

$$h(x, y, t)_{t=0} = h_0 \, (x, y) \qquad (9)$$

$$h(x, y, t)_{\Gamma_1} = h_1 \, (x, y, t) \qquad (10)$$

$$\left[Kh\frac{\partial h}{\partial x}\cos(n, x) + Kh\frac{\partial h}{\partial y}\cos(n, y)\right]_{\Gamma_2} = q \, (x, y, t) \qquad (11)$$

(2) Confined groundwater

Similarly, differential equation for confined groundwater flow will be as follows (Qu H., Zhu X., Zhao J., and Yan J. 1991).

$$T\frac{\partial^2 h_c}{\partial x^2} + T\frac{\partial^2 h_c}{\partial y^2} = S\frac{\partial h_c}{\partial t} - W_c \, (x, y, t) - (h_c - h)K_z \qquad (12)$$

$$h_c \, (x, y, t)_{t=0} = h_{c0} \, (x, y) \qquad (13)$$

$$h_c \, (x, y, t)_{\Gamma_1} = h_{c1} \, (x, y, t) \qquad (14)$$

$$\left[T \frac{\partial h_c}{\partial x} \cos(n, x) + T \frac{\partial h_c}{\partial y} \cos(n, y) \right]_{\Gamma_2} = q_c(x, y, t) \tag{15}$$

K: permeability coefficient of unconfined groundwater
K_z: permeability coefficient in z direction of Confining Bed
T: transmission coefficient of confined groundwater
μ: specific yield of unconfined groundwater
S: storage coefficient of confined groundwater
h: unconfined groundwater level
h_c: confined groundwater head
h_0: initial value of unconfined groundwater level
h_{c0}: initial value of confined groundwater head
h_1: unconfined groundwater level in boundary
h_{c1}: confined groundwater head in boundary
q: flux of unconfined groundwater flow through boundary
q_c: flux of confined groundwater flow through boundary
W_d: budget of recharge and discharge amount in vertical direction of unconfined groundwater
W_c: budget of recharge and discharge amount in vertical direction of confined groundwater
t: time
X, Y: coordinates
$\Delta x, \Delta y$: length of difference lattice blocks
n: flow direction of groundwater

---

6. NUMERICAL CALCULATION OF GROUNDWATER FLOW DIFFERENTIAL EQUATION (ADI METHOD)

Alternating direction implicit (ADI) is one of the effective methods of numerical calculation. In this method, calculating step (k, k+1) is divided into first half $(k, k + 1/2)$ and latter half $(k + 1/2, k + 1)$. As the direction of the implicit method is alternative for the two halves, the calculation is always stable.

Implicit method is applied in x direction and explicit method is applied in y direction in the first half step $(k, k+1/2)$, which means $\partial^2 h / \partial x^2$ is expressed by implicit difference equation, and $\partial^2 h / \partial y^2$ is by explicit difference equation. Thus, a difference equation of groundwater flow is expressed as follows:

$$\frac{h_{i-1,j,k+1/2} - 2h_{i,j,k+1/2} + h_{i+1,j,k+1/2}}{(\Delta x)^2} + \frac{h_{i,j-1,k} - 2h_{i,j,k} + \widehat{h}_{i,j,j+1,k}}{(\Delta y)^2}$$

$$= \frac{\mu}{Kh_{i,j,k+1/2}} \frac{h_{i,j,k+1/2} - h_{i,j,k}}{\Delta t/2} - W_d(i, j, k + 1/2) -$$

$$(h_{k+1/2} - h_{c,k+1/2})K_z \quad (16)$$

Similarly, in calculating the latter step $(k+1/2, k+1)$, explicit method is applied to the x direction, and implicit method, to the y direction, that is $\partial^2 h/\partial x^2$ is expressed by explicit difference equation, and $\partial^2 h/\partial y^2$ is by implicit difference equation. A difference equation of groundwater flow for the latter half step is expressed as follows:

$$\frac{h_{i-1,j,k+1/2} - 2h_{i,j,k+1/2} + h_{i+1,j,k,+1/2}}{(\Delta x)^2}$$

$$+ \frac{h_{i,j-1,k+1} - 2h_{i,j,k+1} + h_{i,j+1,k+1}}{(\Delta y)^2}$$

$$= \frac{\mu}{Kh_{i,j,k+1}} \frac{h_{i,j,k+1} - h_{i,j,k+1/2}}{\Delta t/2} - W_d(i, j, k + 1) - (h_{k+1} - h_{c,K+1})K_z \quad (17)$$

When equations (16) and (17) are expressed by the determinate equation, the solutions of quasi three-dimensional partial differential equation for groundwater flows can be calculated numerically by Gauss elimination method.

7. SIMULATION OF GROUNDWATER CHANGES

Block partitioning method was adopted in the simulation this time. The Hebei Plain with an area of 67,268 km^2 was divided into 16,817 blocks of equal space finite difference lattice of 2 km × 2 km. The data on water head potential was given as the boundary condition. In the Hebei Plain, the groundwater level has been fluctuating significantly during the past 20 years because of the increase in demand for agricultural and industrial use. Three-dimensional simulation of the unconfined and confined groundwater levels for the 11 years from 1985 to 1995 was carried out. (Information and data regarding groundwater, weather, and other relevant factors after 1995 have not been sufficiently organized yet.) Various investigations into the amount of pumped water, irrigated water, precipitation, evaporation and other meteorological data were carried out. One-year step simulation was conducted by using these data and by applying physical parameters obtained from field tests. These data of 1985 was given as initial conditions for the simulation.

The results of the simulation show that, regarding the unconfined water, the error between the observed and the calculated levels was more than 1 m at 2% of the lattice points, and less than 0.5 m at 86% of the lattice points. The observed and simulated data of horizontal distribution of the unconfined groundwater level is shown in Fig. 8. Figure 9 shows those of confined groundwater. In both figures, real

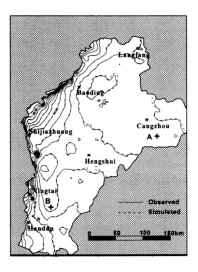

Fig. 8   Contour lines of unconfined groundwater level at 1994 (Hebei Plain)

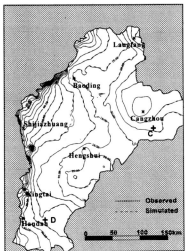

Fig. 9   Contour lines of confined groundwater level at 1994 (Hebei Plain)

lines show observed data, and dotted lines, simulated results. The examples of observed and simulated results of time variation of groundwater level of unconfined aquifer are shown in Fig. 10. Those of confined aquifer are shown in Fig. 11. These proved the accurateness of our digital model of quasi three-dimensional partial differential equation for groundwater flow.

8. FUTURE PROBLEMS

To discuss the future of water resources in the Hebei Plain, it is necessary to estimate the impact of the future land use scenario on the environment, such as the fall of the groundwater level. This will be done by formulating a water-use scenario based on future plans for land use, and to calculate the groundwater level changes in the Hebei Plain with an accuracy of 2 km block (mesh).

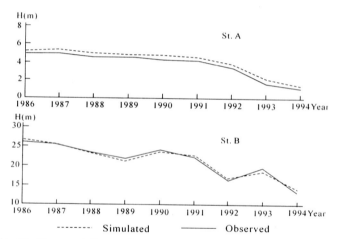

Fig. 10 Time variations of groundwater level of unconfined aquifer at st. A and st. B

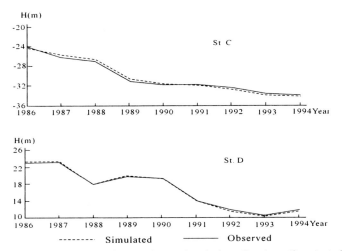

Fig. 11   Time variations of groundwater level of confined aquifer at st. C and st. D

REFERENCES

Guo Y., Shen Z., Zhong Z., and Wang D. 1995. 'The property of deep-lying groundwater resources in Hebei Plain and its reasonable evaluation in view of land subsidence', Earth Science—Journal of China University of Geosciences, 20 4 P. 415-419 (in Chinese).

Jia Y., Lai Q., Wang J., Chen J., and Xin J. 1990. 'Foreground study on the shallow saline groundwater use in the Huabei region', Institute of Hydrogeology & Engineering Geology File, P. 73-97 (In Chinese).

Qu H., Zhu X., Zhao J., and Yan J. 1991. 'Groundwater Hydrodynamics Method' belong to 'Study on Groundwater resources Evaluation in the arid and Semiarid Areas of China', Science Publishing of China, Beijing, P. 30-80. (In Chinese)

Yan J 1991. 'Deep Layer Groundwater Resources Evaluation in the Heilonggang Area of Hebei Province' belong to 'Study on Groundwater resources Evaluation in the arid and Semiarid Areas of China', Science Publishing of China, Beijing, P. 162-179 (In Chinese).

Zhang T. 1990. 'Water conservancy and environment of China', Science Publishing of China, Beijing, P. 52-89 (In Chinese).

Zhu Y., Jia Y., Yan J., Zhang C., Ma B., Ji T., Qi Z., LI M., Li J., Ye H., Xu J., Zhang Z., and Liu J. 1992. 'Comprehensive Hydrogeologic Evaluation of the Huang-Huai-Hai Plain', Geological Publishing House of CHINA, Beijing, P. 5-120 (In Chinese)

Zhu Y., Wenren X., Zhang F., Liao J., He W., Ma Z., Sun J., Cheng D., Liu S., Li B., Li J., and Zhang Z. 1990. 'Evaluation of groundwater resources in Huabei region', Institute of Hydrogeology & Engineering Geology File, P. 69-118 (In Chinese)

CHAPTER 19

Relationship between Agricultural Land Use Change and Socioeconomic Factors in North-East China in Recent Decades

(Qinxue Wang and Kuninori Otsubo[*])

1. INTRODUCTION

The land use/cover change and its driving forces have become an important issue worldwide. Many studies address this subject, in which the socioeconomic driving forces are dealt as most important factors for land use changes (Fischer et al. 1996; Mather, 1996). Land use in China has largely changed in recent decades due to rapid population increase and socioeconomic growth. Several studies on land use/cover changes in north-east China have been conducted by Himiyama et al. (1995, 1997), who reconstructed the digital land use map of the 1930s and compared it with the map of the 1990s. However, the dynamics of land use change have not been well analyzed because of the limitation of time-series database. In this paper, we try to identify both spatial and temporal land use changes and to analyze the relationship between land use change and socioeconomic growth in north-east China using the state statistic data.

2. SPATIAL LAND USE CHANGE

The county-level agricultural statistics (1990 and 1997) for north-east China were used for identifying the spatial changes in the last

[*]National Institute for Environmental Studies, Water and Soil Environmental Division 16-2 Onogawa Tsukuba, Ibaraki 305-0053, Japan

decade. The result of spatial analysis shows that newly cultivated land are located in the mountainous areas along the Xiao Hinggan Ling, Da Hinggan Ling and Changbai Mountain, and at the low plains, such as the Three River and Song-Nen Plains (Fig. 1). On the contrary, the agricultural area around big cities in the north-east plain has decreased. The result implies that urbanization is one of the main causes that led to the decrease of arable land in the north-east Plain over the last decade. Subsequently, local people have moved to mountainous regions or lower marshy basins for reclamation.

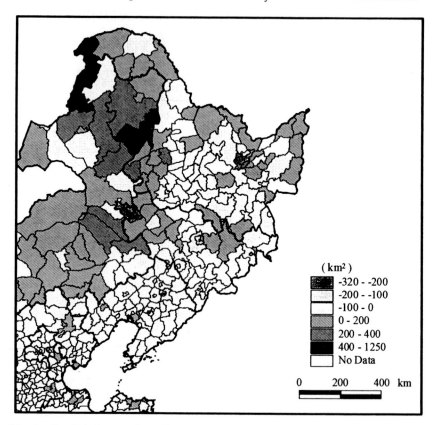

Fig. 1   Spatial changes in cultivated land in north-east China from 1990 to 1997
Data source: *Statistical Yearbook of China,* 1991 and 1998

3.   TEMPORAL LAND USE CHANGE

The statistics from 1953 to 1990 for Jilin Province were used for identifying the temporal agricultural land use changes. Annual variation of each land use pattern shows that the area of total cultivated land and dry fields have decreased year after year and the area of paddy fields and irrigated land have increased to a large extent. (Fig. 2). As a result, grain production has increased rapidly, especially since 1980.

Changes in socioeconomic factors are shown in Fig. 3. We can see that agricultural population has rapidly increased in the 1960s and 1970s, and has stopped increasing since 1980. However, agricultural inputs such as investment, electric application, fertilizer utilization have increased exponentially. As a result, the price of grain has largely risen since 1980. It should be pointed out that the government controlled the price of grain before 1980, when the market economy was not adopted in China. The application of chemicals reached its maximum in the 1970s, and then has been reduced largely because of their harmful after effects.

4. REGRESSION ANALYSIS: SOCIOECONOMIC DRIVING FORCES

The relationship between land use change and socioeconomic change has been analyzed by the stepwise regression method. Stepwise regression method is a semi-automatic process of building a statistic model by successively adding or removing variables, based solely on the t-statistics of their estimated coefficients. Here we choose grain production, cultivated land, dry field, paddy field and irrigation area as the land use factors, and agricultural population, fertilizer application, agricultural chemicals, plastic cover area, electric application, agricultural investment, grain price index and the export of grain, as socioeconomic variables. Table 1 shows the relationship between land use factors and socioeconomic variables obtained by the stepwise analysis.

According to the regression analysis, we are able to sum up following processes as the main mechanisms of land use change in Jilin Province in the last decade (Fig. 4).

(1) Settlement has expended because of population increase, socio-economic development and policy system reform. Before 1980s, the expansion of settlement was mainly policy-driven, but the situation has largely changed since 1980s along with the intro-duction of market economy in China. Now the settlement ex-pansion does not depend only on population increase, socio-economic development and policy system reform, but also on requirement of people's higher living standards.

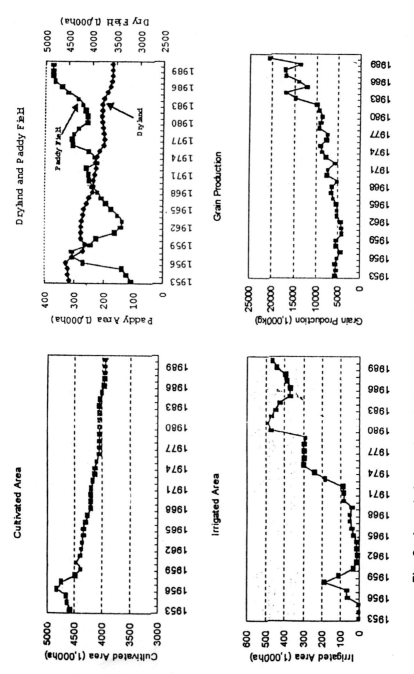

Fig. 2 Annual changes in agricultural land use from 1953 to 1990

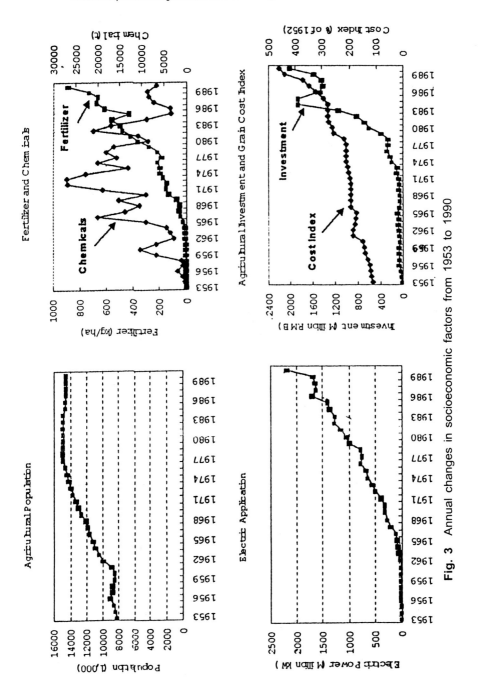

Fig. 3   Annual changes in socioeconomic factors from 1953 to 1990

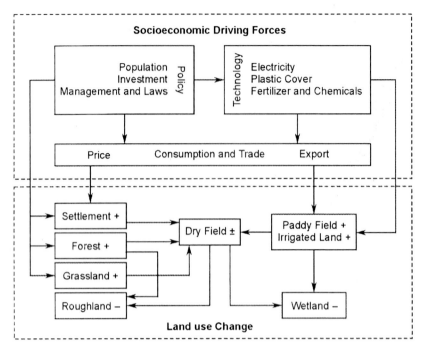

Fig. 4 Diagram of land use change mechanisms in Jilin Province

Table 1 Regression equations between land use factors and socioeconomic variables

Stepwise regression models	Multiple R	Adjusted squared multiple R	Standard error of estimate
Production = 486.920 + 22.591 *Fertilizer* + 0.009 *Plastic* + 0.002 *Investment*	0.968	0.931	112.41
Cultivated Land = 8082.074 – 1.011 *Population* + 7.827 *Fertilizer* – 2.706 *Price*	0.957	0.908	105.98
Dry Field = 7737.119 – 1.060 *Population* – 2.046 *Price*	0.962	0.922	118.80
Paddy Field = 290.590 + 0.001 *Electricity*	0.774	0.588	69.84
Irrigation Area = 97.618 – 0.005 *Chemicals* + 0.005 *Electricity* – 1.441 *Export*	0.953	0.900	84.06

(2) Paddy fields and irrigation area have increased largely because of technological progresses. The stepwise regression result shows that the expansion of paddy fields is mainly related to the degree of utilization of electricity, and irrigation area is related to the amount of exported grain, utilization of electricity and application of chemicals.

(3) Changes in cultivated land are closely related to the increase of population, fertilizer application and grain price.

(4) The increase of grain production is closely related to the amount of application of fertilizer, the area of plastic cover and the amount of agricultural investment.

Finally, it can be concluded that policies, technology developments, consumption and trade are main driving forces of land use changes (Fig. 4). The policies include population policy, agricultural investment policy, and management of agricultural system and laws. The main technological developments include applications of electricity, plastic coverage, fertilizer and chemicals. Consumption is reflected by price index, and trade includes import and export of grain. All these factors are the so-called socioeconomic driving forces, which impact on land use changes synthetically. It should be pointed out that natural driving forces such as climate changes, hydrological changes and disaster, may also affect land use changes. However, these subjects have not been discussed here.

5. CONCLUSIONS

The result of spatial analysis shows that newly cultivated land is located at the mountainous areas along the Xiao Hinggan Ling, Da Hinggan Ling and Changbai Mountain, and at the low plains such as the Three River and Song-Nen Plains. On the contrary, the agricultural areas around big cities in the northeast plain have decreased.

The result of time series analysis shows that the area of total cultivated land and dry field have decreased and the area of paddy field and irrigated field have increased in recent decades. Meanwhile, the grain production has increased rapidly, especially since 1980.

The result of regression analysis shows that the increase of grain production is closely related to the amount of fertilizer application, plastic cover area and agricultural investment, and the decrease of cultivated land is closely related to the amount of population, fertilizer application and the price of grain. The expansion of paddy field is mainly due to the degree of electric application for systematic irrigation. Through this analysis, we come to a conclusion that policy, technology development, and consumption and trade factors are main driving forces of land use changes in this area.

REFERENCES

Fischer, G., Ermoliev, Y., Keyzer, M.A. and C. Rosenzweig. 1996. Simulating the socio-economic and biogeophysical driving forces of land use and land cover change: The IIASA land-use change model, Working Paper WP-96-010, International Institute for Applied Systems Analysis, Laxenburg, Austria.

Himiyama, Y., Ito, H., Honma, T. and. T. Kikuchi. 1995. "Land Use in Northeast China in the 1930s", Reports of the Taisetsuzan Institute of Science, No. 30, 25-35.

Himiyama, Y., Fujisawa, M. and T. Miyakoshi. 1997. "Land Use in Northeast China circa 1980", Reports of the Taisetsuzan Institute of Science, No. 31, 13-24.

Mather, A. 1996. "The Human Drivers of Land Cover change: The Case of Forests", Proceedings of the Open IGBP/BACH-LUCC Joint Inter-Core Projects Symposium on Interactions between the Hydrological Cycle and Land Use/Cover. Kyoto, Japan, November 4-7.

CHAPTER 20

Land Use Controls and Conflicts in Urban-Rural Fringes in Korea — in Relation with the Green Belt Systems

(Manik Hwang[*])

1. INTRODUCTION

Urban growth is a worldwide phenomenon, particularly in many developing countries, such as Korea. There has been rapid urbanization in Korea during the last three decades, unprecedented in the country ever before. Urban sprawl accompanied by the urbanization degrades natural environments and consumes formerly highly productive agricultural lands and open spaces to provide land for the increasing population. The national government imposes various types of land use control policies in both urban and rural areas to provide adequate land resources for economic development, to conserve environments or to stabilize skyrocketing land prices. Today, more than 20 different kinds of land control laws, regulations or ordinances are applied to the land in Korea, causing complications for landowners, property developers or industrial developers, as well as local residents. Of those land control policies, the Green Belt System is the center of debates of reform vs. preservation, particularly since 1997 when the president of Korea had promised to review the Green Belt policy during his presidential election campaign. Since then, it has become a political issue. The national government began to review the policy in 1999 where some of the conflict areas are expected to be freed from the restricted zone in the near future.

*Department of Geography Education, Seoul National University, Seoul 151-742, Korea

This study examines the magnitudes of urban expansion in the Capital region around Seoul and the major problems associated with the restricted zoning policy, originally introduced to prevent urban sprawl in Korea. Specifically, this study presents magnitudes of urbanization, the source of conflicts associated with land use policies for the zones. The study uses Landsat TM data of 1985 and 1996 for Seoul and its surrounding areas. Land uses for the study area are classified into three major classes: urban, agricultural and forest. In fact, the agricultural class includes small farm villages.

2. THE GREEN BELT SYSTEM IN KOREA

The Green Belt is a restricted development zone. Any new development is strictly controlled within the zone. Therefore, it is more apt to call it the Restricted Development Zone (RDZ). The term RDZ is used interchangeably with the Green Belt in this study because the RDZ is a special type of greenbelt. The RDZ is a land use policy defining an area within which a narrow range of changes are allowed for existing facilities and very limited new developments are permitted. The Green Belt systems apply to 14 major urban areas in Korea (Fig. 1). Each Green

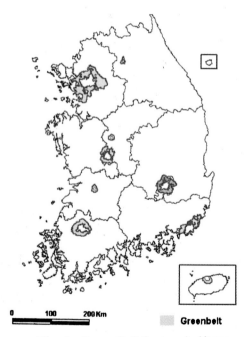

0   100   200 Km

▨ **Greenbelt**

Fig. 1   Green Belt System in Korea

Belt system surrounds its central city. Seoul's Green Belt, for instance, borders 18 cities and 5 counties around Seoul, the capital city. The Green Belt systems of Seoul and 13 other major urban area account about 5.4% (54,000 square kilometers) of the total area of the nation (Table 1). The first establishment of the Green Belt was established in the Capital region in 1971 and it expanded to other metropolitan areas including Pusan, Taegu, Kwangjoo and the remaining large urban areas by 1973. The area covered by the Green Belt in the Capital region is the largest among all 14 designated Green Belts.

Table 1 Central cities and their Green Belts in Korea

Province	Established date	Central City	Area (sq. km)	% of the national total Green Belt
Capital region	1971-1976	Seoul	1,567	29
Pusan	1971	Pusan	597	11
Taegu	1972	Taegu	537	10
Kwang-ju	1973	Kwang-ju	555	10.3
Che-ju	1973	Che-ju	38	1.5
Tae-jon	1973	Tae-jon	441	8.2
Wool-san	1973	Wool-san	284	5.2
Kang-won	1973	Chon-chon	294	5.4
Chung-buk	1973	Chung-ju	180	3.3
Chon-nam	1973	Chun-ju	225	4.2
Kyoung-nam	1973	Ma-san	314	5.8
Kyoung-nam	1973	Chin-ju	203	3.8
Kyoung-nam	1973	Chung-mu	30	0.6
Chon-nam	1973	Yo-su	88	1.6
Total			5,397	100

Source: Ministry of Construction and Transportation, 1998

The original intent of the Green Belt system was to prevent uncontrolled urban sprawl in major metropolitan areas, particularly in the Capital region, limiting population concentration and the unplanned construction of housing and new manufacturing plants in the already congested metropolitan area (Ministry of Construction, 1972). Another purpose for the Green Belt was to preserve the natural environment for urban residents and the supply of drinking water by preventing unauthorized timbering, quarrying or other harmful effects by the degradation of the natural environment in the urban periphery. The Green Belt ordinance was established in 1971-1973 for most parts of the Green Belt today, but the Capital Region expanded its Green Belt further in 1976. The total Green Belt area in the Capital Region increased from 464 square kilometers in 1971 to 1,567 square kilometers in 1976. Since then, there has been no major change. However, there were a very limited number of permits in the Green Belt for construction of large-scale housing projects and such public facilities as public schools, hospitals, and sports and recreation complexes.

The districts of the Green Belt basically form a ring (Fig. 2), instead of disjoint patches of aesthetic natural open spaces. In the Capital region, for instance, the Green Belt ring surrounds Seoul with a width of one to nine kilometers to prevent the coalescence of neighboring small towns and cities with Seoul. At present, Seoul's Green Belt borders 18 cities and 5 counties, consisting of 1,567 square kilometers. Its inner boundary is primarily drawn along a line 100 meters in elevation above sea level.

Fig. 2 Seoul's Green Belt, a ring-shape with many exempt areas

The Capital Region experienced a rapid increase in population by rural-urban movement during the last few decades, with concentration of industries and accompanied social and cultural facilities. The Capital Region, which includes Seoul, Inchon and its surrounding areas, shares about 43% of the nation's total population, 46% of the manufacturing employees, and 54% of the total number of manufacturing firms in the nation at present. As a result, urbanization became very intensive and expanded considerably outward beyond the Green Belt (Fig. 3).

1973

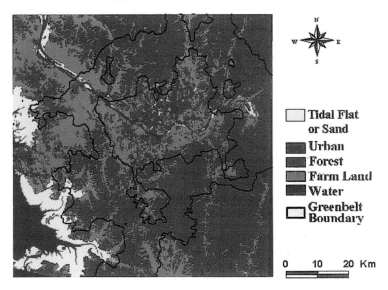

1996

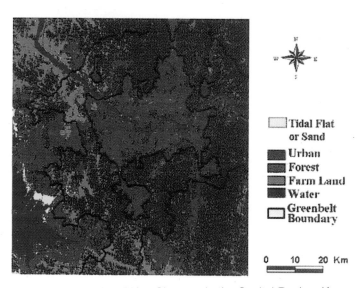

Fig. 3 Urbanization and Land Use Changes in the Capital Region, Korea, 1973-
1996. City of Seoul is located in the center along the Han River, and City
of Inchon is at right along the west coast in the figure.

3. SPATIAL LAND VALUE CHANGES

Land value is a good index of the degree of intensity for urban development. A classic model of urban rent based on accessibility show a typical distance-decay function away from the center of a city. Land use in the urban built-up areas competes for such limited available sites. When a green belt sets limits on the amount of land that can be developed, influences of the green belt on land value will be dependent on the land available inside the boundary (Fig. 4a and b). It will have no effect on the city until the city grows to the inner boundary of the green belt. Once it reaches the boundary, urban land use will be intensified and land values will be higher than the normal distribution curve. Then any new land development will seek cheaper land beyond the outer boundary of the Green Belt or areas in the exempt areas within the zone.

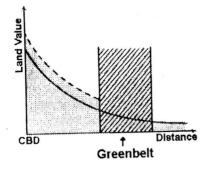

Fig. 4a Land value-distance curve. (Modified from Mills, 1986)   **Fig. 4b** Land value-distance curve with exempt areas within the Green Belt.

4. PRIVATE LAND OWNERS AND CONFLICTS OF THE POLICY

The ring-shaped Green Belt zone must include rural villages where settlements have existed for a long time. While large villages were exempt from the restricted zone, the Green Belt contained many small rural villages (Fig. 5). As a result, this left a large number of holes within the Green Belt, which became exempt from the restricted zone with many un-exempt small villages. Those small villages that were incorporated within the restricted zone were most disadvantaged by the restrictive land use policy. No land use changes other than for agricultural purposes in the zone are allowed. No new facilities or new buildings, even new residential houses are allowed within the restrictive zone. However, landowners and residents within those exempt areas are free from such restrictions. It is argued that the policy impacts unfairly on residents and property owners within the restricted zone.

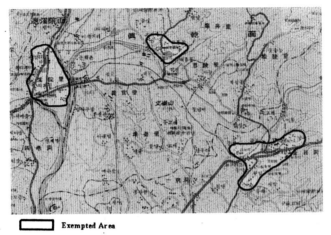

☐ Exempted Area

Fig. 5 Exempt area within the Green Belt.
Many small villages are included within the restricted development zone. The restricted zone is shown here outside of marked heavy lines

5. IMPACTS OF THE GREEN BELT

The Green Belt system brought both positive and negative effects. There are many adverse effects by the restricted land use policy. First, the restricted Green belt failed to reduce population concentration in the metropolitan region. Second, rapid leapfrog of land development appeared beyond the outer boundary of the restrictive zone, despite the availability of real estate within. Development outside of the Green Belt zone caused unnecessary demand for costly infrastructure to connect the inner city and those new outer developing areas. The third and most adverse impact is the economic disadvantage for property owners within the restrictive zone. In fact, land value in the cities inside the inner ring of the Green Belt has been skyrocketing, due to increasing demand by the heavy concentration of population into the major cities. Fourth, village residents within the zone must live with inconveniences because of restricted construction for new infrastructures, transporta-tion facilities, and so on. The government, however, lessened some of the restricted regulations during the last several years, and prepare a major reform at present to reduce those conflicts.

In spite of these adverse effects and problems by the Green Belt, the restricted development zone contributed greatly to preserve open spaces surrounding areas of the metropolitan areas. Without such powerful ordinances, we might have experienced uncontrolled leapfrog urban developments in large metropolitan regions today.

6. LAND USE POLICY

Problems of the Green Belt are two-fold: one is the political pressure from landowners and developers and the other is public concern to improve the present Green Belt system. It needs to incorporate adequate policies for housing and for future economic development and at the same time implement effective preservation of the natural environment. However, there have been strong opposing views to the restrictive development system largely by private landowners because the system restricts private land ownership. Still, some others argue that land under the restricted system will provide enough to preserve natural environment from ever increasing urbanization (Mills, 1986).

The boundary of the Green Belt is under review by the national government. The government is proposing two alternatives: removal of the restricted development zone in areas of low urbanization, and adjustment in areas of the most conflict residential problems or areas of low environmental preservation value (Town and Country Planning Association).

Any efforts to reform the Green Belt system must be firmly founded on the concept of sustainable development by which our generation and following generations can maintain a high quality of life.

7. CONCLUSION

Land use changes by the Landsat data and the land value change model in the Green Belt reflect differences in the intensity of land uses among inner ring areas, Green Belt, and outer ring areas beyond the Belt. A leapfrog of urban land use beyond the inner Green Belt boundary does not occur as long as a considerable amount of property within the Green Belt is available. However, rapid real estate development occurs beyond the inner boundary after the city has considerably evolved. By this time, rapid changes in land use begin to appear in the exempt areas within the Green Belt and beyond the outer boundary of the Green Belt.

No doubt, the Green Belt system's largest contribution has been the preservation of natural environments and of open spaces in metropolitan area in an era of unprecedented rapid urbanization in this country. Although there are many problems related to the restrictive nature of the system, we must maintain this primary goal for the future. At the same time, the central government and metropolitan governments must provide economic compensation for those people in the disadvantaged villages and for private landowners. The ultimate goal for the restricted development system must be based on the concept of sustainable community development.

REFERENCES

Mills, Edwin S. 1986. Korean Government Policies toward Seoul's Greenbelt, Korea Research Institute for Human Settlements: 26.

Ministry of Construction, Republic of Korea. 1972. Urban Planning Ordinance, Article 21.

Ministry of Construction and Transportation, Republic of Korea. 1998. Reform of the Restricted Development Zone System, An unpublished reference report.

CHAPTER 21

Land Use/Cover Changes in Japan Since 1850: A Contribution to the IGU Pilot Atlas of LUCC

(Yukio Himiyama[1], Shoichiro Arizono[2], Yoshihisa Fujita[2] and Takashi Todokoro[3])

1. INTRODUCTION

IGU Study Group on Land Use/Cover Change (IGU-LUCC) plans to publish an atlas tentatively entitled "Land Use/Cover Changes in Selected Regions in the World". The atlas will ultimately contain reports from some twenty-five countries/regions, including Japan. It will be useful for various kinds of comparative studies including those of the processes and mechanisms of land use/cover changes, data sources and processing, analytical and presentation methods, and problems related with the changes. A concrete publication plan was proposed in the IGU-LUCC '98 symposium in Lisbon (Himiyama, 1999), and it was further elaborated in the IGU-LUCC'99 symposium in Hawaii. Table 1 shows the general guideline for a country/regional report and is the outcome of the Hawaii meeting. The present paper proposes the case of Japan as an example of the country/regional report.

2. JAPAN CHAPTER OUTLINE

In Japan, a priority project on environmental changes and GIS was carried out during 1990-1993, and it resulted in the publication of

[1]Hokkaido University of Education, Hokumoncho, Asahikawa 070-8621, Japan
[2]Aichi University, Toyohashi 441-8522, Japan
[3]Takasaki City University of Economics, Takasaki 370-0801, Japan

Table 1   General guideline for a country/regional report

---

1. The atlas will be A3 in size, in vertical position, with about 200 pages.
2. The length of a contribution will be about 6 to 12 pages, with half of them for major maps, and the rest for other maps, tables and text.
3. Major maps should be ideally in colour.
4. Study area can be a region as well as a country, but it should not be too small.
5. Time range can be between 50 and 300 years.
6. The contents include description of data, method, basic facts, processes, driving forces and mechanisms of changes, models of changes, effects of changes, problems of changes, future prospects, etc.
7. There is no common scale for maps.
8. The types of major map include grid map, statistical map, conventional land use map, landscape map, etc.
9. The contribution should be useful for international comparisons, and should aim at not only specialists, but also students, etc.

---

the "Atlas—Environmental Change in Modern Japan" (Himiyama et al. 1995). The highlight of this atlas is a series of computer-generated land use maps covering the whole country for the periods ca. 1850, 1900, 1950 and 1985. The basic data sets are all of raster type, produced from the topographic maps at 1:50,000 based on the methods proposed by Himiyama et al. (1991). They can yield a variety of maps, but the constraint of space in the proposed atlas will allow only a few of them to be presented.

The chapter for Japan in the proposed atlas will have sections on the overview of land use/cover changes in Japan, urbanization, changes in agricultural land use and forest use, including not only the past but the future changes. It will present six pages of major maps as listed in Table 2, together with six pages of text. Generally speaking, major maps in the atlas can be various types such as conventional land use map, statistical map, satellite-based map, or grid map as being demonstrated by Japan. The comparison of different types of map and the related methodologies is one of the objectives of the atlas.

Table 2   Major maps of the Chapter for Japan

Map 1	Land Use/Cover in Japan ca. 1985
Map 2	Land Use/Cover Change in Japan, 1900-1985
Map 3	Land Use/Cover in Japan ca. 1850
Map 4	Urbanization in Japan, 1850-1985
Map 5	Rough Land Use in Mountain Areas before World War II
Map 6	Estimated Land Use/Cover in Japan in the 2020s

---

3. LAND USE/COVER CHANGES IN JAPAN

One of the major roles of the atlas is to show the facts of land use/cover changes in various countries/regions and settings by maps, diagrams, tables and texts. It is noted that long-term land use/cover changes are still grasped inaccurately and understood poorly in most places, though there are various ways to identify and present land use/cover changes, as discussed in Himiyama (1997).

Figure 1 and Table 3 represent two different ways to look at the general trend of land use/cover. The former shows the trend of general land use structure graphically, while the latter shows the magnitude of changes. From these, it is easy to have a general idea about the long term land use/cover changes in Japan. For example, Fig. 1 shows that areas of forest and agricultural land have been fairly stable since the middle of the last century, while the increase of urban land and the decrease of rough land have been rapid, particularly after World War II.

The general understanding as shown above can be refined with appropriate maps, information on qualitative aspects of land use, and explanations of the changes. The strength of the proposed atlas is that it shows fine colour maps, which most other publications on land use/cover changes miss.

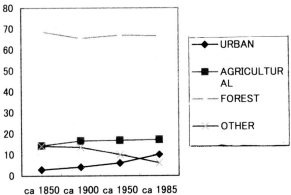

Fig. 1   Land Use Change in Japan, 1850-1985

4. LAND USE/COVER IN JAPAN CA. 1850

The middle of the nineteenth century was the period when the long lasted Edo era (1603-1867) and the policy of seclusion was nearing its end. The year 1850 therefore represents the last days of the closed Japan, i.e. Japan before industrial revolution. During the Edo

Table 3   Land use in Japan ca. 1985 (area ca. 1900 = 100)

Urban	243
Settlement	315
Road	191
Railway	220
Agricultural	103
Paddy field	103
Dry field	94
Mulberry	42
Tea	301
Orchard	1127
Other tree crops	42
Forest	102
Broad-leaved	54
Coniferous	87
Mixed	155
Bamboo	166
Other	45
Rough land	33
Wetland	48
Water	105
Golf course	Infinite
Others	0

era, each locality was highly self-contained in terms of energy and food supply, and the majority of people lived on agriculture, which was then quite sustainable. The land use pattern of ca. 1850 is considered to reflect such circumstances, and is regarded as the initial condition of the increasingly rapid changes that followed. The reconstruction of land use at this period is therefore of fundamental necessity for the study of long-term land use/cover changes in Japan.

1850 differs from the other three time periods in that there was no large-scale topographic map at that time. Arizono (1995) hence used the land use data set for 1900 produced by Himiyama as the basic data, and modified it in order to make the 1850 data set. The main information sources of Arizono's work are numerous historical documents and old local maps. The method of reconstructing past land use can be applied in many countries/regions that have relevant maps.

Table 4 shows the land use structure of Japan ca. 1850, which is based on the 1850 data set. It shows that forest occupied 68.6% of the country, while agricultural land, rough land and settlement occupied 14.4%, 11.8% and 1.7%, respectively. Although settlement occupied much less land than in the later periods, the overall land use pattern was quite similar to that of ca. 1900, except in Hokkaido. The locations of the major urban centres at that time are almost the same as those of today, suggesting that the inter-city system in Japan had been established by then.

Table 4 Land use in Japan ca. 1850

	× 10 km^2	%
Urban	1,064	2.86
Settlement	612	1.65
Road	452	1.22
Railway	0	0.00
Agricultural	5345	14.38
Paddy field	3592	9.66
Dry field	1752	4.71
Mulberry	0	0.00
Tea	0	0.00
Orchard	0	0.00
Other tree crops	1	0.00
Forest	25,497	68.59
Broad-leaved	11,176	30.07
Coniferous	4572	12.30
Mixed	9426	25.36
Bamboo	323	0.87
Other	5265	14.16
Rough land	4401	11.84
Wetland	161	0.43
Water	702	1.89
Golf course	0	0.00
Others	2	0.00
Total	37,171	100.00

Following is the excerpt of detailed observations:

a) Except in Hokkaido, flatlands were dominated by farmland, while the slope lands near settlements were covered with either forest or rough land. The dominant tree in coniferous forests near settlements was pine, which could grow on the land impoverished by the overuse by villagers. Paddy field was prevalent in flat lowlands, while dry field was distributed on the uplands. The total area of dry field in ca. 1850 was only half of paddy field. Dry field, however, existed all over Japan, including high mountain areas where paddy field did not exist.

b) In Hokkaido, which was still largely occupied by the Ainu, most of the flatland was covered with broad-leaved forests, while mountain slopes were largely covered with mixed or coniferous forests. Natural vegetation was still prevalent in Hokkaido at that time.

c) No orchard or other kinds of tree-crop fields are found on the 1850 land use map. Although they actually existed on the ground, e.g. satsuma orange in south-western Japan or mulberry gardens for silkworm in north-central Japan, they were too small and sparsely distributed to be shown on the 1:50,000 maps.

d) Except in Hokkaido, slope land near villages were covered with coniferous forests, mixed forests or rough land, while the heartland of mountains was covered with broad-leaved forest. Slope land, which was covered largely with forest and rough land, was an important source of grass for manure to fields, as well as that of firewood.

e) Rough land was distributed widely throughout the country. It was typically located on the mountain slopes near settlements. Much of the rough land was in use to gather firewood and grass for manure, and it often had an indispensable function for the maintenance of agricultural production and village life at that time.

f) Apart from the four main islands, Sado and Okinawa islands were dominated by forests. In the former, substantial paddy fields were developed in order to feed gold mine workers, while in the latter dry field was widespread in the southern part of the island.

5. CHANGES IN URBAN LAND USE

Urbanization has been one of the most important changes of land use in Japan during the last one hundred years, and it is expected to remain so at least in the coming decades. It includes land use changes inside cities, as well as those associated with urban expansion. Urban land uses and their changes are the products of the complex interaction of various urban functions, population, technological innovations, culture, etc. and they have strong effect on the other land uses and the environment (Todokoro, 1995).

Figure 2 shows rapid increase in the areas of settlement and road. The increase in the area of road was faster than that of settlement till ca. 1950, while by ca. 1985 the increase rates of the two were reversed. This is the result of the rapid economic development and motorization that started in the 1960s, and the improvement of mass-transportation facilities. This fact may be overlooked, as there is widely-held preoccupation that motorization enlarges the area of road more than that of settlement. The expansion of urban areas in the major plains, especially Greater Tokyo, Greater Kei-Han-Shin and Greater Nagoya, has been tremendous. It is also noted that the western half of the country, including Tokyo, has developed far more urban areas than the rest.

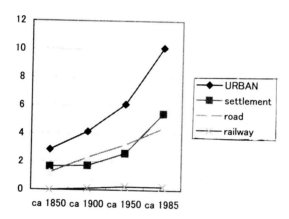

Fig. 2   Change in Urban Land Use, 1850-1985

The growth of manufacturing industries has been one of the major driving forces of the growth of cities during the last hundred years. It resulted in creating new cities that are different in nature from the cities that existed before Meiji era. The construction of railways contributed to the nation-wide networking of cities, and contributed to the development of compact urban areas around railway stations before World War II.

Since the late 1960s, a great number of people moved to the suburbs where land prices and rent were lower and there were less environmental problems than in the built-up areas. This out-migration of people extended urban areas enormously in a very short time.

There are five major types of land use change in urban areas in Japan during the last hundred years.

a) *Intensive concentration*: This is seen in the CBDs of medium or large cities, where high-rise buildings are located.

b) *Concentration plus dispersion*: Manufacturing industries moved out from the inner city to the suburbs particularly since the 1970s, while their previous sites attained central management functions.

c) *Dispersion*: This includes urban expansion fuelled by motorization and dispersion of certain functions such as schools or post offices.

d) *Disappearance and emergence*: There are facilities that once existed but were replaced by new ones, e.g. water mills were still playing important roles 100 years ago, but they were all replaced by smaller number of big power stations and related facilities.

e) *Little change*: The distribution patterns of police offices, tax offices and courthouses have changed little during the last hundred years.

6. CHANGES IN AGRICULTURAL LAND USE

Although the total area of agricultural land use in Japan has been fairly stable over the last century, its distribution and contents have greatly changed. The changes and their backgrounds are outlined.

The percentage of agricultural land increased from 14.4% in ca. 1850 to 16.7% in ca. 1900, but has been stable since then at about 17% (Fig. 3). The increase in agricultural land before ca. 1900 is mainly attributed to that of dry field in Hokkaido. The development of new agricultural land in Hokkaido continued well into the 1980s supported by strong government incentives, but it has been offset by the decrease elsewhere. The Kanto Plain, which is the largest plain in Japan, with Tokyo and many other cities in it, lost large area of agricultural land for the sake of urban expansion, but the new development of agricultural land in other parts of the plain more or less compensated the loss.

The area of paddy field has been stable since the middle of the last century. It is mainly due to the government's policy, at least after World War II. Rice has long been the staple food in Japan, and it has been self-sufficient till today except in some extreme years. Total population more than tripled in the last one and a half century, but due to the increase in per area yield and the decrease in per capita consumption, self-sufficiency has been maintained without enlarging the paddy field.

Mulberry garden spread in the late nineteenth and early twentieth century, and disappeared rapidly afterward. Silk was one of the most important export goods in Japan before World War II, but World War II, which stopped the Japanese silk export to the USA, and the invention of nylon and other synthetic fibres destroyed the industry.

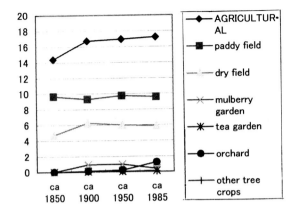

Fig. 3   Change in Agricultural Land Use, 1850-1985

The increase of orchard after World War II is tremendous. It increased about 500% between ca. 1950 and 1985. The increase was partly due to the growing fruits consumption, and partly due to the government's policy.

There is a widespread belief that the rapid industrial development in Japan has reduced the area of cultivated land, especially that in marginal areas, considerably, as is seen in Brown (1995). However, the fact is that the area of cultivated land has not decreased much, and that the cultivated land converted to other uses usually belonged to high-quality land.

7. CHANGES IN FOREST LAND USE

Two-thirds of the land of Japan is occupied by forest. It is important not only as the source of timber, but also for environmental reasons. Environmental consideration, in particular, requires the understanding in the qualitative contents of forest. Figure 4 shows the trend of forest area in Japan. The area of forest has been fairly stable since the middle of the last century. Some forests were converted to agricultural land or settlements, but there were also efforts of afforestation in marginal areas.

Broad-leaved forests decreased markedly, especially after ca. 1950, giving way to mixed forests. This is mainly the result of widespread commercial planting of needle-leaved trees, which was often done in piece-meal, creating an apparent mixture of the existing natural broad-leaved trees and the planted coniferous trees.

Fujita (1995) produced historical forest data sets by a similar method as Arizono (1995), in order to study the change of forest use in detail.

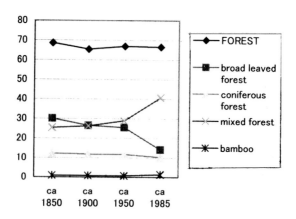

Fig. 4   Change in Forest Use, 1850-1985

Before World War II, the use of forest was fairly stable as a whole, fitting to the local climatic conditions. Traditional shifting cultivation and gathering of grass and fuel wood were commonly practised in broad-leaved forests in mountainous regions. For the farmers in the mountain villages with common or private forests, these were part of their self-support system. Commercial forest was limited, mainly in the mountains near big markets such as Osaka or Edo (current Tokyo). They were developed along with these markets since the late eighteenth century.

There were a lot of slash-and-burn fields, land for grass or fuel wood, pine forests, which are largely the result of the overuse of forest, deforested land and other rough land. Among these, slash-and-burn field was important for the farmers in mountainous areas, particularly for those in moderately deep mountains. Grass was mainly used as fertilizer in paddy fields.

However, these mountains were covered by common land, and a lot of mountains, especially in the western part of Japan, were changed to waste land due to the heavy use by farmers who gathered a lot of grass from these common lands. The overuse and ill management of mountain slopes sometimes resulted in flooding, land degradation and other disasters before World War II.

Under these circumstances, both the national government and farmer landowners in mountainous areas took action in forest rehabilitation after World War II. Many farmer landowners planted needle-leaved trees mainly because of the sharp increase of timber price due to the vast shortage of timber during the post-war period, and because of the governmental subsidies. The boom of afforestation continued into the period of high economic growth, which began in the 1960s, because the development of economic activities created high demand for timber, and the price of timber rose up further.

Thus, the areas deforested before or during World War II had been converted to forest by the 1960s. Furthermore, the broad-leaved forests had been cut and re-planted with needle-leaved trees in the 1970s and the 1980s. Planted forests occupy a large area now, particularly in the mountains along the Pacific coast. Most of them occupy the land that used to be economically marginal.

However, the government thought that the high timber price was the obstacle to the economic development, and it decided in 1963 to start importing cheap timber from other countries. It made the price of the domestic timber go down in the 1970s and 1980s. Thus, many of the farmer forest owners in mountain villages abandoned the management of their planted trees, which need to be cared. Furthermore, the fast economic growth, which started in the 1960s, pushed out many people from mountain villages, and it resulted in the shortage of forest workers. The management of the newly planted areas is a very important issue not only for the maintenance of forest resources, but also for the protection of the mountain environments.

The use of forest or mountain areas is not limited to forestry. Wide-spread development of leisure facilities such as golf courses and ski grounds in the 1980s and the 1990s has added new environmental and economic dimensions in the use of forest areas in Japan.

8. MODELLING AND PREDICTING LAND USE/COVER CHANGES

Though the main task of the atlas is to show and explain land use/cover changes till today, some countries/regions may be sufficiently equipped with data and skill to simulate future land use/cover. The Chapter for Japan may show a predictive land use grid map if space allows. Himiyama (1998) formulated empirical models of land use/

cover changes in Japan after World War II and in the next quarter of a century. The models are schematically represented, and the results of the model simulations are shown in the form of grid maps. It is hoped that the predictive maps, as well as schematic representation of the empirical models, become important ingredients of the atlas.

REFERENCES

Arizono, S. 1995. Land Use in Japan circa 1850, In: Himiyama et al. (Eds) 4-5, 46-51.

Brown, L.R. 1995. *Who Will Feed China?*, W.W. Norton & Company, New York.

Fujita, Y. 1995. Change in the Use of Forest Land in Japan, in Himiyama et. al. (Eds), 75-87.

Himiyama, Y. 1997. How to Identify and Analyse Historical Land Use Changes? In: *Information Bases for Land Use/Cover Change Research*. Himiyama and Crissman (Eds), 42-47.

Himiyama, Y. 1998. Land Use/Cover Changes in Japan: from the Past to the Future, Hydrological Processes, No. 12, 1995-2001.

Himiyama, Y. 1999. Land Use/Cover Changes in Selected Parts of the World, in Proceedings of IGU-LUCC'98, IGU-LUCC (in press).

Himiyama, Y., Iwagami, M. and E. Inoue 1991. Reconstruction of Land Use of Japan circa 1900-1920, Reports of the Taisetsuzan Institute of Science, No. 26, 55-63.

Himiyama, Y., Arai, T. Ota, I. Kubo, S., Tamura, T. Nogami, M., Murayama, Y., Yorifuji, A. and O. Nishikawa (Eds). Atlas Environmental Change in Modern Japan, Asakura Shoten, Tokyo. (in Japanese with English abstract).

Todokoro, T. 1995. Urbanisation in Japan, In Himiyama et al. (Eds) 17-21, 127-131, 143-150, 158-159.

CHAPTER 22

Impact of Climate Change and Other Natural Hazards on Land Use in the Saas and Zermatt Valleys (Switzerland)

(Markus Stoffel[*])

1. INTRODUCTION

Alpine valleys such as the Saas and Zermatt Valleys in the central Swiss Alps have always been influenced by climatic variations and natural catastrophies. The landscape has clearly been marked by several glaciations, torrents and gravitary processes (i.e. landslides, rockslides). Natural hazards have also been driving factors for the settlement of these steep and narrow valleys: as 'secure' space was (and still is) rather rare, places possible for village construction have been limited to restricted areas, limiting the supportable number of inhabitants to a moderate level.

At the end of the last century, English tourists discovered the Zermatt and Saas Fee region. Today, tourism is the main source of income for the area and agriculture—formerly predominant—has lost its importance. As a result, the number of permanent residents has rapidly increased—as well as the number of homes for tourists. But 'secure' space for construction purposes in the Saas and Zermatt Valleys still remains the same, and the growth of those villages has already (or will soon have) reached its limits. Considering the probable changes of our

[*]Department of Geography, University of Fribourg, chemin du Musée 4, 1700 Fribourg, Switzerland.

climate, those involved in planning questions will have to take into account this physical aspect in their considerations of future available areas (Stoffel, 1997). A changing climate can affect land use planning in two different ways:

- On the one hand, changing climate influences land use. The spatial needs of existing uses change and new uses could arise.
- On the other hand, changing climate can influence natural dangers. That can either lead to a decrease or an increase of the available space, depending on whether the danger will increase or decline.

Therefore, this new element leads to new insecurities. The resulting conflicts will especially be grave when existing uses are menaced by new or modified potentials of natural dangers. But predictions of possible changes are very difficult and partly related to major uncertainties. For this reason, one has to underline that the evaluations presented in this paper may be possible, in some cases even probable, but that they never show predictions in 'real time'. In opposition to those predictions, land use planning decisions present resolutions in 'real time' and they thus have important economic consequences. Therefore, this paper essentially tries to answer the following two questions:

- On the one hand, this study tries to analyze and evaluate the existing policy in defining and limiting danger zones by entirety, validity, and appropriateness. At the same time, this method makes it possible to elaborate a nearly complete record of all existing natural hazard areas of the study region.
- On the other hand, possible consequences of a future climate change on natural hazards should be estimated. First, this means detection of future endangered areas. Second, dimensions of such 'new' danger zones should be defined.

The final report of this master thesis has been sponsored and published by the Swiss National Research Program 31 Climate Change and natural hazards) (Bloetzer et al. 1998).

2. GEOGRAPHY OF THE SAAS AND ZERMATT VALLEYS

The Saas and Zermatt valleys form two deep mountain valleys of the Central Swiss Alps. They are surrounded by a large number of some of the highest peaks of the entire Alpine circle. In addition, the test region (520 sq. km) is strongly glaciated (Fig. 1). The number of permanent

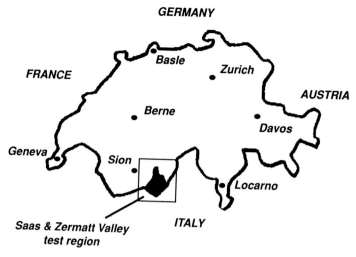

Fig. 1 Geographical situation of the Saas and Zermatt Valleys (Valais, Switzerland)

residents is about 16,810 people, the main source of income is tourism. The tourist centers of Zermatt (Matterhorn) and Saas Fee accommodate nearly 1.5 million tourists per year (Bloetzer and Stoffel, 1998).

Natural hazards often play a key role in the test region by limiting 'secure' space in the valley floors. Nearly all villages in the Saas and Zermatt Valleys are menaced by snow avalanches, rockfalls, land- or rockslides, floods and debris flows. These events are mostly generated at high elevation sites (highest elevation: Dom Peak 4545 m) 13,853 feet (above sea level) before crashing several thousands of feet down into the steep and narrow valleys (lowest elevation: Stalden 710 m) (2164 feet above sea level). Elbow-room for land use planning is therefore rather limited in these valleys (Fig. 2) (Bloetzer and Stoffel, 1998).

3. LAND USE PLANNING AND NATURAL HAZARDS IN SWITZERLAND

3.1 Legal Basis

The goal of land use planning is to guarantee an expedient and economical use of the soil and an orderly development of the country. The Swiss Government has set constitutional articles, several federal laws, statutes and decrees to enforce those targets—namely the Land Use Planning Act (1979). It defines the principles for an appropriate development of the country but gives the Cantons maximum liberty

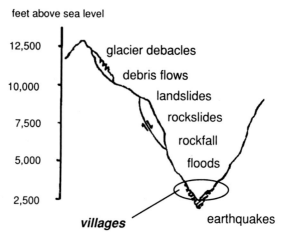

Fig. 2 Almost all catastrophic events in the Saas and Zermatt Valleys start at high elevation sites to reach the narrow valley floor. Note the position of the villages often situated on mountain torrent alluvial fans.

in the definition of the (cantonal) legal articles. Therefore, it can be said that the land use planning statute is strongly influenced locally. In spite of the cantonal and communal differences, a general procedure with three different levels always emerges (Bloetzer et al. 1998).

- At the level of the cantonal general plan, large areas, supraregional functions and criteria for the zoning plan are defined.
- At the level of the communal zoning plan, uses and limitations with obligations for the landowners are determined.
- Finally, the principle of building permits allows the authorities to control and supervise the imposed duties and limits.

Besides this, one has to consider that land use planning measures have long-term effects and that already built residential or industrial zones correspond to practically irreversible types of land use. For this reason, the constitutional principles of lawfulness and appropriateness have to be respected, whenever there are interventions in private property.

3.2 Hazard Mapping

Within these levels, taking natural dangers into account has to be done in several ways. The federal Land Use Planning Act (1979) as well as the federal Forest Act and the federal Hydraulic Engineering

Act (both, 1991) the corresponding decrees and explanations clearly define the guidelines for the elaboration of catastrophy catasters of past events as well as the description of endangered areas (Stoffel, 1999a). Eventually, calculations and simulations of events lead to the creation of hazard maps by distinguishing three degrees of danger (Fig. 3).

What do the different colors mean in terms of danger?

red: People and animals are seriously endangered inside as well as outside buildings

⇒ no constructions allowed in this area.

blue: People and animals are seriously endangered outside buildings

⇒ limited construction possible (reinforced concrete, small or no windows)

yellow: People and animals are lightly endangered outside buildings

⇒ no restrictions.

white: No danger.

For buildings with a temporary or permanent concentration of people (e.g. schools, churches), special regulations are applicable. Such constructions are only possible in the yellow or the white zone.

Fig. 3 Regulations on endangered areas and building space for land use planning purposes in Switzerland (BUWAL, BWW and BRP, 1998 and 1997)

Every municipality has to elaborate maps indicating endangered zones defining future residential or industrial zones. Like this, hazard mapping helps to guarantee long-term planning measures: new buildings may only be constructed in areas where they are (actually) exposed to no or only little danger.

After major events, the hazard maps have to be revised and adapted to the new situation. The Grossgufer rockslide (1991)—an event of about 30 million cube-meters of rock—buried 33 buildings near the village of Randa (Zermatt Valley). For this reason, former residential zones had to be reclassed after the event (Stoffel, 1999a).

4. CHANGING NATURAL HAZARDS BY CLIMATE CHANGES

4.1 Test Region Climate of the 21st Century

In the Climate Change 1995 report, the Intergovernmental Panel on Climate Change (IPCC) estimated the increase of the global mean surface air temperature relative to 1990 of about 2° Celsius by 2100. For the southern part of the Swiss Alps, the increase could be as high as 1.5° Celsius in winter and 0-0.5° Celsius in summer by 2050. Precipitations could diminish during the summer (−10%) and increase during the winter season (+10%) (IPCC, 1996; Ohmura et al. 1996).

With these probable changes of the climate, those involved in planning questions will have to consider this new aspect in their considerations of future available areas: changing climate can influence natural dangers. The resulting conflicts will especially be grave when existing uses are menaced by new or modified potentials of natural dangers. Therefore, climate change and modified natural hazards will lead to new insecurities.

4.2 Modified Natural Hazards

Higher temperatures and a tendency to more extreme weather events will probably influence certain types of hazard found in the Saas and Zermatt Valleys. Even though rockslides, large landslides and snow avalanches will not be much affected by climatic variations, modifications must be expected for (flash) floods, glacier debacles and cryospheric debris flows. They are especially thought to occur more frequently during late summer and fall (Rebetez et al. 1997).

Floods in the Saas and Zermatt Valleys often happen after heavy summer thunderstorms or extended precipitations passing the Southern Alps mountain ridge and touching the dry and leeward test area, more frequently affected by foehn wind situations. Such events seem to increases in number and have recently (1987 and 1993) caused major damages. Maps defining detailed flood menaced areas are in preparation.

Massive destruction of buildings and infrastructures by quick slides of large ice masses known as glacier debacles are rarer than damages by floods or debris flows. Nevertheless, the 1965 Allalin glacier debacle (Saas Almagell) completely destroyed the cabins of the Mattmark dam constructors and buried 88 of them. Many glaciers in the Swiss Alps are regularly controlled, so that the risk of unexpected slides is rather low.

An elevation in the present temperature will probably cause a partial thawing of permafrost soils and rock glacier ice at higher elevations. Like this, loose talus lose their 'natural ice-concrete'. This is the reason why large debris flows could be generated. (Zimmermann et al. 1997). This might lead to an increase in the number and the volume of future debris flows reaching the alluvial fans and the villages of the Saas and Zermatt Valleys. A decrease of the available building land would be the consequence. To get more specified data on future events and menaced zones, general studies on permafrost modification in the departure zone will be necessary. In addition, geomorphological studies on the alluvial fans have to show possible debris flow affected zones.

5. CONCLUSIONS

1. By the determination and the elimination of danger zones as well as the limitation of building areas to 'secure' space, Swiss land use planning authorities possess a good system to provide the population with the best conditions. Nevertheless, there will still remain insecurities in predicting menaced areas, and hazard mapping will always be a continuously ongoing process (Stoffel, 1997).

2. Predictions of possible modifications of natural hazards by climatic changes are a real challenge for those involved in land use planning, very difficult to realize and partly related to major uncertainties. As a precaution, dangerous areas should be designated as 'buffer areas' or areas of expected danger ('Gefahrenerwartungszone'). These potential danger areas possess two indicator functions: on the one hand, construction in such areas can be delayed while carried out elsewhere; on the other hand, these areas and their danger development can be observed carefully (Stoffel, 1999b).

3. But, the functions of land use planning will not change fundamentally due to modified climate conditions, because the uncertainty in estimating the present potential of natural dangers is still considerable, perhaps even bigger than the expected changes caused by the evolution of the climate. Nevertheless, one must absolutely take possible problems into account, when new areas are developed so that both now and in the future only 'secure' areas are used.

4. Much more important than the definition of communal legal principles is a plausible and comprehensible representation of the danger. If the local people are able to understand the danger, appropriate measures required by the constitution will probably be more easily recognized. For dangers that are new and/or influenced by climatic variations, this connection is even stronger and all the more valid.

5. For this reason, risk communication forms a central element in the control of natural dangers. Especially the inhabitants of moun-

tain regions are used to living with natural dangers. They also know that neither absolute security nor predictions free of mistakes can ever exist. The fact that those people on the one hand have to support risk and on the other hand must have a chance to use their living space optimally, gives these people the right of co-determination. It should therefore be a central task of the science to point out possible changes in a clear and intelligible way.

6. ACKNOWLEDGEMENTS

This paper partly reviews the work of the synthesis Group 'Climate Change and Natural Hazards in Land Use Planning' under the National Research Program 31 'Climate Change and Natural Hazards'. The contribution of the following project members are acknowledged: ABW Werner Bloetzer, Visp; Dr. Thomas Egli, St. Galen; Dr. Armin Petrascheck, Biel and Joseph Sauter, Chur. In addition, the author is thankful to all researchers of the National Research Program 31, especially Dr. Pierre Kunz, University of Geneva, Dr. Markus Zimmermann, Bern, as well as to Prof. Michel Monbaron and Prof. Martin Beniston, University of Fribourg.

REFERENCES

BFF and EISLF. 1984. Richtlinien zur Berücksichtigung der Lawinengefahr bei raumwirksamen Tätigkeiten, Bern.

Bloetzer Werner and Markus Stoffel. 1998. Klimawandel als Herausforderung für die Raumplanung der Vispertäler. Final report National Research Program 31 (part IV)-vdf Zurich.

Bloetzer Werner, Thomas Egli, Armin Petrascheck, Joseph Sauter and Markus Stoffel. 1998. Klimaänderung und Naturgefahren in der Raumplanung - Methodische Ansätze und Fallbeispiele; Final report National Research Program 31-vdf Zurich.

BUWAL, BWW and BRP. 1997. Naturgefahren; Empfehlungen zur Berücksichtigung der Hochwassergefahren bei raumwirksamen Tätigkeiten, Bern.

BUWAL, BWW and BRP. 1998. Naturgefahren; Berücksichtigung der Massenbewegungsgefahren bei raumwirksamen Tätigkeiten, Bern.

IPCC. 1996. Climate Change 1995: The Science of Climate Change. Contribution of Working Group I to the Second Assessment Report of the Intergovernmental Panel on Climate Change, Cambridge University Press.

NRP31 (National Research Program 31). 1998. Dangers naturels: Impacts des changements climatiques sur le potentiel d'occurence des catastrophes naturelles; Final report National Research Program 31-vdf Zurich.

Ohmura Atsumu, Beniston Martin, Rotach Matthias, Tschuck Peter, Wild Martin and Maria Rosaria Marinucci. 1996. Simulation of Climate Trends over the Alpine Region; Final report National Research Program 31-vdf Zurich.

Rebetez Martine, Lugon Ralph and Pierre-Alain Baeriswyl. 1997. Climatic Change and Debris Flows in High Mountain Regions: The Case Study of the Ritigraben Torrent (Swiss Alps); In: Climate Change, No. 36, 3/4, 371-389.

Stoffel Markus. 1997. Neue Ansätze zur Berücksichtigung des Klimawandels und der Naturgefahren auf Raumplanungsdokumenten, Department of Geography, University of Fribourg, Fribourg (unpublished).

Stoffel Markus. 1999a. Klimawandel als Herausforderung für die Raumplanung der Vispertäler; Diploma thesis, Department of Geography, University of Fribourg, Fribourg.

Stoffel, Markus. 1999b. Géomorphologie et aménagement du territoire; in: Institut de Géographie, Université de Fribourg, Suisse, Research Report 1998, Department of Geography, University of Fribourg, Fribourg p. 36-37.

Zimmermann Markus, Mani Peter, Gamma Patrick, Gsteiger Peter, Heiniger Olivier and Gabi Hunziker. 1997. Murganggefahr und Klimaänderung - ein GIS-basierter Ansatz; Final report, National Research Program 31- vdf Zurich.

CHAPTER 23

Soil Ecological Function of Grassland Use and its Evaluation for Soil Conservation:
A Comparative Study Based on Chemical Analysis of Andisols in Southwestern Japan

(Nobusuke Iwasaki and Makiko Watanabe*)

1. INTRODUCTION

Susuki (Eulalia, *Miscanthus sinensis*) grassland, distributed on the foot slope of volcanoes in Japan, initially invades devastated regions affected by Quaternary volcanic activities, and develops as a biotic plagioclimax associated with human impact such as harvesting, grazing and burning on a long-term. On the other hand, it is well known that Andisols, volcanic ash soil characterized with thick humic A horizon, develops under continuous use of Susuki grassland.

We may say that human activity has caused the deterioration of the soil resources. For example, the removal of nutrients by harvesting causes obstruction of soil cation circulation and decrease of soil fertility, and the excess of human impact such as overgrazing may also cause soil degradation. Therefore, it is important to understand the soil ecological implication of land use management for the future of our soil resources.

*Dept. of Environmental Science & Technology, Tokyo Institute of Technology, 4259 Nagatuda-cho, Midori-ku, Yokohama 226-8052, Japan

Figure 1 is the statistical data on the changes of grassland area and plantation forest area in Japan from 1951 to 1990, which shows us the decrease of grassland area along with the decrease of livestock numbers and with the increase of artificial forest area. Since a large part of the grassland in the mountainous area has been taken place by plantation forest, the Andisols have been separated from traditional management. This phenomenon recalls not only the local people who traditionally engaged in grassland management but also our concern on the re-evaluation of sustainable grassland use and to enlighten the implication of grassland use from the viewpoint of soil conservation. Therefore, it is required to understand the influence of land use change on soil resources.

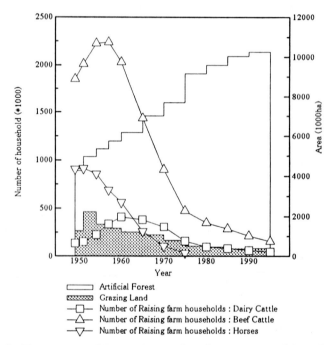

Fig. 1   The change of livestocks number, forest area and grassland area

In this study we attempt to discuss the soil ecological function of grassland use based on chemical analysis of Andisols in Japan. We investigated two conventional grassland areas, Sanbe and Aso, in southwestern Japan (Fig. 2) to compare the properties of Andisols developed under successive grasslands with those under secondary or plantation forests.

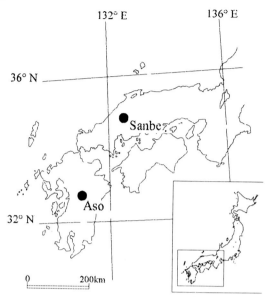

Fig. 2   Map of investigated area

2.   INVESTIGATED FIELD AND METHODS

2.1   Site Description

Sanbe district (35°7′N, 132°38′E) is located in Shimane prefecture. The altitude of the site is about 650 m, and the annual total precipitation and the annual mean temperature are reported as approximately 2000 mm and 8 °C, respectively. The climatic condition of this region is characterized by a relatively large amount of precipitation from December to February. The parent materials of Sanbe pedon are mainly composed of ash fall deposits and dacite pyroclastic flow deposits derived from the activity of Mt. Sanbe, 3,680 y.B.P. In Sanbe district, we investigated Susuki grassland (*Miscanthus sinensis*) and Red pine (*Pinus densiflora*) secondary forest which was 20 years old.

The location of Aso district is in Kumamoto prefecture, Kyusyu Island (35°58′N, 131°10′E). The altitude and the annual mean temperature of the site are 800 m and approximately 10 °C, respectively. The annual total precipitation is approximately 2000 mm and the climatic condition is characterized with heavy precipitation in June and July. The parent material of Aso pedon is composed of fresh basaltic ash fall deposits derived from the activity of Nakadake, Mt. Aso < 1000 y.B.P. In Aso district, we investigated three sites, Susuki grassland (*Miscanthus sinensis*), Japanese cypress

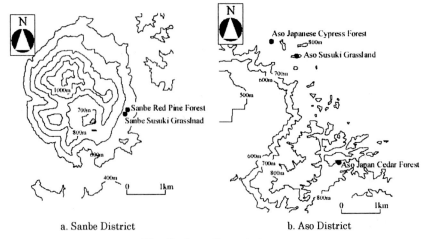

a. Sanbe District   b. Aso District

Fig. 3   Investigated site

(*Chamaecyparis obtusa*) forest approximately 10 years old and Japanese cedar (*Cryptomeria japonica*) forest approximately 50 years old.

2.2   Analytical Method

2.2.1   Carbon content, C/N ratio

The carbon content, C/N ratio in air-dried soil was determined by dried combustion method using an NC analyzer (Sumigraph NC-80).

2.2.2   Properties of humic acid (RF, Δ logK, PQ)

Properties of humic acid were determined according to Nagoya method (Kuwatsuka et al. 1992). The optical properties of humic acid extracted with 0.1 N NaOH were measured by a spectrophotometer (Shimazu UV-2400PC). The following relationship was used to determine the ratio of humic acid to humus (PQ), the relative color intensity of humic acid (RF), and the color coefficient (ΔlogK).

$$PQ = a/(a + b) \times 100\%$$

where a, b are the amounts of humic acid and fulvic acid.

RF = $K600$ sol (the amount (ml) of 0.1N $KMnO_4$ consumed by 30 ml of the humic acid solution for determining absorbance) $\times$ 1000

where K is the absorption coefficient of humic acid at 600 nm.

$$\Delta logK = logK400 - logK600$$

where K is absorption coefficient at 400 or 600 nm.

And humic acid was classified as A, P, B, or Rp type according to Kumada et al. (1967).

2.2.3 Exchangeable base, cation exchangeable capacity, and base saturation degree

Exchangeable bases (Ca^{2+}, Mg^{2+}, Na^+, K^+) were extracted by the Schollenberger method, and the amount of extracted cations were determined using the atomic absorption spectrophotometer (Hitachi Z-8100). Cation exchange capacity (CEC) was measured by the Formal titration methods. Base saturation degree was expressed as exchangeable cation percentage of CEC.

2.2.4 pH(H_2O), pH(KCl) and exchangeable acidity Y1

The values of pH(H_2O) and pH(KCl) were determined with glass electron method in 1:2.5 soil-water. The pH(KCl) value and exchangeable acidity Y1 value were successively measured following the method of Hashimoto (1992).

2.2.5 Clay mineral composition

The clay fraction (< 2 µm) was separated from the H_2O_2-treated sample by sedimentation method. The clay mineral samples were treated by air-dry, Glycerol solvation, K-saturation of air-dried, heating at 300 °C and 550 °C, and Mg-saturation. X-ray diffraction analysis was carried out for these samples with an X-ray diffractometer (Rigaku 2025C).

3. RESULTS AND DISCUSSION

According to the analytical results, we can first recognize the significant differences between the surface horizon of grassland pedon and forest pedon in soil color and soil acidity. The difference of soil acidity is more remarkable for exchangeable acidity Y1 than for the pH value, and more conspicuous in Sanbe district than in Aso district (Fig. 4). Except for Aso Japanese Cedar profile, forest pedon shows a high carbon content, a high CEC, and a low base saturation degree when compared to the grassland pedon. In Aso pedons, the humification degree indicated by ΔlogK and RF value of humic acid has a trend to decrease according to the age of the forest. In Sanbe pedons, the difference of humification degree is not clear between Susuki grassland and Red pine (Fig. 5).

The properties of parent materials differed in districts. Sanbe pedons had shown relatively low clay content and low SiO_2/Al_2O_3 ratio compared with Aso pedons (Table 2). Furthermore, clay

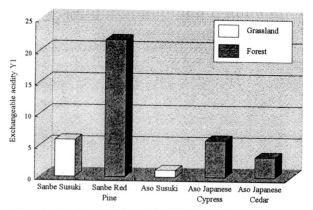

Fig. 4 Exchangeable acidity Y1 in surface horizons

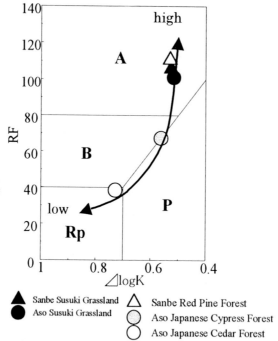

Fig. 5 Humification degree and type of humic acid represented by ΔlogK-RF diagram

mineral composition of Sanbe pedons was characterized with layered silicate clay, while Aso pedons was characterized with dominant amorphous clay (Table 3).

The difference of soil chemical properties between grassland and forest has been discussed by Tamura et al. (1991a, b), Yakimenko (1997), Alfredsson (1998) and others. As for soil acidity, humification degree, and base saturation degree, the results obtained in this study agree

Table 1 Soil properties of C%, humus composition and soil acidity

Pedon	Soil horizon and depth		Carbon content		C/N	Δlog K	RF	PQ	pH		Exchangeable acidity Y1
		cm	Soil color	cm					H₂O	KCl	
Sanbe Susuki Grassland	A11	0-10	7.5YR1.7/1	103	14.3	0.526	106	54	5.31	4.30	5.89
	A12	10-30	7.5YR2/1	65	15.9	0.541	107	66	5.30	4.45	2.90
	A21	30-50	7.5YR1.7/1	147	22.0	0.502	144	78	5.48	4.25	6.88
	AB	50-70	7.5YR1.7/1	113	21.2	0.494	145	72	5.65	4.48	3.23
	BC	70-	7.5YR3/2	17	18.0	—	—	—	5.49	4.89	0.48
Sanbe Red Pine Forest	A11	0-5	7.5YR3/2	208	17.9	0.530	111	70	4.70	3.85	21.73
	A12	5-30	7.5YR1.7/3	195	22.3	0.509	136	81	5.19	4.09	12.68
	A21	30-45	7.5YR1.7/3	200	24.9	0.499	145	80	5.38	4.20	9.35
	A22	45-75	7.5YR1.7/1	134	23.3	0.504	144	65	5.10	4.32	3.87
	BC	75-	7.5YR4/4	38	12.8	—	—	—	5.11	5.10	0.43
Aso Susuki Grassland	A11	0-10	7.5YR1.7/1	129	16.0	0.516	101	54	5.90	4.39	1.12
	A12	10-25	7.5YR1.7/1	134	16.3	0.518	111	52	5.91	4.44	1.08
	A13	25-30	10YR2/1	154	18.1	0.525	100	45	5.69	4.70	0.68
	A14	30-40	10YR2/1	152	19.5	0.509	132	48	5.82	4.70	0.44
	AB1	40-50	10YR2/2	123	21.2	0.519	128	48	5.98	5.01	0.33
	AB2	50-65	10YR3/2	98	22.6	0.530	119	48	5.95	5.02	0.41
	A21	65-80	10YR2/2	123	24.4	0.516	142	60	6.00	4.90	0.37
	A22	80-	10YR2/1	116	22.7	0.514	129	55	6.00	4.91	0.28
Aso Japanese Cypress Forest	A11	0-5	10YR2/2.5	144	14.2	0.562	67	57	5.39	4.25	5.93
	A12	5-20	10YR1.7/1	102	15.1	0.521	87	58	5.50	4.38	4.53
	A13	20-4C	10YR1.7/1	117	16.4	0.473	105	55	5.44	4.40	2.06

Contd.

Table 1 Contd.

Pedon	Soil horizon and depth cm		Soil color	Carbon content cm	C/N	Δlog K	RF	PQ	pH H₂O	KCl	Exchangeable acidity Y1
Aso Japanese Cedar	A21	40-	10YR3/1	207	23.9	0.489	134	69	5.60	4.38	3.68
	A11	0-10	10YR2/2.5	105	16.6	0.728	38	60	5.41	4.23	3.31
Forest	A12	10-25	10YR2/1	74	14.0	0.592	66	48	6.11	4.42	0.87
	A13	25-40	10YR2/1	68	14.2	0.535	86	48	6.00	4.65	0.74
	A14	40-	10YR2/1	84	16.8	0.508	110	59	5.91	4.41	0.67

Table 2 Soil properties of CEC, exchangeable cation, base

Pedon		CEC	Exchangeable cation cmol(+)kg⁻¹ Ca	Mg	K	Na	base amount	Degree of base saturation %	Clay content %	SiO₂/Al₂O₃
Sanbe Susuki	Grassland	27.7	1.24	0.19	0.14	0.10	1.7	6.1	3.0	8.02
Sanbe Red Pine	Forest	71.2	3.69	0.76	0.32	0.21	5.0	7.0	6.1	6.06
Aso Susuki	Grassland	43.0	9.01	0.97	0.42	0.12	10.5	24.5	15.9	3.73
Aso Japanese Cypress	Forest	38.1	4.04	1.07	0.56	0.14	5.8	15.3	6.4	5.96
Aso Japanese Cedar	Forest	40.3	12.00	1.43	0.39	0.15	14.0	34.9	9.7	4.48

Table 3   Composition of layer silicate clay mineral

Pedon		Kt	Ht	Ch	Vt-Ch	Mc	quartz	feldspar	Cr
Sanbe Susuki	Grassland	+++	++	++	++++	+	++++	+++	++++
Sanbe Red Pine	Forest	+++	++	++	++++	+	++++	+++	++++
Aso Susuki	Grassland	–	–	–	–	–	+	–	–
Aso Japanese Cypress	Forest	+	–	–	+	+	+	+	+
Aso Japanese Cedar	Forest	+	–	–	++	++	++	+	+

–: none, +: scarce, ++: common, +++: abundant, +++: predominant

Kt: Kaolinite, Ht: Halloysite, Ch: Chlorite, Vt-Ch: Vermiculite-Chlorite intermediate mineral, Mc Mica, Cr: Cristobalite

with the previous reports mentioned above. Nevertheless, we obtained a contrary result on carbon content. The presentative characteristics of the grassland pedons are recognized as the response of land use management. Human impact such as burning effects on soil to accelerate the circulation of base and the polymerization of humic acid. The acceleration of base circulation raises base saturation degree and lowers the soil acidity. The formation of A type humic acid, the polymerized humic acid stabilized against microbiological decomposition, behave to fix the carbon in soil.

The difference of soil acidity among the land use has shown regionality related to the diverse condition of parent material. Especially, the Sanbe forest pedon has high soil acidity. Probably, the layer silicate in the Andisols of which the origin is known as the aeolian dust supply from continental regions, amplify the difference of soil acidity, particularly exchangeable acidity Y1.

4. CONCLUSION

From this study, we are able to understand the influence of land use changes on chemical properties of Andisols.

Remarkable difference was recognized between the properties of Andisols developed under different land use, grassland and secondary or plantation forest, based on the analysis of humus composition, base saturation degree and exchangeable acidity Y1. The capacity of carbon fixation estimated by the formation of A type humic acid and the capacity of acidity control interpreted by base saturation degree both had a tendency to increase in the grassland Andisols than in the forest Andisols. We inferred that the capacity of acidity control depends on the composition of parent materials regulated by aeolian dust supply.

Consequently, we may say that Andisols which have been developed under continuous grassland use can be recognized as 'soil resource'. That is to say, sustainable grassland use guarantees the potentiality of soil resources in volcanic ash areas. Therefore, we suggest the necessity to re-evaluate sustainable grassland use from the viewpoint of soil conservation. Further experiments are required to discuss soil ecological functions of the grasslands considering the regionality of parent materials and the circulation of soil substance.

REFERENCES

Alfredsson, H., Condron, L.M., Clarholm, M. and M.R. Davis. 1998. Changes in soil acidity and organic matter following the establishment of conifers on former grassland in New Zealand. *Forest ecology and management*, Amsterdam, The Netherlands, 112: 245-252.

Hashimoto, H. 1992. A method of successive measurement for pH(KCl) and Y1. *Diagnostic standard of soil and crop nutrition*, Hokkaidou central experimental farm, Hokkaido, Japan (in Japanese).

Kumada, K., Sato, O., Ohsumi, Y., and S. Ohta. 1967. Humic Composition of Mountain Soil in Central Japan with Special Reference to the Distribution of P Type Humic Acid. *Soil Science and Plant Nutrition*, 13, Tokyo, Japan, 151-158.

Kuwatsuka, S., Watanabe, A., Itoh, K. and S. Arai. 1992. Comparison of Two Methods of Preparation of Humic and Fulvic Acids, HISS Method and NAGOYA Method, *Soil Science and Plant Nutrition*, 38, Tokyo, Japan, 1-13.

Tamura, K., Nagatsuka, S. and Y. Oba. 1991a. Effect of secondary succession on physical and chemical properties of Ando soils in central Japan. *Japanese Journal of Soil Science and Plant Nutrition*, 64, Tokyo, Japan (Japanese and English abstract), 166-176.

Tamura, K., Nagatsuka, S. and Y. Oba. 1991b. Effect of secondary succession on humus properties of Ando soils in central Japan, *Japanese Journal of Soil Science and Plant Nutrition*, 64, Tokyo, Japan (Japanese and English abstract), 177-182.

Yakimenko, E.Y. 1997. Soil comparative evolution under grasslands and woodlands in the forest zone of Russia. In: *Management of carbon sequestration in soil*. R. Lal (Ed.), Boca Raton, Florida, America, 391-404.

➤ **24**

Dynamics of Agriculturally-developed Lands of the Earth

(Vladimir S. Tikunov
and Leniana F. Yanvareva*)

1. BRIEF DESCRIPTION OF THE AGRICULTURAL LAND DISTRIBUTION

Land resources of the planet, as well as its soil cover, are limited in character and their area could not be extended. Before active agricultural development, the area of croppable lands was about 4.5 billion hectares. During the period of cultivation man has lost about 2 billion hectares of productive lands which became badlands and anthropogenic deserts as a result of improper land utilization. The process shows an accelerating trend, the present rates being 30 to 50 times higher than the historical averages.

Geography of agriculture is closely related to the environmental conditions, as well as history of land development and colonization. By the 1930s practically all steppe and forest-steppe plains of Europe, Asia and North America had been already cultivated, while the broad-leaved and mixed forests were partially cleared.

The slight increase of cultivated areas during 1960s and 1980s was replaced by their further decline in all European countries due to arable land withdrawal for industrial and transport construction. Contrary to the general trend, Great Britain experienced the post-war boom of agriculture and the sheep-raising was shifted from the plains to heath lands.

In North America the increase of cultivated areas did not exceed 9% during this period. In Canada the cropping areas on the least

*M.V. Lomonosov Moscow State University, Moscow 119899, Russia

productive podzolic soils in the zone of coniferous forests had decreased, and the area of pastures in the prairies showed a relative increase. The extensive grain cropping was concentrated in the semi-arid zone.

By the end of the 1930s, the Asian countries had cultivated the majority of arable lands. Further increase was mainly through the development of irrigated agriculture.

Within the European part of Russia the cultivation has practically wiped off the zonal boundaries between broad-leaved forests, forest-steppes and steppes. The right banks of the Oka River had been cultivated already in the 16th and 17th centuries. The geography of agriculture had undergone considerable changes during the development of virgin lands in the 1960s. Vast new areas of cultivated lands were formed in Western Siberia (Altai) and Kazakhstan. In the areas of dry regions with unstable agriculture the cultivation had resulted in the sharp increase of pasture loads, causing the accelerated deflation and salinization of soils. A part of cultivated areas were taken out of crop rotation. Virgin lands were developed in northeastern part of China as well. By the 1980s the reserves of arable lands in Asia had been exhausted.

In Africa, South America and Australia the 1930s marked the beginning of the cultivation of land resources. The highly cultivated areas in Africa included the Maghrib countries, the coastal zone of the Gulf of Guinea, the ancient area of cultivation in the Nile River valley and delta, the region around the Victoria Lake, the altitudinal belt of woina-dega in the Abyssinian Highland and the 'maize triangle' of South Africa.

The highest increase of cultivated lands was recorded within the zone of tropical forests and dry savannahs of Western Africa. The main development influenced the red-brown soils of dry savannahs, red mountain soils of seasonally-dry tropical forests and tall-grass savannahs and red-yellow laterite soils of tropical forests.

In South America, the area of cultivated lands was permanently increasing, and the geography of agriculture had changed there. The reddish-black soils and brunizems of humid tropical regions were cultivated in Argentina. During the 1960s and 1970s the areas of cultivation increased mainly through the clearing of seasonally-humid tropical forests in the regions of new development. The improvement of transport stimulated the agricultural development of the evergreen tropical forests and tall-grass savannahs within the Amazon River basin and in Bolivia.

Agriculture in the coastal and high-mountain regions of Peru was very similar to that of the pre-Columbus epoch. Within the Sierra, cultivated areas were mainly in the dry and humid Poona landscapes. The upper line of the agriculture reached 250 m above sea level. The ambitious hydrotechnic projects, realized during 1950-1970s resulted in considerable increase of the area of irrigated lands.

The area of banana plantations in Equador had increased in that period from 1.2 to 200 thousand ha. New region of agriculture was formed along the Pan-American highway in Venezuela.

The spatial pattern of Brazilian agriculture had also undergone considerable transformation. There was an expansion of cultivated areas in the southern regions of the country within the states of Rio Grande do Sol, Parana, San Paolo and Minas Gerais, new areas were developed in the states of Baia, Goiaz, Matu Groso do Sol, Rondonia and Para.

The agricultural development in Australia started in the first half of the nineteenth century. By 1850, the most productive red, red-brown and grey-brown soils of Murray-Murrumbidgee watershed and the foothill plains were cultivated in the southeastern regions. The cropping area of Western Australia was only 9900 ha in 1891. The development of arable lands was very rapid, with the exception of the period of 'gold rush' in the fifties of the nineteenth century and world economic crisis of the thirties. Until now the area of cultivation constantly increases in Australia, the recent rates being about 400,000 ha per year. Agriculture is expanding within the coastal plains of Eastern Australia and the already developed regions of South-Western Australia.

Majority of the countries are experiencing an increase in agricultural intensity usually associated with the growing environmental risk of agroecosystems degradation. As a result, the agricultural activities of humans come into sharp conflict with evolutionary regularities of the biosphere.

In late 1980s the total area of cropland was about 1.5 billion hectares, i.e. 12% of the total land area. Some continents have almost reached the maximum possible area of cultivation, thus transforming the natural ecosystems into less stable agrolandscapes. The reserves of lands with the most favorable soil and climate potential have been nearly exhausted. In North America more than 75% of croppable lands are already under cultivation, the corresponding figures being 50% for South America, 60% for Africa, 80% for Europe, 10% for Australia (Rozanov, 1987). In some regions nearly 80% of steppe, forest-steppe and broad-leaved forest landscapes have been cultivated. It has become imperative to extend agricultural area by cultivation of lands with low natural potential which require radical ameliorative measures.

Shrinking reserves of croppable lands with high natural potential made it urgently necessary to evaluate the degree of fertile soil cultivation and made an account of land resources available for agriculture.

2. INVENTORY OF THE QUALITY OF WORLD LAND RESOURCES

For the first time the rough estimation of qualitative structure of the world land resources was made in 1938 by L.I. Prasolov and N.N. Rozov who used the maps from the Large Soviet Atlas of the World (scale 1:60,000,000), namely Soil Map and Agriculture Map, the latter compiled by I.F. Makarov. The technique of combining the world soil maps with dot maps of agriculture allows to produce quite reliable data on the area of cultivation within the particular type of soils.

In the 1960s, N.N. Rozov had undertaken another attempt to evaluate the share of agricultural use of soils. New maps from the Physiographic Atlas of the World were used for this purpose, namely the soil maps of the continents, as well as the map of agriculture compiled by L.F. Yanvareva at the scale 1:60,000,000 with the same weight of a dot.

In late 1980s, new materials became available, i.e. Soil Map of the World (scale 1:15,000,000) compiled by M.A. Glazovskaya and V.M. Fridland, World Map of Lands (scale 1:15,000,000) compiled by R.S. Narskikh, G.N. Ozerova and L.F. Yanvareva, and the dot Map of Agriculture (scale 1:60,000,000) compiled by the same authors. On their basis it is possible to make a new account of agricultural use of soils applying the advanced geoinformation technologies.

3. GIS DEVELOPMENT

The first stage of such investigation should provide the computer versions of all available cartographic materials and their correlation in order to produce the uniform monitoring GIS with possibilities of its permanent up-dating.

We suppose that this system should meet a number of requirements, especially the completeness, i.e. the comprehensive account of all means of information, program, technical and organization support providing for the system operation and known as hardware, software and humanware (Tikunov and Berdnikov, 1997).

Territorial and conceptual structure of databases should simulate the structure of natural and man-transformed geosystems of which the lands are a part. The core of these structures being the interrelations between the components of geosystems they should necessarily be simulated and represented in the GIS.

The system should be of an integrated nature. The special advantage of geoinformation technologies as against the traditional methods is that they allow one to analyze large groups of interrelated parameters, which is particularly important for studying complex interactions.

Mutual correspondence of the GIS blocks should simulate the procedure of land cover investigation. The system must be open, easy to modify and re-adjust according to current requirements both by its implementator and by user, if necessary. System transformation is needed to provide for its evolution and to solve different kinds of tasks. The GIS must correspond to constantly improving technologies. It is also necessary to support the best possible level of technical and mathematical apparatus and the organization structures.

While choosing software for GIS implementation among functionally similar ones, widely used means are likely to be favored where operating experience could be successfully applied for similar geoinformation projects.

The GIS could form the principal basis for environmental cartographic monitoring of the state of lands, as well as for accumulation, correlation, unification and wide application of large and diverse spatial data on land status, major natural and anthropogenic factors, trends of evolution, etc. Therefore one could expect appreciable environmental and economic effects, particularly in the sphere of ecological assessment and land quality inventory.

The aim of the GIS is to provide for: 1) the unified system of geographical positioning of data from different sources, such as cartographic, statistical, field, remote sensing, etc.; 2) the permanent operating of databases using newly acquired information; 3) the permanent 'land survey' and updating of databases; 4) the production of new 'secondary' information by means of synthesizing of available data; and 5) the decision-making based on advanced geoinformation technologies. GIS could be a multiblock system patterned according to the principles of geographical cartography, i.e. the systematic correlation of information in individual blocks and the interrelations between the blocks. It characterizes land resources in an integral and comprehensive way, thus allowing to solve the problems of land management with due regard to environmental issues.

It would be functional to determine the character and the content of databases for each block (type of graphic and attribute information). Several interlinked databases could be compiled, for example on soil-forming conditions and soil features such as fertility, texture, stoniness, etc. Description of various aspects of soil degradation is also necessary in this case, namely data on dehumification, surface compaction, salinization, hydromorphization and different types of pollution. The database must be systematic with equal importance of information components. It should be based on cartographic materials of similar specification, geographical adequacy and concurrence.

Provision should be made for different types of data visualization, particularly in the form of traditional and computer maps and atlases. Computer maps seem to be the most promising, because they provide for permanent and operative updating, various overlay operations, transformation into 3D images, use of various animations, etc.

In some cases the application of anamorphoses proves to be very illustrative. As an example we refer to the anamorphose of the areas of cultivated lands, based on the GRID-Arendal data, which could be compared with the anamorphoses of the population numbers and GNP of individual countries of the world. These anamorphoses (Figs. 1 and 2) present much higher differentiation of characteristics as compared to the areas of cultivated lands (Fig. 3). Visual correlation of the first and the second anamorphoses is rather good, but their differences are of particular interest. The larger areas of cultivated lands as compared to the population numbers are typical to such countries as Canada, USA, Argentina, former USSR and Australia. The reverse situation is observed for Egypt, Bangladesh, North and South Korea, Japan and other countries. The correlation with the GNP has revealed less pronounced logical links (Figs. 2 and 3).

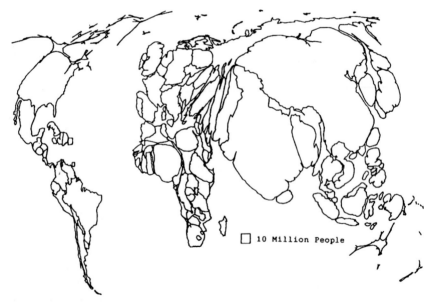

Fig. 1   The anamorphosis of the world based on the numbers of population of countries.

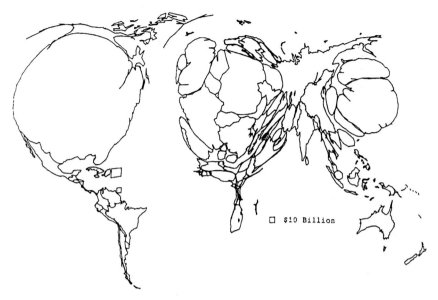

Fig. 2   The anamorphosis of the world based on the gross national product of countries.

In the future, multimedia systems would undoubtedly become particularly useful, for they have various means to describe the current pattern of agricultural lands, show the available land reserves and suggest land use strategies for different regions of the world. GIS and multimedia systems would become the basis for the development of specialized problem-oriented monitoring systems of various thematic content.

REFERENCES

Rozanov, B.G. 1987. Soil Cover of the Earth, Moscow, MSU Press, 231 p.

Tikunov, V.S. and K.V. Berdnikov. 1997. Humanware in Geographic Information Science-Geographical Information'97: From Research to Application through Cooperation. S. Hodgson, M. Rumor and J.J. Harts (Eds), Amsterdam: IOS Press, 271-276.

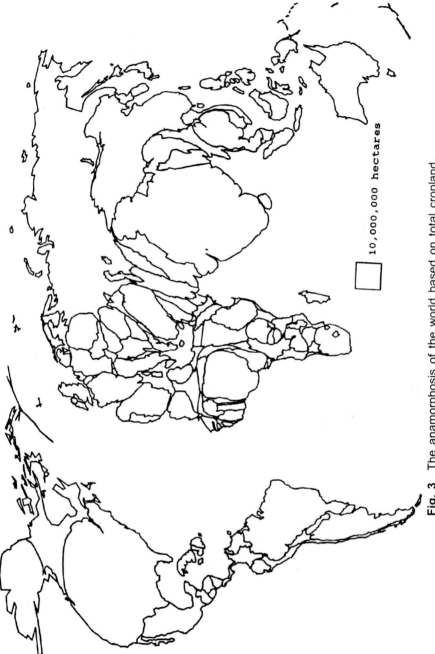

10,000,000 hectares

Fig. 3   The anamorphosis of the world based on total cropland.

Index